CHINA'S HISTORY

CAO DAWEI & SUN YANJING

Translated by Xiao Ying, Li Li & He Yunzhao

CHINA
INTERCONTINENTAL
PRESS

图书在版编目（CIP）数据

中国历史：英文/曹大为，孙燕京著；肖颖，李莉，何云朝译. —北京：五洲传播出版社，2010.1

ISBN 978-7-5085-1302-7

I.中... II.①曹... ②孙... ③肖… ④李… ⑤何… III. 中国－历史－英文 IV. K20

中国版本图书馆CIP数据核字(2008)第058047号

总 顾 问/王　晨

总 策 划/王仲伟

总 监 制/郭长建

出 版 人/李向平

主　　编/吴　伟

中国历史

著　　者/曹大为·孙燕京

翻　　译/肖　颖　李　莉　何云朝

责任编辑/苏　谦

装帧设计/田　林　傅晓斌

制　　作/北京原色印象文化艺术中心

图片提供/Fotoe　CFP　东方IC

出版发行/五洲传播出版社 (北京市海淀区北小马厂6号　邮编：100038)

电　　话/8610－58891281 (发行部)

网　　址/www.cicc.org.cn

承 印 者/北京博海升彩色印刷有限公司

版　　次/2010年1月第1版第1次印刷

开　　本/787×1092毫米　1/16

定　　价/99.00元

Foreword

Through its reform and opening to the outside world, China has worked an economic miracle and boosted its comprehensive strength, enhancing its standing in the international community. As more and more people around the world are eager to know and understand China, we have compiled the China Series, aiming to provide a shortcut for readers to get the basic facts about this country.

The 12 titles in this series cover China's geography, history, politics, economy, culture, law, diplomacy, national defense, and society, as well as its science, technology and education; its environment; and its ethnic groups and religions. These writings will help readers acquire a basic knowledge of China.

It is our hope that this series will enable readers to get a general idea about China:

Chinese history, culture and civilization, which is the oldest continuous major civilization in the world;

China's basic conditions—the world's largest developing country with a huge population, a country that is developing unevenly on a poor economic base; in light of these conditions, China is following its own path to sustainable development while learning from other civilizations; and

China's future—led by the Chinese Communist Party, the Chinese people are focusing their efforts on economic development and carrying on reform and opening-up; they are building a harmonious society in their own country and working for a harmonious world with lasting peace and common prosperity.

We expect that through these books our readers will begin a new journey of discovery—understanding China.

January 2010

Contents

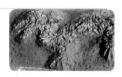

Preface

China is one of the earliest ancient civilizations in the world. Chinese civilization is the only ancient civilization in human history without any interruption.

China's territory ranks No. 3 in the world today and up until the modern age, had always been the largest. China's population had been one-third of the global total over a fairly long time in the history.

China's ancestors lived in the North Temperate Zone in East Asia, nurturing an agriculture-dominant economy. They entered into the threshold of civilization from a stable agriculture community in ancient times, and the clan chiefs transformed into a new ruling class centralizing diverse powers. Thus, the kindred ties and state administrative system fused into an underlying structure of the society, resulting in a trend of inward concentration, human relations, community living and power centralization.

Different from the prevailing slavery system and the serfdoms in the European feudal manors, the intensive cultivation marked with ironware and farm cattle was developed in the basins of the Yellow River and the Yangtze River in ancient China, forging an individual farming economy, private land ownership and tenant contractual relationships.

The natural economy-based centralism, boasting a highly centralized state power and well-organized hierarchy, competently exercises jurisdiction to a large population across a vast territory by professional officials selected through imperial examinations and a smooth and efficient traffic and communication network.

The application of unified characters and the long-term

cultivation of the dominant Confucianism have had a profound influence in the reinforcement of each region's concentration and acceptance to the Chinese civilization, the enhancement of social cohesion and the unity of the country.

Separated from the remote western civilization by mountains, deserts and oceans, China is relatively independent in geography. Acres of fertile farmlands, pasturing prairies and coastal areas for fishing and trading spread over the vast space constitute a distinctive and diverse environment, contributing to social exchanges and complementation.

Relying on advanced productivity, production mode and the Great Unity, ancient China created a brilliant civilization marked with four great inventions, playing a leading role in the world over a long period.

The global historical evolution experienced significant changes in the period of Ming and Qing dynasties (1368–1911). Major European countries entered into the industrial civilization age. The boom of capitalism pushed the whole world into the huge wave of commodity circulation. Western powers swarmed into other continents across the oceans to establish many colonies. Even China reached a new culmination in the farming civilization and sprouted contemporary buds. Then, however, the emperors in the early period of the Qing Dynasty (1644–1991), turning a blind eye on the historic trend and secluding China from the outside world, stubbornly promoted the farming system, withering and even eradicating the industrial civilization buds. Hence, the positions of China and western powers were overwhelmingly reversed, leaving a quick-declining China in the worldwide industrial civilization surge.

The Opium War (1840–1842) interrupted the independent development of China. Three score years from then on, China was invaded and insulted by western powers and forced to ink a series of unequal treaties to cede territory and pay indemnities, falling into a colonial and semi-colonial abysm.

The invasion of imperial powers brought severe tribulations to Chinese people and accelerated the disintegration of the traditional natural economy, producing the national bourgeoisie and proletariat, and bankrupting the peasantry into semi-proletariat through a restricted development of capitalism.

During the one century-odd modernization from the Opium War, Chinese people continuously promoted the development of national industry through the struggles against the imperialism, feudalism and bureaucrat capitalism. The Revolution of 1911 led by Dr. Sun Yat-sen overthrew the Qing Dynasty, profoundly publicized the concepts of democracy and republic. Then the New Democracy Revolution under the leadership of the Communist Party of China pointed a socialist future for the bourgeois revolution and won the great victory of national independence and people's liberation.

October 1, 1949 witnessed the founding of the People's Republic of China, inaugurating a historical new era toward socialist modernization. The reform and opening-up path with Chinese characteristics was finally established after a zig-zagging exploration, strengthening the construction of democracy and laws in the political field, establishing a socialist market economy and actively participating in international competition and cooperation in the economic system, to strive for a sustainable development and an affluent, democratic, cultural and harmonious society.

The Silk Road paved in ancient China played an important role in promoting Sino-foreign exchanges. The introduction of three great inventions to the western world became a powerful leverage for the approaching of the bourgeois society. Meanwhile, the western culture's eastward penetration and the promotion of Marxism significantly influenced the evolution of Chinese history. Today, the Chinese nation, keeping a brand-new philosophy of "facing the direction of modernization, globalization and future construction," has gone global and made contributions in safeguarding the peace and stability of the world and creating a better future for the humankind.

This publication outlines the unique track and evolutionary path of Chinese civilization, represents the demeanor and characteristics of Chinese civilization and interprets the secrecy of the continuity and rejuvenation of the densely populated ancient civilization after several thousand years of vicissitudes.

The Origin of Chinese Culture

Primitive Humans and Tribes

China, a country with the highest number of primitive human sites in the world, has not only preserved the most abundant materials related to the origin of human beings but also had a relatively complete evolutionary progress without serious damage.

In the early Paleolithic Period (about 250,000 to 2 million years ago), the ancient ancestors of humans were scattered in a vast area covering Yunnan, Sichuan, Shanxi, Shaanxi, Henan, Hebei, Jiangsu, Anhui, Hubei, Guizhou, Inner Mongolia, Liaoning and Beijing. Several hundred sites of the late Paleolithic Period, dating to about 10,000 to 40,000 years ago, have been found across China.

The process from Yuanmou Man to Peking Man to Upper Cave Man outlined the evolution of early humans in China.

Yuanmou Man, dating back to 1.7 million years ago, was named after Yuanmou, Yunnan, the site where the fossils were discovered. Fossils of two teeth of ancient humans and some stone instruments processed by manpower were unearthed, and lots of coal dust and burned bones were found in relevant clay layers, too. Yuanmou Man is believed to be the earliest human beings so far confirmed within Chinese territory.

The culture sedimentation layer of the caveman site at Longgu Mountain, Zhoukoudian, Beijing, is above 40 m. Archeological study shows that Peking Man started to live in Zhoukoudian about 700,000 years ago and lived there for about 500,000 years. More than 17,000 pieces of stoneware for picking and hunting, including choppers, scrapers and arrowheads, were unearthed from the area. The 6 m-thick ash layer is the vestige of Peking Man's application of natural fire,

The restored head portrait of Peking Man.

Burned bones unearthed from Peking Man Site, indicating Peking Man's application of natural fire.

The restored head portrait of Upper Cave Man.

which shows that they were able to use fire to cook food, give light, keep themselves warm and drive away beasts, and had mastered the skills of controlling fire. The ability to make and use instruments is an important marker to differentiate human beings from apes.

The usage of fire and eating cooked food helped the physical and mental growth of the primitive humans. Peking Man, while retaining some physical features of apes, could walk upright and had a brain capacity much higher than the ape's, about 76 percent of that of modern humans.

In the caves at the top of Longgu Mountain, the site of Upper Cave Man living about 18,000 years ago was discovered. In addition to three pieces of human skulls and some skeleton fossils, bone needles processed through scratching, cutting, grinding and drilling, and holed stone pearls, clam shells and beast tusks and other adornments were unearthed at the site. These indicated that the Upper Cave Man had mastered the skill of drilling wood to make fire. Manmade fire is deemed to be the beginning of human history. Upper Cave Man had nearly the equivalent brain capacity of modern human beings, as well as a similar physique and appearance.

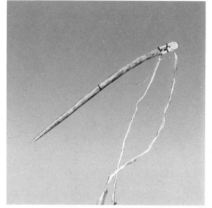

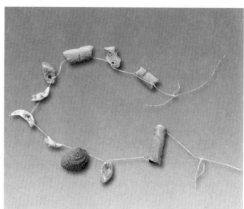

Bone needles and adornments made by Upper Cave Man.

About 10,000 years ago, the Chinese ancestors entered into the Neolithic Period. Most regions were in the prosperous phase of the Neolithic Period about 7,000 years ago. Above 7,000 discovered culture sites, centered around the valleys of the Yangtze River and the Yellow River, are spread over a vast area. Banpo Site of the Yangshao Culture (dating to about 5,000 to 7,000 years ago) and Hemudu Site of the Hemudu Culture (about 5,300 to 7,000 years ago) are representative of the early Neolithic Period, while Longshan Culture (about 4,000 to 4,500 years ago) is a typical site of the late Neolithic Period.

Banpo Site of the Yellow River basin, located in Banpo village of Xi'an, Shaanxi, dates back 6,000 years and covers around 50,000 sq m. The houses where the Banpo men lived were mostly half-buried caves built with wood, branches or grass, in which there were clay-made cookers and heatable brick bed. More than 200 silos were used to reserve food. Tools and bones were excavated from the site. So were colorful porcelains with patterns of humans, animals and geometry.

Millstones and bars of the Neolithic Age, unearthed from Peiligang, Xinzheng County, Henan.

The Hemudu Site, located in Hemudu Village, Yuyao,

Zhejiang, has a history of around 7,000 years and is representative of the Yangtze River basins. The stilt style of architecture that the Hemudu men created has for thousands of years been a major architectural form adopted in the areas south of the Yangtze.

In the Neolithic Period, Chinese ancestors widely used stone-made axes, spades, hoes, knives, millstones and other ground stone tools. They also planted millets, rice, cabbage, mustard and other crops, and raised pigs, dogs, oxen, goats, chicken and other livestock.

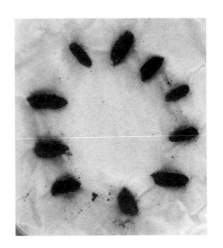

Rice unearthed from Hemudu Culture Site, Yuyao County, Zhejiang.

Xi'an Banpo Site and Lintong Jiangzhai Site of Yangshao Culture have a public activity place in the central area with small residential rooms around it. Kilns for baking pottery are located near the residential quarters. A moat for protection has been excavated around the village. The public tombs are situated outside the village. The Niuheliang Site

Pig-pattern black pottery bowls unearthed from Hemudu Culture Site, Yuyao County, Zhejiang.

A head portrait of an earthen goddess of the Hongshan Culture period, unearthed from Niuheliang, Liaoning.

An altar at
Hongshan Culture
Site, Niuheliang,
Liaoning.

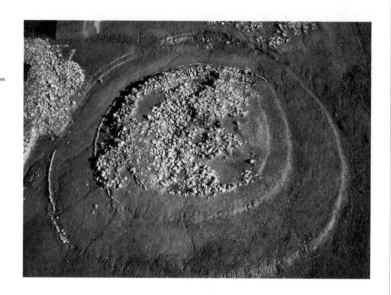

Bone flutes of the
Neolithic Age,
unearthed from
Jiahu, Wuyang
County, Henan.

of Hongshan Culture has a temple to a goddess and a large altar. These sites indicate the existence at that time of the clan, a kin-based community with families as basic components. A tribe normally consisted of a few clans.

From picking, fishing and hunting to primitive agriculture and livestock husbandry and the resulting settlement and clan society, the profound reform of productivity, production mode and social structure promoted cultural leaps, the blooming of talent and prosperous inventions in this heroic age.

Glimmer of Civilization in Legendary Times

Around 3000 BC, the Tigris and Euphrates Valley in West Asia and Egypt in Africa entered the threshold of culture. The Yellow River Valley and the middle and lower reaches of the Yangtze River in China also showed a glimmer of culture.

The history of remote antiquity was passed down mainly through oral myths and legends. Such memories later were recorded in written documents, which narrate the activities of early humans.

Huangdi (Yellow Emperor) and Yandi (Flame Emperor) were the chieftains of tribal groups along the Yellow River Valley in the heroic age some 4,000–5,000 years ago. The later generations, in their efforts to enumerate their ancestors' feats, attributed key inventions to these two leaders.

Yandi, the legendary founder of primitive agriculture and medicine, is also known as Shennong Shi. He is said to have invented pottery-making and established markets for exchange. Huangdi, who taught people sewing and building, as well as invented bows, arrows and vehicles, is also called Xuanyuan Shi. He ordered his subordinates to invent characters, the calendar, arithmetic and music. His wife, Lei Zu, created the skills of planting mulberry, raising silkworm and weaving brocade with the silk produced.

Boat-shaped painted pottery kettles of the Yangshao Culture period, unearthed from Beishouling, Baoji, Shaanxi.

Left: The painted pottery basin of the Neolithic Age, unearthed from Banpo Site, Shaanxi. The decorative pattern features a human face with two fish in the mouth.

Right: The human-shaped pottery pot of the Neolithic Age, unearthed from Dadiwan, Qin'an, Gansu.

The Portrait of Huangdi (copied after the stone sculpture of the Han Dynasty in Wu's Memorial Temple in Jiaxiang, Shandong)

The extant tombs and cultural relics of the Neolithic Period (dating from 4,000–8,000 years ago) provide evidence for these legends. Silkworm cocoons and spinning wheels unearthed in Xiaxian County, Shanxi prove that sericulture and textiles were popular at the time. Colored earthen kettles in the shape of ships unearthed at the Banpo Site indicate shipbuilding was carried out in that period. The symbols discovered at Banpo and other sites also indicate the rudiments of written characters. Clay xun excavated in Banpo and bone flutes in Wuyang, Henan prove the existence of primitive music in the period. Besides, pottery zeng with a hole at the bottom, unearthed in Banpo, shows people cooked food with steam at the time. The room range and pottery patterns illustrate arithmetic progression and symmetric design. The number symbols of I,II, III,X,Λ, ┼ and /\ engraved on potteries unearthed in Wuyang, Henan are the same in meaning with the number symbols in later inscriptions on bones or tortoise shells. Some bone flutes have the half line for drilling holes, indicating the accurate calculation then.

These inventions are the key elements marking Chinese ancestors' entry into the age of civilization and the roots of many great achievements made in modern civilization. Huangdi and Yandi, therefore, are respected as the first ancestors of the Chinese people.

The Huangdi and Yandi tribes, originating from Loess Plateau in North Shaanxi, continued to expand eastward along the Yellow River. They came together and defeated the Chiyou Tribe in the lower stream of the Yellow River. Later,

Huangdi defeated the Yandi in the Banquan campaign to capture the central plains, gradually achieving the integration of the Yandi, Huangdi and Chiyou tribes, thus creating the main part of Chinese nationality.

"Dragons," a combination of multiple animal images, were discovered in the tombs in Puyang, Henan that goes back 6,000 years. The dragon was an integration of the totems of many tribes, reflecting the process from inter-tribal wars to alliances that further led to the formation of the mainstay of the Chinese people.

In the late Neolithic Period, about 4,000 years ago, productivity increased rapidly. Bronze ware unearthed in Gansu, Qinghai and other places indicate that "bronze and stone

The Mausoleum of Huangdi, situated at Huangling County, Shaanxi, is a place for Chinese descendents to offer sacrifices to Huangdi.

ware" were both used in the period. More than 100 pieces of pottery and jade ware were found in some tombs of the period. In other tombs, only one or two pieces, or no pieces, were found, indicating the emergence of private property, the polarization of the rich and the poor, and the confrontation of classes with the development of production.

The heroes during this period were Yao, Shun and Yu, famous chieftains of the tribes in the Yellow River Valley after Yandi and Huangdi. The area suffered severe floods during the times of Yao and Shun. At such a critical moment, Yu led people to dredge rivers. After 13 years of hard work, such disasters were finally conquered and the people lived a happy life. He also led the people to build irrigation projects. Thus, production in the Central Plains developed rapidly and Yu's influence extended to the Yangtze River and the Huaihe River basins.

The dragon laid with conches unearthed from the tombs in Puyang, Henan is honored the "First Dragon in China."

Yu's feats of large-scale water control facilitated the development of social organizations and management institutions, as well as the presence of state apparatuses and the Chinese civilization. According to such historical books as *Annals of the Xia Dynasty from The Records of the Grand Historian*, Yu had "removed numerous mountains and dug

The stone carving of Yu's water control in Yuwangtai, Kaifeng.

numerous channels" to get rid of the obstacles to the water-control work. That helped break the tribal boundaries and promoted the integration of various tribes into a unified social community. Yu also gave instructions on production based on the geological features of different regions, asked

○ Data Link

Features of China's Primitive Agriculture

Three core origins of agriculture exist around the world: West Asia, Central and South America, and East Asia. China was the agricultural origin of East Asia. Chinese agriculture can be traced back to 10,000 years or so, and its primitive agriculture had developed very well 7,000–8,000 years ago.

China's primitive agriculture had its distinctive features when compared to those in other parts of the world. In terms of planting, China saw the dominance of millet in the North and rice in the South, a pattern different from that in West Asia, where wheat and barley were the major crops. The pattern was also different from Central and South America, where potatoes and corn were widely planted. In terms of Chinese livestock husbandry, dogs, pigs, chickens and buffalo were among those first raised and the list later included the "six domestic animals" (horses, cattle, sheep, pigs, dogs and chickens). In West Asia, sheep and goats were dominant and alpacas were the only livestock raised in Central and South America.

the regions to pay tributes, and distributed grain among the regions for an overall balance. Yu's extraordinary capabilities and enormous achievements helped him establish authority over the whole region. The tribal union headed by Yu was described as "a magnificent and grand occasion" in Chinese history.

Generally speaking, Chinese civilization, as one of the independent civilization sources, has a clear evolutionary track, indicating a diversified development with the central plain as the core and resulting in the feature of mutual penetration and integration.

The Xia, Shang and Western Zhou Dynasties: Early States and Bronze Civilization

Presence of the State and Changes of Dynasties

The Xia, Shang and Western Zhou dynasties were an important period for the formation and development of early states.

Around BC 2070, Yu set up Xia, the first dynasty in Chinese history.

Yu divided the whole country into "nine regions" and established the capital in Yangcheng (today's Dengfeng). The administrative regions included today's Henan, Hebei, Shanxi, Shandong, Shaanxi, Jiangsu, Zhejiang, Anhui, Hubei, etc. Yu also collected all the bronze in the state to make nine huge "dings" (an ancient cooking vessel), symbolizing its supreme authority.

The Xia Dynasty built palaces and cities with walls and moats for protection, established management institutions for different matters as well as the official posts at different levels. Furthermore, it also defined tributes and taxes, set up military forces, formulated ritualism and criminal laws, built jails and carried out other functions of a sovereign state.

The succession of authority from Yao and Shun to Yu was originally performed through peaceful abdication with the atmosphere of primitive democracy. Yu, by means of his

A drawing of restored palaces at Erlitou Site.

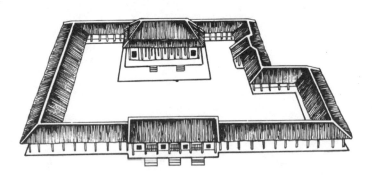

authority, used his son Qi's power to defeat the Dongyi Tribe Chieftain Yi, the planned successor of Yu, and conquered other rebellious tribes. From then on, the hereditary system replaced the abdication system and this was followed by the later dynasties.

There are few historical records of the Xia Dynasty. However, the archeological excavations complement the historical records, presenting a relatively complete cultural view of the dynasty.

The area and period of existence suggested by the Erlitou Cultural Relics from Yanshi, Henan generally match the location of the Xia Dynasty. At the site, the earliest palace cluster in China to date was discovered. They were standard and orderly in layout, symmetrical along the central line, equipped with roads and pottery-pipe ditches, as well as a temple for offering sacrifices to ancestors. Jade, pottery and bronze ritual ware were also excavated at the site. Cast bronze and pottery mills were distributed around the city, indicating social division of labor. The difference in tomb systems and funereal articles, and more than 30 skeletons with signs of binding and execution, are indicative of the gap between the rich and the poor, social hierarchy and class confrontation. All these indicate the establishment of the rudiments of a country in the Xia Dynasty.

Jade person of the Shang Dynasty, unearthed in Fuhao Tomb of Yin Ruins, Anyang, Henan, represents the image of the Shang people.

The Xia Dynasty lasted more than 470 years. The final ruler of the dynasty was cruel and extravagant, and was opposed by the masses and deserted by his followers. Around BC 1600, Tang, the chieftain of the Shang Tribe living in the lower reaches of the Yellow River, united numerous tribes to terminate the Xia Dynasty and establish the Shang Dynasty with Bo as its capital (Yanshi, Henan). The capital was later relocated several times. In BC 1300, Pangeng, the ruler of Shang, moved the capital to Yin (today's Anyang, Henan) and stayed there from then on. Thus, the Shang Dynasty is also called the Yin Dynasty.

The sovereignty of the Shang Dynasty lasted more than 500 years, until the Zhou Tribe rose from the Weishui River and replaced it. In BC 1046, King Wuwang of the Zhou Fief, together with more than 800 tribes, defeated the troops of Zhouwang of the Shang Dynasty and established the Zhou Dynasty with its capital in Haojing (west of today's Xi'an, Shaanxi). It is called the Western Zhou in history. At the end of the Western Zhou Dynasty, the vassals were strong while the court declined. In BC 771, the northwestern Quanrong ethnic group captured Haojing and killed Emperor Youwang, marking the end of the Western Zhou Dynasty.

Early States and Religious Society

China's early regime had features that were distinctive

Li Bronze *Gui* of the Western Zhou Dynasty, having a 32-character inscription, recorded the historical event of the punitive expedition to the Shang Dynasty by Emperor Wuwang of the Zhou Dynasty.

from that in ancient Greece, the origin of western civilization. In ancient Greece, crisscrossing mountains and rivers led to diverse production and living styles, and the development of navigation and trade increased interpersonal communications, which further led to disintegration of family organizations. When entering the class society, Greece saw a separation among political authorities, financial power and theocracy as well as their alliance to overthrow the unitary clan leadership. Greece also established a regime on the basis of a slavery system and implemented citizen politics. The Chinese civilization primarily originates in the central plains, where an intensive agricultural economy prevailed and the blood ties didn't collapse even in the civilization of society. The needs from water control, external wars and other public affairs increasingly strengthened the blood relation-based family organizations that connected the single, separated natural agricultural economies. This further consolidated the rights and positions of clan leaders, who later turned into members of the new ruling class that integrated political power, religious authority, financial and military power as well as theocracy. Consanguineous organizations melted into state forms, shaping basic patterns for the patriarchal and fief society.

The Xia and Shang dynasties saw backward traffic conditions and group inhabitation of people based on blood relations. The clustering tribes were called "Fangguo" (Clan State). The ruling of the country depended more on traditional clans and ties of kinship and the country was ruled on the basis of the relationship of subordination among clans. This kind of relationship was actually a union of Clan States whose influence didn't directly penetrate into the

Bronze Yu *Ding* (tripod caldron) of the Western Zhou Dynasty. In the inner wall of the Ding, 291 characters in 19 lines were engraved, describing the conferment of the aristocratic Yu in the 23rd year under the reign of Emperor Kangwang of the Zhou Dynasty and the awarding of subjects and slaves to him. It is an important historical material to study the fief system of the Western Zhou Dynasty.

neighboring kingdoms.

In the early Western Zhou Dynasty, Zhougong established ritualism as well as patriarchal and fief systems to beef up the state's rule over neighboring regions. That resulted in further intensified state administrative functions.

The patriarchal system based inheritance of land, property and position on blood relations. The King of Zhou called himself the "son of Heaven." The throne of the Zhou Dynasty would be inherited by the eldest son of the legal wife, who was called "Dazong" of the state. The brothers of the eldest son inherited part of the king's property and were honored as vassals, who were "Xiaozong" of the state but "Dazong" within their own jurisdiction. The same principle would apply to the lower ministers, scholars and ordinary people.

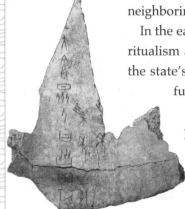

Oracle inscription on ox bones saying "farming together" records the Monarch of Shang Dynasty ordered his subjects to till lands jointly.

Based on the patriarchal principle, the fief system was designed to enfeoff the royal relatives to cement the rule of Zhou Dynasty. The awarded vassals would be given "both citizens and land" and were supposed to manage local affairs, pay visits and tributes regularly and offer services to fulfill their liability of safeguarding the court. The fief system based on the vassals of the same surname broke the old kin-based state borders, helped establish authority in some rich regions, key strategic areas and military places, resulting in a network from the central government to the local areas. This contributed to the country's stability and pushed the economic and cultural development of peripheral areas. While in neighboring areas, a small number of relatives-in-law, heroic ministers and descendants of nobles were awarded with a view to unifying other tribes and stabilizing political situations.

The Xia, Shang and Western Zhou dynasties, which differentiated political positions based on kin relationships, were class societies with stringent hierarchies. As *The Commentary by Zuo on the Spring and Autumn Annals* goes, "There are 10 social hierarchies, just as there are different days in life." The king ruled over ministers, who were superior to scholars who were followed by servants at lower levels. Nobles with various privileges were often administrative officials at all levels, constituting the ruling class. The imperial family and nobles owned many slaves who were prisoners or criminals, and could be given away or sold. In addition to being used for hard labor, slaves were also killed as sacrifices to ancestors or buried alive with deceased nobles. More than 500 slaves were offered as sacrifices in a festival during the Shang Dynasty. However, strict patriarchal ties of kinship ensured that ordinary clansmen did not decline as "speaking tools." The ordinary clansmen had their own families and production tools. As the main laborers of the agricultural and handicraft industry, they belonged to the civilian class and undertook services for the court and for nobles.

In order to conquer those outside and oppress those inside their kingdom, the Shang and Zhou dynasties regarded a powerful army as a major issue. Jails and cruel criminal

Bronze Zhao *You* of the Western Zhou Dynasty, has an inscription of 44 characters inside the ware, describing the Monarch of Zhou's awarding a land 50 square *li* in Bi Area to Zhao. It is an important evidence to study the square-fields system.

laws involving execution, burying alive, and cutting off noses and feet were established as important means to maintain the reign of the nobles.

In Xia, Shang and Western Zhou dynasties, both nobles and civilians were living in the social networks weaved by clan or patriarchal ties. In addition to the establishment of the kin and region-integrated patriarchal clan system and the fief system, a series of ritual and musical systems regulating behavior were formulated to "differentiate and rank the nobles and the commoners" and maintain hierarchy and social order.

In the Western Zhou Dynasty, offering sacrifice to ancestors had equal importance with wars, and was an important rite to safeguard the patriarchal clan system and enhance national integration. Guided by the idea of "destiny is conditional and favors those with virtues," the Zhou abandoned the Shang's blind belief in ghosts and gods and promoted the morality of respecting ancestors and the thought of "holding moral and caring people in high esteem." That helped enlighten the masses and safeguard the hierarchical system and social orders, showing a certain degree of rationalism.

○ Data Link

The Square-fields System

The square-fields system was a kind of land ownership system adopted in the Shang and Zhou dynasties. The "square fields" refer to the farmland that was divided into patches of square-shaped fields. With boundaries outside and crisscross ditches and paths inside, the field looks like the Chinese character of "Jin" (well). The square fields were state-owned fields in name but owned by royal families and nobles in reality. They were distributed to civilians only for their use, who had to pay certain tributes in return. No sales or transfers were allowed. A square field was divided into nine square-shaped areas, with the outer eight patches being private ones and the central one public. Village members were allowed to work in the "private fields" that only after finishing the work in "public fields" for the nobles.

By adopting a chain of innovative measures regarding regime construction, Western Zhou Dynasty leaders cleverly combined kinship with the state regime, which played a significant role in stabilizing the society, maintaining social order and enhancing national cohesion. In the meantime, breaking the old pattern in the Xia and Shang dynasties that saw conflicts among numerous independent clans also strengthened the king's control over all parts of the state and pushed forward the economic and cultural development in remote areas.

Brilliant Bronze Civilization

Both the Shang Dynasty and the Western Zhou Dynasty had territories that were much more extensive than that of the Xia Dynasty. They were the biggest country in the world. With the rapid social and economic growth and the gradual maturity of state mechanism, the civilization during the Shang and Zhou made a great leap, mainly indicated through the development of cities, inscriptions on bones or tortoise shells and bronze ware, etc.

A piece of complete tortoise shell.

The capital of the Shang covered an area of 30 million sq m, and boasted a population of 140,000 and a thriving commercial sector with "nine markets," The Western Zhou had 3 million citizens nationwide and saw even more development in urban cities, traffic, accommodations and post services.

Ghosts and gods worship was popular in the Shang Dynasty. The nobles always cast lots in cases of sacrifices, wars, fishing and hunting, diseases and others. They engraved the results, i.e. "oracle inscriptions," on tortoise shells or bones.

Bronze *Jue* of
the Xia Dynasty,
unearthed at
Erlitou, Yanshi
County, Henan, is
the earliest bronze
vessel discovered
in China up to now.

The ancient characters used in oracle inscriptions are called *Jiaguwen* (inscriptions on bones or tortoise shell). Since the 19th century, more than 150,000 pieces of bones and shells with inscriptions have been unearthed from such places as the Yin Ruins in Henan, indicating the wide use of *Jiaguwen* in the Shang Dynasty. The application of *Jiaguwen* also marked the start of China's recorded history.

More characters cast on bronze ware from the Western Zhou Dynasty are preserved, which are called *Jinwen* (inscriptions on bronze). *Jiaguwen* and *Jinwen* had incorporated six kinds of character-shaping principles including pictography, pictophonetic compounds, ideography, logical aggregates, and associative transformation and borrowing, paving the way for the development of the Chinese characters. A total of 4,500 *Jiaguwen* characters have been found so far. While the number of *Jinwen* characters increased greatly, so did the passage lengths. For example, a long inscription with nearly 500 words has been found. *Jiaguwen* and *Jinwen* are the only ancient words with vitality. Chinese characters used today were developed based on *Jiaguwen* and *Jinwen*. The extensive application of characters is a symbol of social development reaching a higher stage. It goes beyond time and space, recording the thoughts, languages and experiences of humans as well as intricate natural and social phenomena. That enabled the communication of culture and tradition and greatly drove cultural development forward.

The development of the bronze casting industry during the Shang and Zhou dynasties greatly improved social production and living quality. About 10,000 pieces of bronze ware cast in the Shang Dynasty have so far been unearthed. More than 5,000 pieces of bronze ware were excavated from the tombs of Guo Kingdom of the Western Zhou Dynasty alone. The bronze ware unearthed were mainly ritual ware, weapons like daggers, spears, battle-axes and arrowheads and tools like knives and axes, as well as a few fittings for carriages and farm tools.

The bronze mining, smelting and casting techniques were rather mature in the Shang Dynasty. The site of an ancient bronze mine from the Western Zhou Dynasty, located in Tonglv Mountain, Daye, Hubei, covers an area of around 2 sq km, with the mine as deep as 60 m. Various ways to excavate for silos, inclined alleys and flat valleys were adopted. Drainage systems were built and ventilation inside the mine was primarily solved as well. The residue from the ancient mine contains a bronze content of only 0.7 percent. The craftsmen of the Shang Dynasty could accurately prepare the proportion between bronze and tin and made bronze ware of different hardness.

The bronze ware of the Shang and Zhou dynasties were

Simuwu Bronze *Ding* of the Shang Dynasty, unearthed in Wuguan Village, Anyang, Henan, is the heaviest bronze ware made in ancient China discovered up to date.

Bronze bell
chimes of the
Western Zhou
Dynasty. Chimes
are the main ritual
instruments played
in sacrifices,
banquets and other
events of nobles in
the Zhou Dynasty.

famous not only for their great number and diverse categories, but for their spectacular shapes and superb craftsmanship. Simuwu *Ding*, unearthed in the Yin Ruins, is grand in size and exquisite in pattern. As the largest extant bronze ware in the world, it is 133cm high and weighs more than 800kg. Its output and casting technology reflect the power of a country. The majestic bronze *Ding* is a symbol of the brilliant civilization of the Shang and Zhou dynasties.

Ancient Egypt, ancient Babylon and the Harappan Culture in the Indus River Valley, which once coexisted with China's Xia and Shang dynasties, successively declined after creating splendid civilizations. However, the rise and fall of the Xia, Shang and Zhou dynasties accumulated the successive genes of Chinese culture, in terms of production technology with bronze ware, and the culture structure with *Jiaguwen* as the carrier. The gradually maturing political system, social structure and ritualism of the early countries had a profound influence on later generations.

The Spring & Autumn and Warring States Periods: Vassals Contend for Hegemony and Social Reform

The Five Powers in the Spring and Autumn Period and the Seven States in the Warring States Period

In BC 770, the second year after the Western Zhou Dynasty ended, Emperor Pingwang of the Zhou Dynasty relocated the capital to Luoyi (today's Luoyang, Henan), which is known as the Eastern Zhou in history. The Spring and Autumn Period (770–477 BC) was named after the State of Lu's chronicle Spring & Autumn, and the Warring States Period (477–221 BC), was named after the conflicts among states for the throne.

During this 550-year period, the power of the court declined and retreated to a small vicinity of 600 *Li*. Vassals stopped paying visits or tributes to the court, and the king, therefore, had to "announce a state of hunger" and "beg for money and chariots" and thus became highly dependent on vassals. King Huanwang of the Zhou Dynasty was even shot by troops of the Zheng and lost his dignity as a king.

Vassals waged hundreds of wars against each other in order to make expansion. China successively underwent two historical periods, for example, the Spring and Autumn Period with five hegemonies, and the Warring States Period with seven powers.

Duke Huan of Qi took the lead to seek hegemony in the Spring and Autumn Period. After taking power, he named Guan Zhong as the prime minister, who later launched

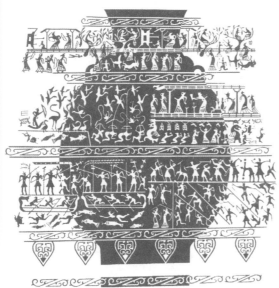

The Land and Water Battle Scenes inscribed on the bronze kettle from the Warring States Period, which shows the life scenes in the Warring States Period like entertaining, hunting and fighting (unearthed from Chengdu, Sichuan).

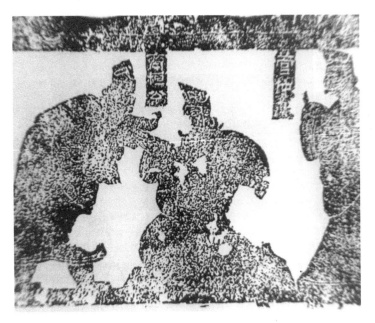

A portrait brick of Duke Huan of Qi and his minister Guan Zhong.

large-scale reforms. Economically, Guan Zhong encouraged reclaiming barren land and trading businesses. Militarily, he organized strong armies, and politically, he highlighted the slogan of "respecting the king and dispelling aliens," joining hands with all the states in the central plains and working to safeguard advanced Chinese culture. In BC 651, the State of Qi initiated a meeting of all the vassals in Kuiqiu, which the king of the Zhou Dynasty sent a representative to attend. That established the hegemonic position of Duke Huan of Qi in the central plains.

The states of Jin and Chu rose successively after the State of Qi. After decades of exile, Duke Wen of Jin returned to his home state, taking the throne and making vigorous effort to rejuvenate his country. Defeating the troops of Chu in Chengpu Battle in BC 632, he organized a meeting of all vassals where his hegemonic position was established. The

The sword of Gou
Jian, King of Yue.

State of Chu in the South thrived once again after Duke Zhuang took the office. In BC 606, the troops of Chu threatened Luoyi, capital of the Zhou Dynasty, and brazenly asked about the size and weight of the Ding of Zhou, which apparently showed his ambition to replace the king of Zhou. Before long, his troops marched northward once again, defeating the troops of Jin at Bi and resulting in the hegemony of Duke Zhuang of Chu.

In the late Spring and Autumn Period, the states of Wu and Yue in the South rose to hegemony in succession. The State of Wu in the lower reaches of the Yangtze River captured the capital of the State of Chu in BC 506. It also later swallowed the State of Yue in the Qiantang River basins, defeated the troops of Qi in the North and met all the vassals at Huangchi, Henan. King Goujian of Yue, after being defeated and captured, endured much humiliation and hardships for 20 years. But he finally conquered Gusu, the capital of Wu, by dispatching troops at a time when King Fuchai of Wu had squandered all the national wealth. He further merged the State of Wu years later and marched into the central plains, becoming the last hegemony in the Spring and Autumn Period.

In the early Warring States Period, the patriarchal and fief system was destroyed and the king's privileges were transferred to lower levels. Some ministers and senior officials who grew to be important players because of implementing reforms gradually carved up and replaced the privileges and positions of former vassals, paving the way for them to come into power. In BC 403, the states of Han, Zhao and Wei divided the State of Jin, and Tianshi, a senior official of Qi, replaced Jiangshi to become the vassal. The wars among vassals got more frequent, resulting in the pattern where seven powers, known as the states of Han, Zhao, Wei, Qi, Chu, Yan and Qin, coexisted and fought against each other to seek hegemony. Following the dominance of Marquis Wen of Wei in the central plains, the hegemony-seeking war between Qi and Wei, and the confrontation between Qin and Qi, the State of Qin grew strong through Shang Yang's reforms. Qin defeated the troops of Zhao at Changping in BC 260, which led to the rise of Qin and the chaotic situation of "vertical alliance and horizontal collaboration."

The wars in the Spring and Autumn and Warring States periods brought serious disasters to the people and broke the old social order to pave the way for a new system. The five powers of the Spring and Autumn Period—namely Qi, Jin, Chu, Wu and Yue (or Qi, Song, Jin, Qin and Chu)—and the seven states of the Warring States—namely Qi, Chu, Yan, Qin, Han, Zhao and Wei—all strived for reform and rose toward a new reunification.

The bronze mirror with patterns of a warrior of the Qin State during the Warring States Period fighting against a beast, unearthed from Yunmeng, Hubei, showing the warrior spirit of the people of Qin after Shang Yang's reform.

○ Data Link

Vertical Alliance and Horizontal Collaboration

Seven powers strove to seek hegemony in the Warring States Period. Besides using military force, each state also carried out political and diplomatic policies. The six eastern states joined hands to form a south-north vertical alliance to confront the State of Qin, called the "vertical alliance." Meanwhile, the State of Qin, located in the West, took advantage of the conflicts among the eastern states, and tactically went into collaboration with part of the six states and finally attacked all of them one by one, called a "horizontal collaboration." The eastern states sometimes followed the State of Qin and sometimes followed the State of Chu for the sake of their own interests. Some advisors like Su Qin and Zhang Yi traveled around the states, persuading vassals to adopt a vertical alliance or horizontal collaboration and were called "Men of Alliance."

The History of China

Social Reform Triggered by Ironware and Ox-led Plowing

The Spring and Autumn Period witnessed profound re-forms and changes in ancient Chinese society. Production tool improvement and technical renovation were the under-lying motivation for the large-scale social reform.

The Iron Age starts from the Spring and Autumn Period. Hard and sharp ironware replaced wood and stone instru-ments and was extensively applied in agricultural produc-tion. In the Warring States Period, iron plows drawn by two oxen were used. New tools and improved plows promoted cultivation technology. However, traditional mass cultiva-tion seriously hindered the popularization of new technol-ogy. The historical records of "slow for collective cultivation while quick for private land" reflect the profound reform of large-scale compulsory collective cultivation replaced by in-dividual plowing. Thanks to the efficiency of iron tools and ox-led plowing, a great deal of barren land was reclaimed in this period. The products reaped from the extra private land were no longer presented to the kings. Owners of these pri-vate lands leased their lands to peasants for collecting rent, resulting in a new production management mode, which greatly aroused the production enthusiasm of individual peasants. Low-efficient, backward collective cultivation for "public fields" was strongly opposed, leading to stretches of uncultivated land with widespread weeds. The vassals, therefore, had to lease the "public fields" to peasants for cul-tivation, marking the collapse of the "square-fields system." Landowner economy, based on land privatization and indi-vidual cultivation, rapidly expanded.

The booming landocracy intensively required to break the old system of the patriarchal nobles' hereditary occupa-tion of fiefs and military and political power, abolish their hereditary privileges in position and salary and initiate reforms aimed at developing a landocracy economy, enriching the country and forging a mighty army.

Guan Zhong of the State of Qi in the Spring and Autumn Period initiated the policy of "collecting tributes and taxes according to the size and quality of land." The State of Lu implemented the policy of "initial tax on land per-*mu*," which provided that taxes should be levied based on actual land size regardless of ownership of the land. These tax reforms, in nature, confirmed land privately owned in the form of state laws. Later on, the State of Qin launched the land policy of "destroying square fields and allowing land sales," which further legalized and popularized the privately-owned land and paved the way for the state's ruling over land owners.

Li Kui, named by Marquis Wen of the State of Wei in the Warring States Period, worked out *The Book of Law* to beef up

An iron sword with gold nose and head of the Spring and Autumn Period, unearthed from Shanxian.

Mould for simultaneous casting of two iron sickles of the Warring States Period, unearthed from Gudonggou, Xinglong County, Hebei.

Zenghouyi *Zun* tray of the Warring States Period, unearthed from Zenghouyi's Tomb in Suixian County, Hubei, represents the sophisticated bronze technology through the remarkable casting process.

the landocracy ruling legally. King Dao of the State of Chu appointed Wu Qi to carry out a renovation with the goal of changing the old hereditary fief and official administration systems and consolidating the centralized monarchy. The reform confronted fierce resistance due to the damage to the interests of the old nobles. For instance, after King Daowang of the State of Chu passed away, the conservative side killed Wu Qi with arrows. Wu had been hiding at the side of the King's body for shelter, He was killed despite the penalty of family extermination for damaging the king's body. However, after many setbacks, reforms won obvious effects in Qi, Jin, Zheng, Wu, Yue, Wei, Chu, Qin, Han, Zhao, Yan and other vassal states, including Shang Yang's Political Reform in the State of Qin in the middle Warring States Period.

In BC 356, Marquis of Xiao of the State of Qin appointed Shang Yang to launch a political reform. The main contents of the reform included awarding cultivation and battle feats,

abolishing the square-fields system and
the field boundaries and establishing
a county system. The new law abolished the hereditary position and salary system and set up 20 ranks for cor-

responding political and economic privileges to be awarded
equally according to feats. The reform attacked the nobles'
privileges and improved the morale and battle-effectiveness
of the army. It also ruled that those having high output of
grain and cloth would be exempt from duty service and taxes, playing the function of inspiring production activity and
improving state power. "Abolishing the square-fields system
and the field boundaries" refers to opening the boundaries
of the square-fields occupied by the nobles and admitting
the legality of private land to promote the development of
landocracy. The new law also divided the State of Qin into
31(or 41) counties to replace the fief system. The county
magistrates and assistants were appointed and dismissed by
the king and no heredity was allowed. The State of Qin also
compiled household registration and implemented penalties to implicate others related to the one charged or found
guilty. Normally five or 10 families formed a unit for super-
vising each other. In addition, Shang Yang formulated Qin
Rules and promulgated uniform metrology standards, making great contributions to unification.

The Square
Bronze *Sheng*
made by Shang
Yang is a standard
bronze measuring
instrument to unify
the metrology of
the Qin State.

Shang Yang performed two stages of reform in the State of
Qin for 20 years, making Qin gradually powerful and rich.
Shang Yang executed laws rigidly and cut off the nose and
tattooed the face of the Prince's tutor of anyone who sub-
orned the Prince to block the reform. When the Prince came
into power, Shang Yang was torn asunder by five carts. But
the laws continued and the new policies prevailed. The rapid rise of Qin in the remote western areas in the later period
of the Warring States was largely attributed to the profound

influence of Shang Yang's new policy. A century after the death of Shang Yang, King Ying Zheng of Qin took advantage of the influence of Shang Yang's reform that helped accelerate the pace of national unification.

First, Qin paid great attention to agriculture, laying a solid economic foundation for unification. The Dujiangyan Irrigation Project built by Qin's Shu County Major Li Bing is still irrigating thousands of *mu* of land and making the Chengdu Plain a fertile place where people no longer suffer starvation caused by drought and flood. The Zhengguo Channel, constructed in the Weihe River Plain under the leadership of Zheng Guo, irrigated 2.8 million *mu* of farmland, creating another enormous granary in the central Shanxi Plain.

The policy of honoring military exploits forged a brave army. The tri-ridge arrows unearthed from the Qin's terracotta warriors and horses pit had the sharpness to penetrate armors, which is proof of the brave Qin army's fine range of weapons. The six states' military force had a reputation for never escaping in the face of the Qin's army, as it was like "putting a heavy weight on bird's eggs."

Opening and enterprising policies and absorbing the merits of other states were important reasons for Qin's unification. In BC 238, a time shortly after King Ying Zheng of Qin came into power, the state of Han sent Zheng Guo to persuade Ying Zheng to dig a channel in the Jinghe basins to divert water for irrigation. This request was actually intended to exhaust the national strength of Qin and hinder its pace of marching eastward. But the plot failed before the channel was built. Facing the penalty, Zheng Guo said building the channel could do nothing but offer a few years more for the State of Han even though it consumed lots of fiscal revenue. But for the State of Qin, the great project would benefit later generations. Hearing this, the king of Qin changed his mind and let Zheng Guo continue its construction. However, patriarchal ministers argued that Qin's alien ministers should be dismissed since they came to Qin for persuasion and alienation. Li Si, an alien minister from Chu, submitted *Remonstrance on Dispelling Alien Ministers* to disprove them with the instances that the kings of Qin utilized alien ministers to build Qin. Then Ying Zheng became aware of the importance of alien ministers and cancelled the order for dispelling ministers and called Li Si back. He and other alien ministers played an active role in helping Ying Zheng unify the other six states into one country.

From BC 230 to BC 221, Ying Zheng directed his army to conquer six states and established the first centralized empire in Chinese history.

Instances of vassals contending for hegemony and progress in social reform were interwoven into the period. Collapsed ritualism and musical systems and social turmoil offered an open space for reform in states. Reform was the only way to make the country and army powerful and win the competition in the chaotic situation. Warfare for merging and seizing power was endowed with the added significance of expanding reform and new policy. On the basis of destroying the old system, the new unification made by the emerging landocracy showed the people's will and promoted the huge progress of society.

Cultural Awakening and Contention of a Hundred Schools of Thought

In the late Spring and Autumn Period and the Warring States Period, the iron tools and ox-led farming enhanced rapid development of productivity, boosted commerce and town prosperity, and seriously impacted the traditional ritual order. In the reform fever of various kingdoms, a batch of scholars broke the parochial clan network and moved freely.

They maneuvered among various political groups and gave lectures here and there, greatly enlarging their field of vision and enhancing cultural awakening.

In the Spring and Autumn Period, the pattern of "cultural learning exclusive to officials and nobles" was broken, and "private schools" for spreading culture established by scholars gradually prevailed. For instance, Confucius of the State of Lu vigorously promoted the thought of "education for all," with more than 3,000 disciples, including 72 famous ones, some of whom were of humble birth. Widespread education paved the way for the booming culture in that period of transformation.

An intensive yeoman economy showed much more benefits than the simple and extensive farming, which further

aroused the enthusiasm inside the producers. Furthermore, the highly-developed handicrafts and commercial sectors and the reforms in all kingdoms aimed at building a more prosperous society helped achieve great scientific and technological progresses in the Spring and Autumn and Warring States periods. Bronze casting techniques were extremely mature, resulting in a vast number of superb bronze artworks. Raw iron could be smelted as early as the Spring and Autumn Period, and cast iron techniques were invented in the Warring States Period, which was 2,000 years earlier than those in the West. The Spring and Autumn Period saw the production of the world's earliest cementite steel. The Warring States Period witnessed the accomplishment of the Dujiangyan Irrigation System, built by the masses and led

Dujiangyan Irrigation System, constructed under the leadership of Li Bing and his son, still plays the roles of anti-flood and irrigation today.

by Li Bing and his son. The irrigation system, consisting of the fish-mouth water diversion dike, bottleneck and flying, and weir, was able to prevent and drain floods, as well as irrigate and carry boats. It helped the Chengdu Plain develop into a land of abundance and can irrigate tens of millions *mu* of land even today.

Astronomically, *The Shi Star Catalogue* recorded the world's earliest observations of comets in BC 613. *The Shi Star Catalogue*, the world's first star catalogue, recorded the positions of more than 120 stars. Arithmetically, the 9x9 Formula for Multiplication and the Method of Count Calculating were invented. Physically, the *Mohist Canon*, written in the Warring States Period, includes the Lever Principle and the Theory of Buoyancy, as well as knowledge about acoustics and optics—proof of outstanding achievements made in ancient China. Medically, Bian Que, a famous doctor in the Warring States Period, established a theory of four diagnostic procedures, namely inspection, auscultation and olfaction, inquiry, and pulse-taking and palpation. These procedures have been adopted by Chinese doctors for 2,000 years and Bian Que was thus reputed as the "ancestor of Chinese pulse-taking science."

Portrait of Qu Yuan.

Great scientific advances sped up the awakening of rationalism and cultural spirit.

The Spring and Autumn Period saw the emergence of China's first poetry collection, *The Book of Odes*, which is a compilation of 305 odes written in the 500 years from the early Western Zhou to the middle Spring and Autumn Period. The book has three parts, namely *Feng*, *Ya* and *Song*. The *Feng* section (also named *Guofeng*) is of the highest quality, with records of folk songs in the Spring and Autumn Period that include satires on the ruling class, praises for the protesting spirit of the masses, and wishes for beautiful love. With simple and rich languages, *The Book of Odes* mainly contains four-character sentences and many overlapping sentence forms, marking the formation of Chinese poetry. The inclination toward realism and rhetoric means of Fu, Bi and Xing had a far-reaching influence on poets of later generations. In the subsequent Warring States Period, Chu odes, a new form of poetry based on folk songs in the state of Chu in the south, emerged and became popular. With free-style sentences, they are more suitable for expressing complicated feelings. *The Lament*, written by Qu Yuan, was a collection of famous works in Chu odes expressing his political hopes and patriotic feelings. The poems feature the repeated use of symbol and metaphor, and combine myth, legend, historical figures and natural scenes with magnificent words, distinctive imagination, strong feelings and profound concepts.

Portrait of Confucius.

The Book of Odes, with *Guofeng* as its representative, and Chu odes, with *The Lament* as their representative, are usually combined and called Feng Sao, which reflect the emergence of early cultural spirits and respectively started the realistic and romanticist styles of ancient Chinese poetry.

Two great thinkers with far-reaching influence on Chinese history emerged in the Spring and Autumn Period—Confucius and Lao Tze.

Confucius, named Qiu and style-named Zhongni, was a thinker of the State of Lu. His thoughts were mainly recorded in The Analects of Confucius, a book compiled by his disciples. The essence of Confucianism is Ren (benevolence)

and Li (ritual norms). He advocated the idea that "the benevolent loves his fellow people," and requested the rulers experience and observe the situation of the people. He was against tyranny and arbitrary punishment. He advocated the behavior codes of loyalty and tolerance, and called for "not doing to others what you don't want to be done to you" and understanding others to adjust personal relationships and stabilize social order. Confucius also held the opinions of "ruling by morality" and "ruling with the ritual norms" and maintaining the political and educational system of the country by restraining oneself and restoring the ritual system and practice of moral norms. He attempted to correct the confused social class orders in accordance with the ritual system of the Zhou Dynasty and make it perfectly justifiable. This reflected Confucius' conservative political ideology. However, Confucius was not against improving and reforming some obsolete ritual customs and political orders on the basis of maintaining the old system based on social classes. Mencius and Xun Zi in the Warring States Period inherited and developed Confucius' theory and made the political ideals and moral norms of Confucianism the mainstream of traditional thought in China for more than two millennia.

Lao Tze on an Ox. It is said that Lao Tze, at the sight of the decline of the Zhou Dynasty, rode an ox out of the Pass and vanished from the earthly life.

Lao Tze, surnamed Li, named Er and style-named Ran, was a thinker of the State of Chu. Erudite and knowledgeable, he was once the historical official in the royal court of Eastern Zhou, responsible for managing collections.

Confucius once asked Lao Tze about the knowledge about "ritual norms." *Tao Te Ching*, a book compiled by the followers of Taoism in the Warring States Period, records all the thoughts of Lao Tze and is full of philosophy and wisdom typical of the oriental world. Lao Tze denied the absolute authority of destiny, advocated following natural laws and ruling without intervention. "Ruling without intervention" stands for not intervening arbitrarily. Lao Tze warned the rulers not to oppress the common people too much. However, his ideal that "though the noises made by the chickens and dogs can be heard, the people do not contact each other until death" and his opinion "making the people ignorant and without desire" led to some negative effects. His philosophy contains rich dialectic thinking. Lao Tze pointed out that everything has two contradictory sides, for example—high and low, front and rear, existence and void, difficult and easy, life and death, noble and humble—and both parties could transfer to the opposite. Lao Tze has been regarded by later generations as the founder of Taoism, whose thoughts imposed great influence upon Chinese culture, including philosophy and ethics, as well as the mode of thinking, morality and personality of the Chinese people.

Portrait of Mencius.

The increasingly intense competition among all vassal states for hegemony in the Warring States Period led to a more urgent need for talents. The profound social reforms offered scholars with improving consciousness a broad stage for independent thinking and creative exploration.

King Xuan of Qi once had hotels near Jimen, Linzi, capital of Qi, expanded to accommodate literators and persuasive talkers, and awarded such scholars as Zou Yan, Tian Pian and Shen Dao mansions and official titles to encourage them write books and establish theories. The academic house at Ji-men then grew into a center for communication among various sorts of academic cultures. Under such a background, representatives from different class and schools offered different opinions towards different issues and held discussions with each other, resulting in the situation of "contention of a hundred schools of thought."

Among the active schools of thought were Confucianism, Mohist School, Taoism, Legalism, Yin-Yang School, the School of Names, Military School and the School of Eclectics.

Mencius and Xun Zi were the representatives of Confucianism in the Warring States Period. Mencius further developed the "benevolence" thought of Confucius into a systematic political doctrine, proposing the concept of "The people are the most important element in a state; next are the gods of land and grain; least is the ruler himself." He also stressed "righteousness comes first and then the benefit" and "giving one's life for righteousness," and advocated the spirit of "never to be corrupted by wealth or title, never depart from your principles when in poverty and hardship, and surrender never to power and force." Xun Zi said that ruling a state should be based on ritual norms and supplemented by laws. He also held the opinion that "nature has its laws" that wouldn't be changed by humans' wills, but humans should give play to their abilities to "make use of the objective laws" and thus benefit themselves.

Portrait of Zhuang Tzu.

The founder of Mohist School was Mo Tzu, a man of humble birth in the State of Lu. He was once a craftsman and later became a senior official of the Song State. Mo Tzu advocated "universal love," going far beyond the concept of "benevolence" proposed by Confucius that was based on different classes. He considered all the people are equal, no matter they are nobles or commoners. He also upheld "respecting the wise," employing talented people regardless of which class they come from, and proposed "respecting the working people," stressing the position of labor in the society. Meanwhile, Mo Tzu opposed extravagance and waste, advocated "thrift in daily life and funerals." The book *Mo Tzu* that has been passed down for generations also greatly contributes to natural science and logical science. The Mohist School highlights the interests of the working class, especially those of craftsmen. It was once prominent and widely adopted and cited by other schools.

Zhuang Tzu inherited and developed the thoughts of Lao Tze and was the representative of Taoism in the Warring States Period. He was named Zhou and born in the State of Song. He despised wealth and fame, hated the unfair social phenomena of "stealing ideas from one person is plagiarism, and stealing ideas from many is research." He once refused the request of the King of Chu to be a senior official, and earned a living by making grass shoes and wrote books for recreation instead. Zhuang Tzu upheld the idea that "natural law" has its own roots and everything is the same in nature. On such a basis, he put forward a playful living attitude of pondering over nothing, and worrying about nothing. He pointed out that "dimensions are limitless, and time is endless." He recognized the infinity of time and space and believed that humans should obey the natural laws. Politically, Zhuang Tzu upheld the thought of ruling without intervention.

Han Fei, a philosopher of the late Warring States Period, was an integrator of Legalism. In his philosophy, the ruler firmly controls the state with the help of three concepts: his position of power (*Shi*), certain techniques (*Shu*), and laws (*Fa*) to set up a monarchic despotism. He believed laws were the basis of handling state affairs, techniques were the tools for the emperor to control the ministers, and power was the regime and influence of the emperor. He advocated "ruling a state according to law" and "laws don't protect the powerful persons," which was of positive significance for attacking the privileges of former nobles and maintaining the centralized system of emerging landocracy. He believed that the society keeps developing and changing, and history will never reverse itself. He was against the historical concept of Confucians, "confirming the ancient practice and denying today's practice" and advocated reform. In his opinion, ruling the people with the politics of ancient kings was as ridiculous as standing by a tree stump waiting for a hare to dash itself against it. Han Fei's philosophy met the requirements of establishing a centralized regime and was advocated by Ying Zheng, which made Han's philosophy the guiding concept of ruling the country.

Portrait of Han Fei.

In the more than one millennium since the Western Han Dynasty, his thought and Confucianism supported each other and became the theoretical foundation of the ruling thought of ancient China. The spirit of reform became the theoretical weapon for progressive thinkers and politicians in the following generations to implement reform.

Yin-Yang School was a school of thought emerging in the late Warring States Period. They socialized the Five-Element Theory known as "Metal, Wood, Water, Fire and Earth," and believed that social evolution is just like changes of the five elements and the "natural laws" that control everything move in cycles. Representatives include Zou Yan of the State of Qi, who had great influence upon the social ideology in the Qin and Han dynasties.

The School of Names was a school that analyzed and "rectified" the turbulent situation of mixing names with realities in the times of social reforms. Representatives were Hui Shi and Gongsun Long. The followers viewed the similarity-difference relations from a philosophical perspective, and pointed out the distinctions between feelings and objective facts, as well as entities and attributes. This helped develop logic in China.

The founder of the Military School was Sun Wu, a militarist in the Spring and Autumn Period. His *Art of War* reveals many tactics of deploying troops as well as military laws such as the systematic and overall way of controlling. He also created a complete system of military theories. It has been considered a classic book of military science that can ensure "fighting a hundred battles with no danger of defeat" and enjoyed an extremely high reputation worldwide. The representative of the Military School in the Warring States Period was Sun Bin, the descendant of Sun Wu. As the military advisor of Qi, Sun Bin once directed the classic battle known as "saving the Zhao by besieging the capital of the Wei." Inheriting the thoughts of Sun Wu, he stressed commanding the rules of war and creating favorable situations for oneself and highlighted the role of people. His military thoughts were compiled into the book entitled *Sun Bin's Art of War*, which had bamboo-slip versions from the Han Dynasty.

The thoughts of the School of Eclectics were a combination of the above. It was a school shaped in the late Warring States Period, with *Lu's Spring and Autumn Annals* as the most famous representative work. Focusing on the idea of "acting according to the ways of nature," the book was about state-governing politics that integrate the diverse thoughts of many schools. The Eclectics held that kings should respect teachers and advocate education, put public interests in front of their own, employ talented people and rule the state without arbitrary intervention. Kings should also follow the wills of the people and unify the country with righteous armies.

The argument among the pre-Qin schools and their mutual influence greatly helped promote the prosperity of thoughts and culture. The creative concepts and theories established in all the representative works cover a wide range of fields, including politics, economy, military science, laws, education, philosophy, history, literature, art and natural science, jointly constituting the original classics that guide Chinese ideology and the fundamental spirit of traditional Chinese culture.

Around 5th century BC, both the eastern civilization and western civilization reached a very high level of development. They affected each other and jointly created a spectacle that marked the start of a brand-new era in human history. The city-state democratic politics of ancient Greece, established on the basis of a slavery economy, gave rise to such great thinkers as Socrates, Plato and Aristotle. Meanwhile the profound yeoman reforms and social transformation in China's Spring and Autumn and Warring States periods offered the environment for the rise of many cultural masters like Confucius and Lao Tze. The philosophers in both the east and west jointly built numerous lofty monuments for human civilization.

Qin and Han Dynasties: Establishment and Development of a Great Unified Country

Qin Dynasty Lay the Foundation for Great Unification

The Qin and Han dynasties, from BC 221 to 220 AD, were the first unified multiethnic centralized states in Chinese history, laying the foundation for a great united empire.

In BC 221, Qin continued expansion outward after merging the six states. It suppressed Baiyue in the southeastern coast and southern China and the ethnic groups in southwestern areas and established administrative organs there for unified management. Qin's troops also attacked the Huns in the north, regained the Great Bend of the Yellow River to migrate and cultivate, and constructed the Great Wall to consolidate the northern defense. Finally, Qin established an unprecedented vast empire with a population of 20 million multiethnic people.

Portrait of Emperor Shihuang of the Qin Dynasty.

Ying Zheng, after unifying the six states, called himself "Shihuangdi" (the first emperor) because he thought "his merits are better than the Five Emperors (Huangdi, Zhuan Xu, Di Ku, Tang Yao and Yu Shun) and the land under his rule is larger than those of Three Kings (Fu Xi, Nu Wa and Shen Nong)" and established supreme power. Emperor Shihuang of the Qin Dynasty, insisting on and developing the social reform evolving from the Spring and Autumn and the Warring States periods, implemented a series of measures to intensify the centralized sovereignty.

With respect to the political system, Emperor Shihuang of the Qin Dynasty believed the fief system was the source of the ceaseless wars since the Spring and Autumn Period and thought "it's time to set up armies because peace has returned and the country is unified." He accepted the suggestion of Li Si to award his sons and the officials who performed deeds of great merit but not enfeoff them, and further established a complete set of bureaucratic administration systems at both central and local levels.

The emperor controlled the country's military power, and the throne was inherited by his descendants from generation to generation. At the central level, there were three chief ministers and nine departments. The "three chief ministers" referred to the prime minister, military minister and supervision minister. The prime minister assisted the emperor in handling political affairs and led all the other officials. The military minister assisted the emperor in military affairs, and the supervision minister was responsible for supervision and law enforcement as well as literature management. The three ministers were not subject to one another and all obeyed the emperor's orders. The nine departments included the administrative organizations at the central level and those in charge of royal affairs. The system established imperial power as supreme, and the prime minister as the leading official. All the officials were responsible for their own business, and for laying a foundation for the organizational pattern of ancient Chinese central government.

Qin's bronze weight. On its body, "eight *Jin*" and the imperial decree for unifying metrology promulgated on the 26th year of Qin are engraved.

Two levels of administrative organizations, namely prefectures and counties, were established nationwide, shaping local bureaucratic administration systems. A prefecture was the higher-level administration organization for the central government directly governing the local. The supreme executive of the prefecture was named the prefecture governor (*Junshou*). The *Juncheng* (prefecture governor's assistant)

Sketch for unified coin. Upon the unification of Emperor Shihuang of the Qin Dynasty, the spade-shaped coins, knife-shaped coins and bronze shells circulated in previous kingdoms were unified into a kind of round coin with a square hole.

helped the prefecture governor handle administrative affairs, criminal punishment and prison affairs, while the *Junwei* (prefecture governor's assistant officer) was in charge of military affairs and public security of the prefecture. Under the prefecture, county governments were set up. The responsibilities of the county executive, county executive's assistant and county executive's assistant officer were similar to those of the officials at the prefectural level. The officials of the prefecture and the county were assessed, appointed and dismissed by the central government. Under the county level, there were the basic organization township and Li (administrative units of 25 neighboring households). Among the township officials, *Sanlao* was responsible for education, *Sefu* was responsible for case hearing and taxation and *Youjiao* was responsible for public security.

The country governed the people and levied taxes through the three chief ministers and nine departments as well as administrative organizations at various local levels, and the individual household became the basic unit of society in the country.

In the economic sphere, Emperor Shihuang ordered land-lords and yeomen who owned land to make household reg-istrations based on the actual land occupation situation. The country then practiced area-based taxation. Thus, private ownership of land was confirmed by law to protect the ad-vanced landocracy economy mode. Before the unification of the Qin Dynasty, the currencies of different vassal states had different shapes, sizes and weights, and the measuring units were not the same, which hindered the development of na-tionwide commodity exchange and tax collection. In BC 221, Emperor Shihuang unified the currency and promulgated metrological standards to strengthen the economic ties among regions and promote commodity economy develop-ment, which was helpful for the country's economic unity.

After unification, Qin removed the barricades built by the six states, unified vehicle specifications and built a network centered around its capital Xianyang (northeast of today's Xianyang, Shaanxi). During the unification of the south of the Five Ridges, the Lingqu Canal was dug to link the Yang-tze River and the Pearl River systems. A "five-*Chi*-wide" valley road was built in the hills from today's Yibin, Sichuan to Qujing, Yunnan. These measures ensured the smooth communication of political decrees and army dispatch, pro-moted economic and cultural exchanges among the regions and ethnic groups and forged solid material foundation for a unified state.

Before unification, the languages and characters of the state areas were different. After unification, Emperor Shihuang regulated the *Xiaozuan* font as the standard for the whole country. It helped the country in terms of political decree implementation and cultural exchange and greatly intensi-fied the regions and ethnic groups' sense of identification and belonging to Chinese culture. In the succeeding 2,000 years, written Chinese maintained a unified form, having an extremely profound influence on the concentration and consolidation of a unified multiethnic country.

After the unification, the Qin Dynasty also absorbed relevant rules and regulations of the former six states to formulate a legal system of Qin, which covered a wide range of areas including criminal laws, procedure laws, civil laws, economic laws and administrative laws.

In BC 213, some conservative Confucians insisted "no sustainable governance would be achieved without imitating ancient people and following long-established rules." Li Si firmly criticized those opponents. Emperor Shihuang accepted the suggestion of Li Si and further strengthened ideological control. He only allowed public schools and prohibited private schools, ordered the historiographers to burn historical records and all folk books including *The Book of Odes, The Book of History* and other books of all schools except *The History of Qin* and the books on medicine and forestation. He also regulated that those participating in private discussions on *The Book of Odes* and *The Book of History* shall be executed and the entire family of those disagreeing with the current situation and politics shall be exterminated. In BC 212, some scholars and alchemists blamed Emperor Shihuang of being "greedy for power" and "glad at severe penalty." More than 400 people were arrested and buried alive under the crime of defamation. Although the action of burning books and burying scholars alive suppressed opposition and safeguarded the centralized reign, the cruel manner caused a huge loss to Chinese culture and had a negative political influence.

Most of the wars and projects initiated by Emperor Shihuang had great and progressive significance. However, the urgent deployment, heavy taxation, rigid penalties, especially the construction of palaces and tombs, brought a heavy burden and suffering to the people. In BC 210, Emperor Shihuang died of illness during a tour of inspection. Emperor Ershi of the Qin Dynasty succeeded to the throne. The ruling classes struggled with each other, resulting in heavier taxation, crueler punishment and a rapidly intensifying social division. In BC 209, a large-scale peasant uprising led by Chen Sheng and Wu Guang took place, which heavily shook the rule of the Qin Dynasty. In BC 207, the Qin Dynasty ended under the attack of Xiang Yu, Liu Bang and other forces. After the four-year Chu-Han War, Liu Band defeated Xiang Yu in BC 202 and set up the Han Dynasty in Chang'an (today's Xi'an), known as the Western Han Dynasty in history.

Though the Qin Dynasty ended only after the ruling of two emperors, the new systems established by Emperor Shihuang made pioneering contributions to the development of China as a unified multiethnic country and took Chinese history on a new path in the following 2,000 years.

A tiger-shaped tally issued by Emperor Shihuang of the Qin Dynasty to generals stationed in Yangling is divided into two halves with a 12-character inscription on both parts saying "the tally for troop movement with the emperor holds the right part and the generals in Yangliang the left." The left and right half must match each other for troop dispatch.

Western Han Dynasty's Strategies on Consolidating Centralized Ruling

The tyranny and turmoil at the end of the Qin Dynasty had left a poor economic situation for the early Han Dynasty. The rulers of the early Han Dynasty learned the lessons from the extermination of Qin and applied a rehabilitation policy. During the period of Emperor Wendi and Emperor Jingdi, the economy recovered and society stabilized, beginning the first peaceful period in Chinese ancient history. Based on this, Emperor Wudi of the Han Dynasty displayed his grand talents for further exploitation and development and reached the culmination of the Western Han.

The Western Han continued Qin's basic grand unification policy while abolishing its tyranny. Moreover, some adjustments and renewals were made, further consolidating and developing the layout of the unified multiethnic country initiated by Qin.

Economically, rehabilitation was practiced with policies of reducing taxation and corvee, and awarding production. Liu Bang, Emperor Gaozu of the Han Dynasty, promulgated a range of favored measures including releasing soldiers to farming fields, offering amnesty and enlistment of refugees, freeing servants and maids to suitable places, reducing and exempting corvee and setting the land rent at 1/15, resulting in a mass movement of population back to agricultural production. Emperor Wendi applied agricultural and textile development to evaluate local officials and reduced the land rent to 1/30. These measures pushed the rapid recovery and development of agriculture. Emperor Wudi further promoted the official monopoly of salt and iron, collected industrial and commercial taxes, established buffer institutions to control prices, unified the currency, prohibited private coin casting and implemented other financial reforms. Thus, the country firmly grasped the economy and increased financial income, laying a solid economic foundation for a grand unified empire.

Eaves tile saying "Han's dominance over China," unearthed from Chang'an site, Xi'an, Shaanxi.

As for the state regime, the Western Han Dynasty experienced a process of ups and downs. In the early Han Dynasty, Liu Bang awarded some ministers with grand feats as vassals from different families. Fief and prefecture organization coexisted. The area of seven vassals' fiefs equaled half of the territory of the Western Han Dynasty. They had their own troops and constituted a threat to the imperial power.

Liu Bang exterminated the vassals successively and subin-feudated his nephews. He hoped to rely on Liu's families to defend the borders. With the passing of time, the vassals of the same surname gradually became more powerful and did things in their own way. They established laws, collected taxes and tributes and cast coins without permission from the central government and were richer than the emperor. They even organized armed rebellions to challenge the central authority. Emperor Jingdi's acceptance of Minister Cao Cuo's suggestion on "removing monarchs" aroused the joint rebellion of Wu, Chu and five other states. Emperor Jiingdi was forced to kill Cao Cuo to apologize to the seven states, but that didn't stop the attack from the rebel forces. Finally, General Zhou Yafu received the orders in face of danger and defeated the enemies. After putting down the rebellions, the court concentrated the vassals' power to the central government. Emperor Wudi learned the lesson from the rebellion caused by feoffing and promulgated the "fief expansion order" for further distribution of fief to greatly reduce the vassals' might. He also divested 106 marquises of their ranks at one sacrifice ceremony on the pretext that the gold they presented was of insufficient weight and poor quality.

Meanwhile, Emperor Wudi also strengthened imperial power in controlling the central and local administrative institutions. To firmly control the country's supreme power, he promoted some middle and lower officials to form a "central court" to assist the emperor in decision-making, while the "outer court" led by the prime minister only took care of political affairs. The supervision system was an important part of the centralized political system and was greatly strengthened in the Han Dynasty. Emperor Wudi of the Han Dynasty established a position of *Silixiaowei* at the central level to supervise the behavior of officials and imperial members. He also divided the country into 13 supervision areas, which were called "13 state-departments," and sent one *Cishi* to each state-department to inspect local officials, curb and attack the illegally rich people on behalf of the central government. Thus, the centralized regime was enhanced.

The rulers of the Han Dynasty practiced the recommendation system. The local officials recommended talents to the court, which appointed the recommended persons according to their capabilities with examination. The government enrolled persons with special reputations and capabilities to officiate in the court, which was named *Zheng* (enrollment). The practice under which a senior official recruited his subordinates was named *Pi*. The official selection system attached more importance to the capabilities of the recommended but could easily cause cronyism, consequently giving rise to phenomena such as the recommended scholar could not read and the recommended *Xiaolian* (filial to one's parents and clean as an official) did not live with his parents.

To avoid decades of governance of an official in a local place that might resulted in corruption or setup of a separate regime, the Han Dynasty set years of terms for major local officials, and the officials' origins and any blood relations with their superior leaders would be considered as well.

The prevailing quiet and inactive Huangdi and Lao Tze Doctrine in early Han Dynasty had a loose ideological space, which was a departure from the growing centralization. The political situation during the reign of Emperor Wudi was stable, and the national power was strong. Hence, ideological control was strengthened. Emperor Wudi adopted Dong Zhongshu's suggestion of "rejection of various philosophical schools and exclusive reverence of Confucianism." Confucianism, which propagated centralized rule, obtained the position of the dominant official ideology. The policy penetrated into politics, ideology, culture and education, helping consolidate the centralization and attack local regimes.

It had a far-reaching influence on intensifying the power of concentration of Chinese culture and the monarch's control of popular thought.

The renovation measures concerning politics, economy, ideology and other aspects implemented by Emperor Wudi based on actual situation proved quite fruitful and drove forward the development of the unified multiethnic country initiated by Qin.

Consolidating Northern Borders and Developing Western Regions

The Qin and Han dynasties saw the rise of nomad Huns living in northern Mongolian Plateau. The oases west of Yumen Pass and Yangguan Pass, including present-day Xinjiang, Central Asia and even further areas, were called Western Regions, where "36 kingdoms" including Wusun and Cheshi were created. The Western Regions were conquered by the Huns in the early Han Dynasty. Hun and the Qin and

The Site of Western Han's Great Wall, Yumen Pass, Dunhuang, Gansu.

Zhaojun to the Border Area by Qiu Ying in the Ming Dynasty.

Han dynasties were confronted with each other along the natural agricultural boundary respectively in the North and South. The relationship between both parties had a direct effect on the stability and development of the river bends, the Western Regions and even the unified multiethnic country.

In BC 215, General Meng Tian, dispatched by Emperor Shihuang of the Qin Dynasty, led a troop of 300,000 to attack the Huns, regaining the previously-occupied river bends and establishing counties there. To defend intrusion from the Huns, Qin kept and cemented the old walls along the northern borders built by the former states of Yan, Zhao and Qin. The effort resulted in the initial formation of the world-famous Great Wall that extends from Lintao, Gansu in the west and ends in Liaodong in the east. Twelve prefectures were set up along the walls and a vast number of people immigrated there to consolidate the border areas. That laid a foundation for stabilizing the northern borders and developing the Western Regions.

The early Han Dynasty saw a depressed economy and failures in its defending wars against the Huns. Even peace-making marriages and bribery couldn't stop the Huns from a large-scale intrusion. Relying on stronger national strength, Emperor Wudi waged two great battles successively in places south and north of the Yellow River, driving the Huns out of South Desert. He further sent Wei Qing and Huo Qubing to chase the Huns in the North Desert. Meanwhile, a vigorous effort was made to build the walls along the areas west of the Yellow River, with beacon towers at short intervals extending west to the Lop Nur in Xinjiang.

Before long, the Huns broke up into several parts. Huhanxie, Khan of Hun led his troops to submit to the Han Dynasty and agreed "the Han Dynasty and Hun are in one family and no cheating or attacking is allowed." Emperor Yuandi of the Han Dynasty accepted the request of the Huns for a peace-making marriage and married Wang Zhaojun, a court lady, to Huhanxie as a princess. That resulted in decades of peace and stability in northern border areas. Consolidating borders with walls, reclaiming land, developing traffic accompanied the peace-making marriages between the Han Dynasty and the Huns and the bilateral trade. That not only facilitated the social and economic development in the central plains, but also helped spread advanced culture and tap the border areas, and paved way for the rise of the frontiers. Livestock in the early Han Dynasty were few, and officials had to take oxcarts to travel around. While under the regime of Emperor Wudi, the areas south of the Great Wall saw "widespread horses and cattle in fields." Lots of

The fresco from the tomb of the Han Dynasty in Helinge'er, the Inner Mongolia, reflecting the farming life of the northern nomadic people at the time.

A piece of Dunhuang fresco: Zhang Qian bids farewell to Emperor Wudi of the Han Dynasty.

livestock were applied to farming and transportation, greatly enhancing the social productivity in the central plains. In the meantime, the Huns traded horses and cattle with inland merchants, getting large quantities of daily necessities and pushing forward the development of a livestock economy. Numerous unearthed cultural relics serve as proof that the iron plows, currencies, weighing and measuring instruments used in such areas as Gansu, Ordos of Inner Mongolia and Liaoyang of Northeast China had little difference with those adopted in inland areas.

The Hans' exploitation of the Western Regions was best reflected in the development of the Silk Road that started from Chang'an, through Hexi Corridor, present-day Xinjiang, to Central Asia and West Asia and finally to Europe. Along the land route that spanned across Asian and European continents, techniques concerning iron-casting, well-digging, iron-plowing and ox-led farming, silkworm-raising and silk-reeling as well as large quantities of metal tools and silk fabrics were transported from the east to west, speeding up the social progress of the western areas. In return, Akhal-Teke, camels, fur goods, grapes, megranates, benne, walnuts and other products of the Western Regions, as well as the wonderful alien music and dances, were introduced into inland areas, offering fresh impetus to the traditional Chinese culture. The trade road also connected the Han Dynasty with countries of ancient civilization like Kushan, Arsacid and Rome. In BC 1st century, the Roman emperor Caesar was once dressed in a "coat of Heaven" made of Chinese silk, and the Europeans called the Han Dynasty "Seres," which meant "the country of silk." Plinius, a Roman natural historian, mentioned in his book *Natural History* that "despite the variety of iron, none could be paralleled with the iron from China (the Han Dynasty)." Furthermore, Buddhism of ancient India, magic of Rome and some alien sculpturing and painting art were also introduced from the west to east. The opening of the Asia-Europe passageway, called "Silk Road" by later generations, tightly connected the Western Regions with the central plains and imposed a far-reaching influence on the cultural exchanges between the east and west and the development of human civilization.

The territory under Emperor Wudi was twice as large as that of the Qin Dynasty. The population reached 60 million at the peak of his rule. The establishment of such a vast and populous empire required mature political and economic systems and operation mechanisms, efficient management, harmonious relationships between the central and local governments and among ethnic groups, and a concentrated power based on consistent cultural concepts and value orientation. Although territories changed, dynasties were replaced and regime divisions and mergers were constant occurrences, the grand trend of unity was never reversed. An important factor in

The gold coin of the Eastern Roman unearthed from the Silk Road.

The bronze
galloping horse
from the Eastern
Han Dynasty,
unearthed from
Wuwei, Gansu.

ancient China was overcoming its divided status to create a
unique continuous civilization.

At the end of the Western Han Dynasty, Wang Mang, a
relative of the emperor on the side of his wife, seized power
and crowned himself in 9 AD, starting the Xin Dynasty to
replace the Western Han. But, 14 years later, uprising peasants called Lulin and Chimei captured Chang'an and exterminated Xin. In 25 AD, Liu Xiu resumed the Han Dynasty
in Luoyang, known as the Eastern Han Dynasty. Liu Xiu
released the servants and maids and reduced taxation. Thus,
the society and economy recovered and developed. The
power of local despots that he relied on also expanded ac-
cordingly. At the end of the Eastern Han Dynasty, the court
was controlled by eunuchs and the relatives of the emperor
on his wife's side. The struggle and strife led to social turbulence. Under the onslaught of the Huangjin Peasant Uprising, imperial power declined and passed into the hands of
scattered warlords. In 220 AD, Cao Pi dethroned Emperor
Xiandi of the Han Dynasty and established the Wei Dynasty
in Luoyang, indicating the end of the Eastern Han.

Booming Culture in Qin and Han Dynasties

The establishment of the unified country offered a fundamental foundation for sustainable cultural growth. The Qin and Han dynasties witnessed further advances of science and culture based on the great leap in pre-Qin period and the consequent prosperous situation featuring all-around cultural development.

The invention of the paper-making technique was the most prominent contribution made to human civilization. Chinese characters first appeared on pottery, tortoise shells and bronze ware, and later on bamboo slips and silk cloth, which were either heavy or expensive and made cultural spreading difficult. In the early Western Han Dynasty, workmen, while beating pods into silk, occasionally found that characters could be written on the remaining silk

The manilla paper map from the Western Han Dynasty, unearthed from Fangmatan, Tianshui, Gansu.

Pottery Boat
of the Eastern
Han Dynasty,
unearthed in
Guangzhou,
Guangdong.

membranes. Enlightened by the process, the Chinese people adopted flax as raw materials to produce the earliest plant fiber paper, which was still rough and not suitable for writing. In the Eastern Han Dynasty, the eunuch Cai Lun resorted to tree barks, flax cloth, rags, old fishing nets and other raw materials that were easy to acquire to make quality but cheap paper, which were called "Marquis Cai Paper." From then on, paper was produced on a large scale and became the most popular material for writing.

China's paper-making technique was first exported to Korea and Vietnam, and then to Japan in the 7th century, to Arabian counties in the 8th century and further to Europe in the 12th century. That played a significant role in worldwide cultural spreading, accumulation and communication, and had a profound impact upon the progress of world civilization.

The iron-smelting sector of the Han Dynasty remained as advanced as before. Quenching techniques were invented and coal was used as the fuel for smelting. In the Eastern Han Dynasty, wind power was utilized in metal smelting, and a low-temperature steel-making technique was invented and popularized as well. With regard to ship-making, more efficient sculls, more flexible stern steering wheels, cloth sails relying on wind power and firmer anchors were invented, leading to improved navigation techniques. With regard to the handicraft sector, the superb black porcelains made in the late Eastern Han Dynasty marked the maturity of porcelain-making techniques that were first initiated in China. Improving silk embroidery workmanship resulted in more diversified categories of embroideries with exquisite patterns and bright colors that were exported to East Asia and Europe in large quantities and reputed by the Romans as "the world's No.1 fabrics." With regard to measuring celestial bodies, Zhang Heng of the Eastern Han Dynasty invented the earliest "armillary sphere" that revolved with hydraulic power. He also invented a seismograph that could precisely measure the direction of earthquakes that occurred thousands of miles away—more than 1,700 years earlier than similar devices invented in Europe.

Seismograph invented by Zhang Heng (mould).

The book photograph of Liu Hui's *The Nine Chapters on Mathematical Art*.

Unlike Greek classical mathematics that focused on theorem proving, ancient Chinese mathematics centered on algorithm creating, especially algorithms on solving equations. The *Zhou Bi Mathematical Manual* finished in the Western Han Dynasty, first records a special case in geometry known as Pythagorean Theorem, about 500 years earlier than that proposed in the west. *The Nine Chapters on Mathematical Art* written during the Eastern Han Dynasty was a collection of mathematical achievements

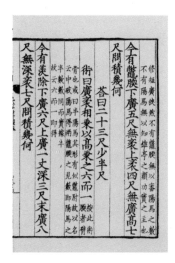

Portrait of Hua Tuo.

from pre-Qin to the Han Dynasty, and was respected as the most important book of algorithms. The book records all the algorithms on practical problems closely related to production, including those about land areas, grains, trade, warehouse sizes, earthwork and tax, and summarizes ways of calculating positive and negative numbers and solutions of quadratic equation. Its presence marked the formation of the ancient Chinese mathematical system in which counting rods were used as the calculation tool and the decimal system was adopted. The book was introduced to Japan in the Sui and Tang dynasties, and some parts of the book were spread to India and the Arab world, and even to Europe.

Many famous doctors and classic books emerged in the Han Dynasty. *The Yellow Emperor's Classic of Internal Medicine* during the Western Han Dynasty was a fundamental book of traditional Chinese medical theory. The book, which was comprised of two parts, had 162 articles in 18 volumes. It discussed basic theories concerning the body, physiology, causes of diseases, and diagnosis, as well as acupuncture, channels and collaterals, and health care. *Emperor Shen Nong's Materia Medica* written during the Eastern Han Dynasty was a summary of drug use since the Warring States Period and laid a foundation for subsequent Chinese pharmacology. Zhang Zhongjing, known as the "Medicine Saint" in the Eastern Han Dynasty, proposed a set of traditional Chinese theories in *The Treatise on Febrile Diseases*, including the three causes of diseases, and treatment according to syndrome differentiation. Hua Tuo, a highly skilled doctor in the Eastern Han, invented *Mafeisan*, the earliest surgical anesthetic, performed the first abdominal cavity operation in China, and invented the five-animal health care exercise.

Against the backdrop of unification, the official mainstream ideology in the Qin and Han dynasties experienced a transformation process from "contention of a hundred schools of thought" to "paying supreme tribute to one thought while banning all ways of spreading other schools of thought." The thought of legalists in the Warring States was adopted by Emperor Ying Zheng as a sharp tool pushing for the reform and, based on abandoning Confucianism and absorbing part of the diverse thoughts of many schools, further became the dominant ideology guiding the politics of the Qin Dynasty after the unification.

Stone Carvings of the Han Dynasty: Sermon.

In the early western Han Dynasty, the economy was seriously damaged and a host of neglected tasks cried for attention. Faced with the rehabilitation policy, the intellectual field was relatively loose and the philosophy of Huang Di and Lao Tze prevailed. During the term of Emperor Wudi, ideological control intensified as the political situation became more stable and the economy prospered. Dong Zhongshu, a representative of Confucianism, put forward the opinion of "paying supreme tribute to Confucianism while banning all other schools of thought" and "banning all ways of spreading other schools of thought" except Confucianism, which he believed could make the people know what to obey and thus safeguard the ruling of the emperor. Emperor Wudi accepted his suggestion and established it as a national strategy. The new Confucianism of Dong Zhongshu, in fact, was a new ideological

Portrait of Sima Qian.

system shaped by combining many schools of thought like Yin-Yang School, Taoism and Legalism, based on Confucius' political outlook of maintaining the hierarchical system and the thought of unification highlighted in *The Kung-Yang Commentary of the Spring and Autumn Annals*. Dong Zhongshu claimed that "social norms originate in the nature, and no changes in social norms shall happen without changes in the nature." He advocated that "regality is awarded by the heaven" based on the theory of "induction between the heaven and man." He also warned that if the emperor was brutal in his rule, the heavens would send calamities to condemn and deter the emperor. Therefore, the emperor must observe the way of the heavens and exercise benevolent rule. Dong emphasized that the emperor should rule the country with benevolence at its core and punishment as supplementary, and put forward the ethical norms of benevolence, righteousness, propriety, wisdom and fidelity. The three cardinal guides—the ruler guides his subjects, the father guides his son, and the husband guides his wife—were the cardinal guides that could not be changed.

"Paying supreme tribute to Confucianism while banning all other schools of thought" is an important event in the history of China. Confucianism occupied a dominant position in politics, which was conducive to consolidating the unified country and stabilizing the ruling order. Since then, Confucianism became the required course of all schools and the assessment standard for the court to select officials. Thus the dominant position of Confucianism was established in the traditional culture of China.

The Records of the Grand Historian, written by Sima Qian, and *The Book of Han*, written by Ban Gu, were two famous historical books arising from the time of unification. Sima Qian, once the Prefect of the Grand Scribes and the Chief of the Secretariat during the regime of Emperor Wudi,

compiled the first general history of biography in Chinese history by absorbing part of previous historical books and thought of many schools, making use of the files collected by the State and conducting field investigations and interviews. The book includes 130 chapters and more than 500,000 words, recording all the major historical events during the past 3,000 years from the legendary Huangdi to Emperor Wudi. It could be used to "study the relationship between humans and nature, understand the changes both in the past and at present and thus help shape unique and deep insight." *The Records of the Grand Historian* marked the fresh start of narrating historical events, systems, human activities and social changes by combining multiple ways of recording, including *Benji* (biographical sketches of kings), *Biao* (tables), *Shu* (records of systems), *Shijia* (records of vassals) and *Liezhuan* (biographies), and thus became the model for compiling historical books. *The Book of Han* written by Ban Gu was the first book of dynastic history, offering detailed and in-depth descriptions about the social evolution of the Han Dynasty.

The achievements of literature in the Han Dynasty were best reflected in the creation of Fu of the Han Dynasty and *Yuefu*. Fu is a kind of rhyme that combines the rational spirit of *The Book of Odes* before the Qin Dynasty with the romantic

Terracotta warriors and horses in the tombs escorting the Mausoleum of Emperor Shihuang of the Qin Dynasty.

expression of the Chu odes. Fu attaches importance to expatiation, parataxis and magnificent wording. Sima Xiangru and Yang Xiong were the most notable writers of Fu. Their works reflected the spirit of aggressive union of the Han Dynasty.

Yuefu was the musical department established during the reign of Emperor Wudi of the Han Dynasty. Poems collected, sorted and recorded by *Yuefu* department were called *Yuefu* poetry, which inherited and developed the excellent tradition of the folk songs in *The Book of Odes* and had lively language and various forms.

The Terracotta Warriors and Horses of Emperor Shihuang of the Qin Dynasty manifested the outstanding artistic achievements made in the Qin and Han dynasties with their exquisite artistic shapes and spectacular scale. Nearly 10,000 pieces of terracotta warriors and horses, all the same size as real ones, have different appearances and postures and were extremely vivid and lively. Inside the 14,000-square-meters No.1 pit is a huge army consisting of 6,000 terracotta warriors and horses, more than 40 chariots and 160 driving war horses. The army is "marching" eastward with the momentum of an avalanche like a living army, reproducing the gallant manner of the troops of Qin that bravely fought against the other six states in the central plains and manifesting the pioneering spirit of the time and the grandness of the unified empire.

Wei, Jin and Southern and Northern Dynasties: Regime Division and Ethnic Concentration

The Three Kingdoms Period and the Southern and Northern Dynasties

The period from 220 AD to 589 AD witnessed the rise and fall of the Wei, Jin, Southern and Northern Dynasties in Chinese history. A turbulent political situation, the rise of multiple hegemonies and the entry of northern ethnic groups into the central plains resulted in long-tem disunity of the country and confrontation between the south and north.

The main reason for the struggles among local warlords was the malignant expansion of local despots since the Eastern Han Dynasty. Upon the establishment of the Eastern Han, Liu Xiu awarded ministers and relatives greatly. Some famed families monopolized the key offices of the court for several generations. They greedily merged land by means of political privileges and set up nationwide manors. Bankrupted and exiled peasants were forced to attach themselves to the despots and landlords as tenant peasants. These landlords had political privileges and tyrannized the local areas. They had economic power over the tenant peasants. They also built high walls, moats and private armed forces. Seizing the opportunity of the turbulent situation, they crazily expanded their power, growing into warlord groups that monopolized local places and initiating wars against others for hegemony. That finally resulted in the rise of three powers, known as Caowei, Shuhan and Sunwu.

Cao Cao was once the Commander for Military Standards during the regime of Emperor Lingdi at the end of the Han Dynasty and participated in the allied troop crusading against the rebellious minister Dong Zhuo. He later defeated the Yellow Turbans Uprising at Qingzhou, incorporated more than 300,000 soldiers and further established a valiant army called "Qingzhou Troops." In 196 AD, Cao Cao took back Emperor Xiandi, who had been held under duress by

Dong Zhuo, and moved the capital to Xuxian (present-day Xuchang, Henan), gaining a favorable position of "coercing the king to control all his vassals." In 200 AD, he won the battle at Guandu against the troops of Yuan Shao and gained control over areas both north and south of the Yellow River. Cao Cao further conquered Wuhuan of Liaoxi, basically unifying the northern part of China. In 208 AD, he led a troop southward but was defeated by the allied army of Sun Quan and Liu Bei at Chibi, resulting in the pattern of separatist regimes among three kingdoms. Retreating to the north, Cao Cao successively occupied Guanzhong and Liangzhou and expanded the scope of his power in the northwest areas. Politically, Cao Cao respected the wise and believed talent was the only criterion for official selections. He also beefed up centralized ruling and attacked those who were getting rich or powerful through illegal means. Economically, he prohibited land merging, implemented the *Tuntian* System (a kind of government-encouraged agricultural system) and *Zudiao* System (a kind of tax system) and recruited exiled peasants

Painting of Chibi. The War at Chibi is decisive to the establishment of the confrontation of Three Kingdoms.

to reclaim barren land on a large scale. That greatly promoted the development of northern economy, which was once damaged by ceaseless wars, and helped the widespread desolate fields change into a land of harvest and abundance. After Cao Cao's death in 220 AD, Cao Pi dethroned Emperor Xiandi and established the Wei Dynasty, which was historically called Caowei.

Liu Bei was a descendant of the royal family of the Han Dynasty. After the family fortunes declined in his early years, he went to his relative, Liu Biao, the governor of Jinzhou, for help. As a man of ambition, Liu Bei always hoped for hegemony and went everywhere for talents who could assist him. It is said he once paid three visits to the thatched cottage in Longzhong, Jinzhou to invite Zhuge Liang, who had retreated for refuge. Following the death of Liu Biao, Liu Bei controlled Jinzhou. In 211 AD, he attacked Hanzhong and further occupied Yizhou in Sichuan, consolidating his rule over the southwestern regions. In 221 AD, Liu Bei declared himself a descendant of the former imperial family and established a state, historically called Shuhan, with the capital in Chengdu. Assisted by Prime Minister Zhuge Liang, Liu Bei implemented clean politics and paid particular attention to the state's relations with local ethnic groups. Economically, he also made a vigorous effort to popularize raising silkworms, and to develop iron-smelting, textile and other handicraft sectors, leading to the rapid development of the southwestern regions and close ties with the central plains.

Relying on rich and powerful landlords and inheriting his family fortunes in areas south of the Yangtze, Sun Quan was confronted with Caowei across the Yangtze

Terracotta figure with sword, unearthed in Changsha, Hunan, presents the image of a military official or soldier of the Western Jin Dynasty.

Brick carving of the
Southern Dynasty:
Ladies' Outing.

and energetically expanded in areas south of the river. He
later eliminated the forces of Liu Bei from Jinzhou and occupied Lingnan, extending his scope of power southeastward.
In 229 AD, Sun Quan ascended the throne, established Ji-
anye (present-day Nanjing) as the capital and changed the
state tile to Wu, which was historically called Sunwu. Sun
Quan had outstanding achievements in developing the
economy in the backward areas south of the Yangtze.

Wu, Shu and Wu each achieved a regional unification, respectively making significant contributions to local society.
Caowei was the strongest of all. Upon Zhuge Liang's death,
the Shuhan regime was monopolized by eunuchs, resulting
in political corruption and waning national strength. The
regime was finally eliminated by Caowei in 263 AD. After
Emperor Mingdi of Caowei died, the regime was seized by
the minister Sima Yan, who later came into power in 266 AD
and changed the state title to Jin, historically called the Western Jin. At the end of the regime of Sunwu, the tyranny and
extravagance of Emperor Sun Hao aroused widespread complaints and anger among the people. In 280 AD, the Western
Jin ended Sunwu and thus unified the whole country. Due

to bureaucratic corruption, the "Rebellion of Eight Princes" resulted from fief and the consequent sharpened class contradictions and ethnic conflicts, the Western Jin lasted for only 30 years and was ended by the northern ethnic regime in 316. In 317, the remaining royal family of the Western Jin moved to areas south of the Yangtze and established Jiankang (present-day Nanjing, Jiangsu) as the capital of the state, historically called Eastern Jin, which lasted about 100 years. In 420 AD, Liu Yu ended the Eastern Jin and changed the state title to Song. Since then, the areas south of the Yangtze witnessed frequent changes of regimes from Song (420–479), Qi (479–502) to Liang (502–557) and Chen (557–589), which were collectively called the Southern Dynasties in Chinese history.

A dozen ethnic regimes took root in the north from 304, generally called the 16 States Period. In 439, the Northern Wei, led by Tuoba from the Xianbei ethnic group, unified the Yellow River Valley. Later on, after divisions and replacements, the Eastern Wei (534–550), the Northern Qi (550–577), the Western Wei (535–556) and the Northern Zhou (557–581) came out and were called the Northern Dynasties. The Northern and Southern Dynasties confronted each other and are collectively called the Southern and Northern Dynasties in Chinese history.

Drastic social turmoil and long-term wars led to the division of the state, economic decline and destruction of social civilization. After more than three centuries of chaos, many northern ethnic groups gradually merged during the regime conflicts and exchanges. The southern areas made unprecedented economic development and laid a solid foundation for reunification at a higher level.

Development of the Areas South of the Yangtze

Due to ecological diversity in ancient China, three major economic zones, namely the stockbreeding zone north of Jieshi, Longmen, the traditional agricultural zone in the central plains in the Yellow River basins and the areas south of the Yangtze, had taken shape as early as the Qin and Han dynasties. Different regions had their distinctive economic features and complemented each other. The central plains, including present-day Henan, Shandong and Hebei, as well as South Shanxi, North Jiangsu and North Anhui, enjoyed superior natural conditions and were developed earlier. The region is home to Chinese civilization and has long been the economic center of China. While areas south of the Yangtze, with hot and wet weather and widespread forests and wetland, saw the dominance of hunting, fishing and lumbering. In the Qin and Han dynasties, parts of the areas south of the Yangtze were preliminarily developed, while areas like Chuyue still featured vast land and a sparsely-distributed population. But the backward situation was soon changed in the Eastern Jin and Southern Dynasties, with a national

The clay brick with ox-cart patterns from the Southern Dynasty,

economic center starting to move southward.

The Wei and Jin dynasties experienced the second freezing period in ancient China. The freezing weather, excessive reclamation and wars rapidly destroyed the agricultural environment in the Yellow River Valley. By contrast, the areas south of the Yangtze saw huge potential for economic development with better weather conditions and abundant resources.

After moving southward, the Western Jin effectively prevented the invasion of northern nomads relying on the natural moat of the Yangtze. In 383, an 800,000-soldier troop of the Di ethnic group marched southward but was defeated by the 80,000-soldier troop of the Eastern Jin, which resolutely waged a counterattack at Feishui. That prevented the areas south of the Yangtze from being invaded and offered a relatively stable environment for local economic development.

The "Rebellion of Eight Princes" in the Western Jin Dynasty and the immigration of northern nomads to inland areas led to decades of chaos in North China and large-scale migration from the central plains to southern areas. During the 170 years from the end of the Western Jin to the early Southern Dynasties, up to 900,000 people moved to the south, making up one-sixth of the total population in the south. That helped export both labor and advanced tools and production techniques to the south, offering a powerful impetus to the economic growth of the areas south of the Yangtze. Stretches of barren land were reclaimed, and many water conservancy projects were constructed. Iron plows and ox-led farming were adopted and a crop system combining paddy rice and wheat planting were created. Craftsmen also moved from the north to the south on a large scale, helping create a boom in the handicraft sectors like silk-weaving, iron-smelting and pottery-making and the prosperity of commerce and cities. According to *The Book of Song*, the southern area had become the most prosperous place in the country during the Eastern Jin and Southern dynasties. Ancient China's economic center started to shift from the northern Yellow River Valley to the southern Yangtze River's middle and lower reaches.

Gathering of Northern Ethnic Groups

The relationship between the northern ethnic group and the Han group is an important factor that affects the development of ancient Chinese history. Since the Eastern Han Dynasty, the northern and northwestern ethnic groups like Hun, Xianbei, Jie, Di and Qiang had been forced to move into the hinterlands and become tenant peasants, soldiers or even servants, further sharpening the divisions between ethnic groups. Some ethnic regimes were set up during the struggle against the Han rulers. They continuously advanced to the central plains when the Han reign was under chaos.

At the time of Wei and Jin dynasties, the northern ethnic groups' migration resulted in a "half population in northwestern prefectures." They still kept the original clan organization and set up an ethnic regime in the chaos. They revolted against oppression, strengthened power, struggled for wealth and attacked each other, intensifying social turbulences and wars. On the other hand, the ethnic groups were registered as national households mainly engaged in agriculture. They lived together and married local people. The frequent exchanges showed a harmonizing trend.

After decades of living together, mutual conflicts and exchanges, most of the ethnic groups acknowledged the culture of central plains, regarding themselves as offspring of Yangdi and Huangdi and imitating the political and economic policies of the central plains developed since the

Han and Wei dynasties with varying degrees. For instance, Liu Yuan, an aristocrat of Hun, was quite acquainted with classical works on Confucianism as well as *The Records of the Grand Historian*, *The Book of Han* and *The Art of War*. He claimed himself the nephew of the emperor of the Han Dynasty and established a state with the title of Han. His successor Liu Cong was equally acquainted with literature and history and was good at calligraphy like cursive handwriting and official script, with hundreds of poems and odes. Fu Jian of the Pre-Qin Dynasty declared to "mix all the ethnic groups into one family." He attached great importance to officials of the Han Dynasty, courteously treated celebrities of all ethnic groups and worked to popularize Confucianism and the systems of Han in an all-around way. After the Northern Wei built by the Xianbei ethnic group unified the north, the ethnic group permeation was sped up.

Above: Carving bricks of the Wei and Jin dynasties: Land harrowing.

Below: Wei and Jin's murals: estafette.

At the beginning of the Northern Wei's reunification, many outdated traditions were still in existence. For instance, in the wars, persons from Han and other ethnic groups were infantries for assaults while the Xianbei cavalries supervised them from behind. Economically, the ruler's cruel oppression aroused intense resistance. Queen Mother Feng from Han with the edification of central plains culture instigated Tuoba Hong, Emperor Xiaowendi of the Northern Wei who succeeded to the throne at five, to reform. In order to smoothly promote reform and better learn the culture of the central plains, Emperor Xiaowendi moved his capital from the remote Ping Cheng (to-day's Datong, Shanxi) to Luoyang, the capital, for several dynasties. After the move, Emperor Xiaowendi greatly promoted Han-oriented policies, regime organization, rituals and codes. For life and customs, Hu-style clothes and Xianbei language were prohibited. Xianbei persons were to change their surnames to the Han style. He also advocated marriage between the Xianbei and Han and forbade it

The portrait of Emperor Xiaowendi dressed in the Han clothes on an imperial inspection in Longmen Grottoes, Luoyang.

between Xianbei persons of the same surname. During the reform, Emperor Xiaowendi set himself an example to others by changing the royal surname from "Tuoba" to "Yuan" and renamed himself as "Yuan Hong." He also married the daughter of a minister of Han and married his daughter to a person of Han. After the all-around reform in politics, economy, culture and customs, the Northern Dynasty completed the ethnic group permeation.

During the Wei, Jin and Southern and Northern dynasties, the world also experienced a huge change. The Gupta Empire rose in India. The Arsacid Dynasty was ended by the Persian Empire. The brilliant ancient culture of Rome was interrupted by the invasion of other countries. Although experiencing prolonged disunity and wars, Chinese culture continued and developed along a winding way. Not only did the southern economy achieve an unprecedented boom, the northern ethnic groups gradually gathered together in the conflicts and converted to the civilization of the central plains. Without shaking landlords' occupation over land, the System of Equal Distribution of Land practiced in the Northern Wei area distributed land to peasants according to household population. That properly solved the problem of combining land with labor and significantly pushed forward the means of production in the central plains, having

Dunhuan fresco in the Northern Zhou Dynasty represents the business brigade flow in the Silk Road.

far-reaching influence on Chinese history. Hu-style food, clothing, beds, music and dances with unique features of northern ethnic groups, as well as other prairie cultural elements like advanced techniques concerning livestock breed selection, and disease prevention and treating, were gradually merged into the Han daily life, enriching the culture of the central plains. The ethnic group permeation, with Emperor Xiaowendi's reform as a mark, laid a solid foundation for reunification at a broader and higher level.

Colorful and Diverse Culture in the Wei, Jin and Southern and Northern Dynasties

The extension and development of Chinese culture during the period were also expressed in science, technology and culture. Agronomy, medicine, mathematics, geology, calligraphy, painting and sculpture surpassed the Qin and Han dynasties and reached a new peak.

The period saw the invention of the perfusing steel method that was used to produce steel by combining pig iron and wrought iron, the creation of a rotating water cart, a kind of high-efficient tool for irrigation, as well as the cultivation of a superior silkworm breed that could produce pods eight times a year. In addition, oil and natural gas were also used for lighting or even fire attacking.

The book *Essential Techniques for the Peasantry*, written by Jia Sixie in the Wei State, systematically summarized the experiences in farming, stock-raising, fishing and other production activities of the people in the middle and lower reaches of the Yellow River, as well as the ways to process and store food. It is the first available complete agricultural book in China and the first agricultural encyclopedia in the world as well.

The book photograph of *Essential Techniques for the Peasantry*.

The Commentary on the Waterways Classic, written by the geographer Li Daoyuan, is a book of notes to previous works. With more than 300,000 words, it goes into details about 1,250 rivers as well as the mountains, landscapes, evolution of counties, local products, customs, history and legendaries in areas along the waterways. *The Commentary on the Waterways Classic* is more than an excellent comprehensive geographical work; it is of great significance in both history and literature.

Zu Chongzhi, a mathematician in the Southern Dynasty, concluded that the value of *pi* falls between 3.1415926 to 3.1415927, an achievement 1,000 years earlier than that worked out in the west. He formulated *The*

Portrait of Zu
Chongzhi.

Daming Calendar, concluding a year actually
includes 365.24281481 days, with an error of no
more than 50 seconds. Zu Chongzhi was also
good at making mechanical instruments, successfully duplicating the compass cart, even
though its creation techniques had been lost for
generations. Zu also created the "thousand-*li*
ship" that could travel hundreds of *li* per day
and water mills. To commemorate his great
contributions to world science and culture, the
International Astronomical Union named a ring
mountain on the moon as the "Mountain of Zu
Chongzhi" in the 1960s.

The collapse of the Eastern Han and the ensuing severe
turbulences destroyed the overwhelming supremacy of
Confucianism and led to a flourishing of legalism and metaphysics. The local Taoism and Buddhism introduced between the Han dynasties were particularly prosperous, pos-
ing a challenge to the Confucianism that they believed was
all about ridiculous words and unchanging doctrines.

The metaphysics that emerged between Wei and Jin dynasties respected Lao Tze and Zhuang Tzu, and advocated
"void is the nature of everything" and "acting in accordance
with the natural laws." The representatives like Ji Kang and
Ruan Ji brazenly declared that "he despises the King Tang-
wang of the Shang Dynasty and King Wuwang of the Zhou
Dynasty, and belittles Zhougong and Confucius," speaking
and behaving beyond established ritual and legal norms.
Metaphysics grew as the dominant school of thought at that
time, driving forward the development of philosophical
thinking and liberation of individuals. But it later developed
into empty talks that didn't make sense.

Buddhism was introduced into the central plains from
ancient India during the Western and Eastern Han dynasties

and prospered in the Wei and Jin dynasties. Buddhism emphasizes the karma and samsara, telling people they could attain happiness in their afterlife so long as they tolerate pains and earnestly practice Buddhist rules. The doctrines allowed the maintainance of the hierarchical orders, offered converts spiritual support and was particularly attractive to the poor who were struggling in the turbulent world. The Southern and Northern dynasties saw the peak of Buddhism. As the poems of Du Fu, a poet of the Tang Dynasty, described, "Many of the 480 temples in the Southern and Northern dynasties are shrouded in mist and drizzle." In the Northern Dynasties, the number of Buddhist temples increased to more than 30,000, and monks and nuns to three million. The spread of Buddhism injected fresh elements and had a huge impact on traditional Chinese culture in such aspects as ideology, culture, art and literature.

Taoism, established at the end of the Eastern Han Dynasty, is a local religion of China combining Taoist thought and supernatural art. It was reconstructed by Ge Hong in the Eastern Jin Dynasty and enhanced to an official position. It advocated harmony between heaven and human beings, attainment of the highest state of spiritual enlightenment and becoming immortal with cultivation and immortality pill making according to the Taoist doctrine. Tao Hongjing of the Southern Dynasties further established a system of immortals from Jade Emperor to City God and Kitchen God, having far-reaching influence upon ancient Chinese people.

The successive rise of metaphysics, Buddhism and Taoism greatly attacked the hackneyed Confucianism, creating an open, diverse and lively atmosphere in the ideological world and leading to competition among Confucianism, Buddhism and Taoism.

The Wei, Jin and Southern and Northern dynasties saw the collapse of ritual norms and social turbulence. That gave rise to calligraphy as an ideal form for scholars to express their thoughts and pursuits. Chinese character writing gradually evolved into a self-conscious calligraphic art. Wang Xizhi, who was known as the Saint of Calligraphers in the Eastern Jin Dynasty, had exquisite style and hard strokes like floating clouds and flowing water. His *Preface to the Orchid Pavilion* represents the spirit of calligraphic art in the Jin Dynasty and is called the "best-running script works."

The Wei and Jin dynasties were the first important developmental period for traditional Chinese painting, with the creation of paintings with marked individuality by scholars. Scholar-bureaucrats of the time admired inane disputes and stressed the spirit while evaluating a person. Gu Kaizhi, a famous artist in the Eastern Jin Dynasty, was a representative of the spirit-oriented style. He insisted that the "spirit of a figure shall be expressed through outer appearances" and especially highlighted the traits of figures. While painting a Buddhist image for the Waguan Temple in Jiankang, Gu didn't draw the eyes until the rest of the painting was finished, immediately making the image extremely vivid and winning praise and adoration from all the witnesses who later gave alms to the temple in succession.

Frequent exchanges with the ethnic groups in the Western

Preface to the Orchid Pavilion by Wang Xizhi in the Eastern Jin Dynasty.

regions and foreign nations helped enrich the art forms like music, dance and grotto sculptures in the Wei, Jin and Southern and Northern dynasties. The grotto sculptures that combine sculpture and painting art particularly reflect the highest achievements of the time. Yungang Grottoes in Pingcheng (present-day Datong, Shanxi), initiated in the early Northern Wei Dynasty, boasts spectacular scale with more than 50,000 Buddhist statues and Flying Apsaras. The largest Buddhist statue among them is 13.7 m high and was carved with superb craftsmanship. Affected by the Indian

The painting of Ode to the Goddess in Luo (part) by Gu Kaizhi in the Eastern Jin Dynasty.

Yungang Grottoes, situated at Datong, Shanxi, were carved from the 2nd year of Xing'an Period, Northern Wei and mostly completed previous to the dynasty's capital relocation in Luoyang.

Buddhist art styles, the Buddhist statues have high noses, deep eyes and serious facial expressions, showing traits typical of the Hu people in the Western Regions. Longmen Grottoes in Luoyang, Henan, were created after Emperor Wendi of the Northern Wei Dynasty moved the capital there, with one-third of the thousands of grottoes and habitats excavated during the Northern Wei Dynasty. The Buddhist statues, serious and kindly, are dressed in exquisitely carved clothes with smooth veins, and show cultural features of the central plains.

The thoughts and culture of the Wei, Jin and Southern and Northern dynasties hadn't been interrupted either during the Three Kingdoms Period or in the confrontation between the South and North dynasties. On the contrary, they thrived because of the awakening of scholars and showed a pattern featuring the dominance of the culture of the central plains and a merging of diverse elements, leaving unique marks on ancient Chinese history.

Sui and Tang Dynasties:
a Prosperous and Open Age

Reunification and Rise and Fall of the Sui Dynasty

From the end of the 6th century to the early 10th century, a unified empire was rebuilt in China and entered into its heyday.

In 581, Yang Jian, a female-side relative of the emperor of the Northern Zhou, replaced the dynasty and renamed the nation as Sui with the capital in Chang'an (today's Xi'an, Shaanxi). Yang Jian, Emperor Wendi of the Sui Dynasty from a military noble group of Han, was the son-in-law of a noble of Xianbei and the maternal grandfather of Emperor Jingdi of the Northern Zhou Dynasty, who succeeded to the throne at age 7. His family itself was the epitome of the time featuring merging of ethnic groups. Yang Jian was encircled by a group of Han officials and Xianbei nobles deeply influenced by Han culture. Furthermore, his position as a royal relative who was entrusted to assist handling politics rendered him great power and privileges. That facilitated Sui's smooth replacement of Zhou and the subsequent establishment of the Sui Dynasty, the first dynasty ruled by Han people accepted by the minorities in the Northern Dynasties, indicating the shift from an ethnic war to a reunification war.

In 589, the Sui troops crossed the Yangtze River and ended the Chen Dynasty, capturing Jiankang within eight days and reuniting China after 400 years of separation. Sui achieved unification based on a broader and deeper base, such as the integration of the Yellow River and Yangtze River economic areas, greatly intensified the political, economic and cultural ties between the north and south, and promoted the rapid growth of social economy.

After reunification, Emperor Wendi and his successor Emperor Yangdi promulgated a series of political and economic reforms to further intensify the centralized sovereignty and develop social economy. At the beginning of Emperor Yangdi's reign, he started to build Luoyang to better display its function as an economic center. Meanwhile, a 2000-km-long canal from Zhuojun (today's Tongzhou District, Beijing) in the north to Yuhang (today's Hangzhou, Zhejiang) in the south was also being built. The Grand Canal, linking five rivers—the Haihe River, the Yellow River, the Huaihe River, the Yangtze River and the Qiantang River—became an important artery closely linking politics, economy and culture, and played an important role in consolidating and promoting development along the river banks.

The period from the start of the Sui Dynasty to the early regime of the Emperor Yangdi saw vast expanses of territory and powerful national strength. With substantial increases of the population and land reclaiming areas, the state's official granaries could contain grains totaling millions to thousands of millions of *shi* (one *shi* equals 50 kg). Extra granaries were built for relief in times of harvest failure. At the end of the regime of Emperor Wendi, "the grain storage nationwide could meet needs of the people for the next 50 to 60 years." In the term of Emperor Yangdi, the cloth and silk in Dongdu piled up like mountains. Part of the storage of

Gongchen Bridge in Hangzhou, the first bridge over the Grand Canal.

the Sui Dynasty still remained until the 20th year of the reign of the Tang Dynasty. This was why Ma Duanlin, a historian of the Yuan Dynasty, said "no other dynasties in history could be compared with the Sui."

Emperor Yangdi determinedly and dauntlessly pursued his policy of reform, with great achievements. Most of the projects and political and economic reforms initiated by him were of strategic significance, contributing to the flourishing of the later Tang Dynasty. However, he paid little attention to the people's burden and continuously engaged in civil works with millions of people and wars against Koryo, resulting in desolated lands and starving people everywhere. Civilians even broke their own hands and feet to escape from labor and army service. Emperor Yangdi's tyranny gave rise to nationwide peasant uprisings. Sui rapidly perished. In 618, Li Yuan seized the opportunity and established the Tang Dynasty in Chang'an.

The portrait of Emperor Taizong of the Tang Dynasty.

Splendid Times of the Early Tang Dynasty

In 626, Li Shimin, honored with great feats in building Tang and reunification, changed the title to Zhenguan. The powerful Sui Dynasty's quick collapse deeply shocked Li Shimin, Emperor Taizong of the Tang Dynasty. He realized emperors "will be the head if honest and upright, and isolated if brutal and tyrannical." So, he successively freed 6,000 court girls and promised not to hold grand ceremonies of worship of heaven on mountains, pray for celestial beings or conduct large-scale touring around. He was also open to advice and tolerant toward his ministers' comments. His minister, Wei Zheng, often cited the end of the Sui Dynasty as an example to criticize his faults in public. Emperor Taizong, when extremely angered by the criticism, once told the empress that he would kill Wei Zheng sooner or later, but he eventually accepted Wei's suggestions tolerantly. That gave rise to an open and loose political atmosphere between the emperor and his ministers.

Emperor Taizong believed that "winning talented people is fundamental to the national prosperity." With an open mind and unique insight, he didn't stick to fixed patterns for appointing talents. He chose from former leaders of the insurgent troops, former ministers of the Sui Dynasty, favorite ministers of his political opponents and ordinary people of humble birth. Those wise or brave people later played a big role in formulating and implementing the new reforms, expanding the ruling foundation and stabilizing the political situation.

During the regime of Emperor Taizong, he earnestly drew from the experiences and lessons from the Sui Dynasty, establishing a series of policies aimed to stabilize society and develop the economy. He vigorously adjusted productive relations, social relations and the relations inside the ruling group. That resulted in clean politics and a recovering economy, and the period was thus called the "Peaceful and Prosperous Zhenguan Period" in history, paving the way for the prosperity of the Tang Dynasty.

Wu Zetian, the only female emperor in Chinese history, has been sitting on the throne for 15 years and actually controlled the country for nearly half a century.

Li Zhi, Emperor Gaozong, the successor of Emperor Taizong, was a coward and weak in health. Wu Zetian, the queen, was actively engaged in political affairs. After he passed away, Wu Zetian ascended the throne in 690, becoming the only female emperor in Chinese history. Wu controlled the empire for half a century. Wu Zetian's father was a nouveau riche, who rose with Li Yuan, Emperor Gaozu,

The Kaiyuan Iron Ox from the Tang Dynasty at Pujindu. During the Kaiyuan Period, the Tang government cast 0.8 million kilograms of iron into oxen, humans, mountains and columns as ground anchors to build a pontoon bridge between the banks of the Yellow River at Pujindu. The salt, iron and coal in Shanxi were subsequently transported across the Yellow River to Chang'an, Shaanxi Province.

but was regarded as humble by the hereditary noble families. Emperor Gaozong's replacement of Wang with Wu as his empress was once strongly opposed by his senior ministers. The support of the ministers of non-scholar birth helped Wu Zetian step on the political stage as an empress. After Wu seized power, she regulated that all officials including soldiers promoted to fifth-ranking officials due to feats should be enlisted in the name catalogs previously meant exclusively for hereditary officials. She also put cruel officials in important positions for framing crimes and killing noted families and ministers embracing resistances to break the tradition of prestigious families' monopoly of high ranks and politics. Moreover, Wu held examinations and questioned applicants herself. She selected talents from common landlords without restriction of rank or family. Luo Binwang, one of the four outstanding poets of the early Tang Dynasty, once wrote *A Call to Crusade against Wu Zetian*, condemning that she was ruthless and rapacious, and "is hated by both people and the god, and can't be tolerated by the heaven and earth." Instead of flying into a rage, Wu spoke highly of Luo's talent and chided the prime minister for not adopting such talented people like him.

During her regime, Wu followed the policies of the Zhenguan Period to award farming and sericulture, and reduce labor service and taxation. Being prudent in wars resulted in continuous economic development. According to *Assembled Essentials of the Song Dynasty*, households nationwide rose from 3.8 million in 652 AD, a time right before she came into power, to 6.15 million in 705 AD, when she abdicated from the crown.

In 712, Li Longji ascended the throne and was called Emperor Xuanzong. During his early term, he stuck to implementing reforms, adjusting official systems and developing production. That led to a highly stable society and a thriving economy with years of harvests, quality and cheap grain and up to 10 million households. The period also saw an unprecedented development of handicrafts like porcelain-making, textile and iron-smelting in product categories, production scale and techniques. The state power of the Tang Dynasty had reached its culmination, and the period was thus honored as the noted Kaiyuan Flourishing Age and was another peak time in ancient China.

New Reforms of the Sui and Tang Dynasties

The prosperity of the early Tang came from contemporary economic and social development. The reclamation of land and irrigation marked with bending shaft ploughs and scoop waterwheels gave higher freedom to individual peasants, leading to the rapid development of intensively cultivated small land blocks and produced a great number of middle and small landlords. Meanwhile the decadent gentry or landlords crushed by the widespread peasant wars at the end of the Sui Dynasty, gradually declined. The individual cultivation-based landlord broke the fetters of those gentry families and started to get full play in state politics, initiating a range of far-reaching innovations in the prevailing systems.

Establishment of the Three-Ministry and Six-Department System in the Sui and Tang dynasties was a significant change in the ancient Chinese official system. Zhongshu Ministry, Menxia Ministry and Shangshu Ministry were the supreme administrative organizations of the country, in charge of decision-making and drafting orders, and the review and execution of state affairs respectively. Under

Shangshu Ministry, six departments were set up. The Organization Department was in charge of the appointment and assessment of officials. The Hu Department was in charge of land resources, household registry, taxation, and financial affairs. The Li Department was in charge of ritual affairs, celebrations, sacrifices, schools and imperial examinations. The Bing Department was in charge of officer selection, serviceman registry, military orders and weapons. The Xing Department was in charge of laws, orders, the judiciary, criminal punishment and prisons. The Gong Department was in charge of civil engineering, irrigation and flood control, arable land, traffic, etc. The heads of these three ministries were prime minister. They discussed state affairs and assisted the emperor in ruling the country, sharing the power of prime minister while supplementing each other and checking each other. The works of the six departments were well divided, peeled off the functions of managing affairs of the imperial family of Nine *Qing* before and became the formal administrative institutes of the country.

The expostulation system was designed to supervise and correct major policies of the court. Even the orders of the emperors were intensified in the Tang Dynasty, and Menxia Ministry had the exclusive right to review and return the orders of the emperor and reject reports of the officials. During the Zhenguan Period, the "Wuhua Panshi" system was also implemented, allowing officials of concerned departments to overview all the major military events and present

Civilian (left) and warrior figures (right) of the Tang Dynasty.

their views to the emperor for the final decision. To ensure administrative efficiency, officials who intentionally delayed the deadline of the joint signature would be punished.

The Wei, Jin and Southern and Northern dynasties highlighted family background when selecting officials. Descendants of noble birth could get promoted to ministers and monopolize the positions for generations even though they sometimes were ignorant, incompetent and unenterprising. But things had changed in the Sui and Tang dynasties with the increasingly bigger role of emerging commoner-landlord class, hence the establishment of the official selection system with imperial examinations. Under the system, the central government chose officials with regular imperial examinations and emphasized that capabilities were the standard

The Big Wild Goose Pagoda in Xi'an, built in the third year of the reign of Emperor Gaozong (652). The newly presented candidates of the imperial examinations of the Tang Dynasty carved their names on the tablets of the Big Wild Goose Pagoda, which were considered as the supreme honor for scholars.

The rubbing inscriptions of names of the successful candidates of the imperial examinations on the tablets of the Wild Goose Pagoda.

for official selection. The imperial examinations were divided into *Jinshi* and *Mingjing*. *Mingjing* was designed to test the capability of reciting classics. *Jinshi* mainly focused on poetry and ode writing and strategies on current affairs, aimed at testing the person's capability of governing political affairs and solving social problems. The scholars had to pass further examinations of the organization department and the outstanding ones would be chosen and appointed. Another way to be appointed was to first act as assistant in the local government and then be recommended by senior officials.

The official selection system with imperial examinations broke the monopoly of the rich and powerful families, expanded the social foundation for the central regime and injected a fresh force into social development. It created a relatively objective, equitable and fair official selection mechanism, ensuring the continuous introduction of talented people and providing the state organization with a systematic guarantee for vigorous, stable and efficient performance.

Tang's laws simplified the system of the Sui and had lighter penalties. Execution was very prudently applied, and five-time review was required before any execution. *Comment on Law of Tang Dynasty* is the earliest extant code in China, having great influences on Asian countries throughout history.

The Early Tang Dynasty made certain adjustments based on the System of Equal Distribution of Land adopted since the Northern Wei and Sui dynasties. Provisions on awarding land according to numbers of slaves and maids, *buqu* (a social class between slaves and ordinary people) and cattle were canceled, keeping the despotic economy in check to some extent. Officials with five-rank or higher and those honored due to feats of arms were also awarded a certain size parcel of land based on respective ranks and levels of merits, which served as an important way to support the emerging landlord class. Restrictions on sales of some types of land, like permanently-held land and bestowed land, were loosened, facilitating the development of private ownership of land. With regard to tax and corvee system, Tax-Labor-Substitution System was implemented widely, which allowed replacement of corve with silk or cloth. In the middle Tang Dynasty, the merging of land and false reporting of household population led to the collapse of the System of Equal Distribution of Land. The court also changed the Tax-Labor-Substitution System to the Dual-Tax System, speeding up the process of land privatization and the development of the commoner-landlord economy. The Dual-Tax Law stipulated

The Fresco of Farming in Dunhuang from the Tang Dynasty.

that taxes would be levied based on the size of property and land of each household—and not based on population—which released the control over peasants. In addition, coins largely replaced physical goods in tax paying, and nobles, bureaucrats and merchants were all required to pay tax, too. That expanded the government's tax sources and increased its revenue. Those principles were mostly inherited by later generations.

These significant systematic reforms implemented in the Sui and Tang dynasties reflected the development of the emerging commoner-landlord system and their political pursuits as well. They initiated a new trend for future social development and made the Sui and Tang dynasties a critical turning point in ancient Chinese history.

Hu and Han are "Members of One Family"

The Tang Dynasty was witness to another grand unification. The Central Government and the bordering ethnic groups developed closer relations. Emperor Taizong announced that, "I love the Han and ethnic groups equally though most favor the former all along." After defeating the Eastern Turks in the South Desert during the Zhenguan Period, the Tang Dynasty adopted the policy of "all tribes following their local customs." Turkish aristocrats were still the governors, and generals had the jurisdiction over tribal members. All the previous ethnic customs and ways of life were retained. In the meantime, nearly 10,000 Turks moved to Chang'an, including more than 100 Turkish chieftains who were honored as senior officials with five-rank or above. Before long, the Tang Dynasty set up the Protectorate General of Anxi in the Western Regions, and the Protectorate General of Beijing was further established during the regime of Wu Zetian, respectively governing areas south and north of the Tianshan Mountain.

Moved by the open policy, chieftains of northwestern tribes addressed Emperor Taizong respectfully as Tian Khan (the great heavenly Khan) and supported him as the mutual leader. During the later Zhenguan Period, more than 10 tribes in North Desert, including Huihe, submitted to the Tang Dynasty in succession, and opened a "road of Khan" in the desert. The court set up 68 posthouses along the path to receive emissaries and offer services for traveling businessmen. After that, Emperor Suzong, Emperor Dezong and Emperor Muzong all married one of their princesses to the Huihe Khan for peace-making marriages.

Emperor Taizong also accepted the request of Songzan Gambo, the chieftain of Tubo on the Tibetan Plateau, to marry Princess Wencheng to him. When the princess entered Tibet, she also brought along lots of handiworks, grains, vegetable seeds, herbal medicines and tea, as well as more than 100 kinds of production techniques and medical books, making Tubo "gradually affected by the advanced culture" and greatly driving forward local economic and cultural

Emperor Taizong of the Tang Dynasty Meeting Tibetan Emissaries (part) by Yan Liben delineates Tibetan King Songzan Gambo dispatched envoys to Chang'an for a marriage alliance with the Tang Dynasty.

Dunhuang fresco from the Tang Dynasty represents the integration of Han and the northern ethnic group's music and dance.

growth. After succeeding to the throne, Emperor Gaozong conferred the title of Chief Commandant of Escorting Cavalry upon Songzan Gambo and honored him as the King of Xihai Jun. During the regime of Emperor Zhongzong, he further married Princess Jincheng to Chidai Zhudan, the king of Tubo, who called himself the "nephew" of the emperor and said "Tubo and Han are members of one family." In 823, the Tang Dynasty and Tubo entered into an alliance in Changqing, and the Monument to the Tang-Tubo Alliance still stands in front of the Jokhang Temple in Lhasa today, serving as witness to the friendly relations between the Tang Dynasty and Tibet.

The middle seventh century saw the rise of Heishui and Sumo tribes of the Mohe ethnic group in the Songhua River and Heilongjiang River basins. During the Zhenguan Period, Heishui Mohe started to pay tribute to the Tang Dynasty.

In the early eighth century, the Tang Dynasty established Heishui Governor-General Mansion and appointed its chieftain as the governor. In the beginning of Kaiyuan Period, Emperor Xuanzong conferred the title of King of Bohai upon Dazuorong and honored him as the Governor of Huhan Prefecture. Bohai had close relations with the central plains, with the buildings in its capital, Shangjing Longquanfu (present-day Bohai Town, Anning City, Heilongjiang Province), similar to those in Chang'an of the Tang Dynasty. The prefecture and county system were also copied, as well as the advanced production techniques in the central plains.

There were six tribes—Six Zhaos—in the Erhai area during the Sui and Tang dynasties. In the early eighth century, the Tang Dynasty supported South Zhao to unify the Six Zhaos, and Emperor Xuanzong honored its chieftain as the King of Yunnan. The advanced techniques taken by craftsmen from the central plains promoted the development of the local economy. When growing stronger, South Zhao came into conflict with the Tang Dynasty, resulting in alternating wars and peace. At the end of the eighth century, South Zhao once again submitted to the Tang Dynasty. In 794, the King of South Zhao met the emissary team of the Tang Dynasty at the Divine Temple in Diancang Mountain. From then on, South Zhao has been deeply affected by the Tang Dynasty in a wide range of aspects like administrative organization, production techniques, and social lives, making great contributions to the development of the southwestern regions.

With more than 800 provinces, prefectures and counties were established in bordering ethnic group areas, the early Tang Dynasty boasted a territory reaching the sea in the east, the Anxi and Congling Mountain areas in the west, the Mongol Plateau in the north and the South Sea in the south, and was characterized by unprecedented affluence and power. Such aspects as folk customs and art also showed features of communication and the merging of Hu and Han cultures. Food like dumplings, and the silks and porcelains of the central plains were deeply loved by the ethnic groups, and tea became an important material for exchange. Meanwhile, the central plains saw the popularity of Hu clothes and food. The frescoes and sculptures from the Tang Dynasty also reflect a distinct glamour of the Western Regions, either in expression or artistic style. The dancers and bands mostly were from diverse ethnic groups, and the musical instruments include those of both Hu and Han styles, manifesting the characteristics of the time when Hu and Han were members of one family and diverse elements mixed together.

Openness and Communication

The Sui and Tang dynasties boasted developed outbound traffic. The land route ran from present-day North Korea in the east, through the Silk Road, to present-day India, Pakistan, Afghanistan, Iran and the Persian Gulf in the west. It further extended to many European and African countries through Central Asia and the Mediterranean Sea. The sea route started from today's South Korea and Japan in the east and ended in the Persian Gulf in the west. The Tang Dynasty's policies that encouraged openness and communication, as well as the smooth land and sea routes, gave rise to extremely frequent Sino-foreign exchanges.

Japan had sent its emissaries to the Tang Dynasty 13 successive times, with Japanese students going with each emissary mission numbering into the hundreds. In 645, Japan launched Taika Reform, taking the Tang Dynasty as a model in many aspects including political, legal, land and tax systems and even construction of the capital city. Ku Kai, a Japanese scholar monk who once went to the Tang Dynasty to study Buddhism, adopted the components of

Chinese characters to create Japanese letters called Kataka-na. Jianzhen, a monk of the Tang Dynasty, tried to cross the ocean eastward to Japan but failed multiple times. He finally did it at the age of 66, which was his sixth attempt. Jianzhen himself carried out monkhood initiation for the Japanese emperor, empress and prince, as well as ordinary people from various circles. He gave lectures on Buddhism and introduced Chinese medicine, architecture, sculpture, calligraphy, painting and other knowledge to the Japanese people, which had a significant influence upon the Japanese culture. In the late seventh century, Silla on the Korean Peninsula also sent groups of students to the Tang Dynasty, and imitated such Tang systems as the six departments and official selection through imperial examinations. Deeply affected by the Tang Dynasty, Silla displayed a strong flavor of the Tang style in a wide range of areas from science and technology

Left: Statute of Jianzhen.

Right: Portrait of Xuanzang.

to art, literature, and folk customs.

During the early Zhenguan Period, the senior monk Xuanzang made an arduous journey west to India, where he earnestly studied Buddhism for five years. Then he toured around many other counties to give Buddhist lectures. Seventeen years later, he returned to Chang'an, where he devoted himself to translating Buddhism records and had *The Buddhist Records of The Western World* compiled, which described what he saw and heard along his westward journey. He systematically introduced Buddhism, history, geography and customs of India. He was also entrusted by Emperor Taizong to translate the *Tao Te Ching* into Sanskrit. Xuanzang's efforts with Buddhist scriptures promoted Sino-Indian cultural exchanges and imposed a great influence on history.

Tang Tri-colored Pottery Figures. The persons on the camel are bandsmen, singers and dancers from the Middle Asia.

The Tang Dynasty opened itself to the outside world in an all-around way and carried out extensive communication with foreign countries, keeping commercial ties with more than 70 countries, including countries in West Asia, Europe and Africa. The government permitted foreigners to live in China, marry Chinese people and take part in Chinese examinations for official selection. Some foreigners even acted as military officials of the court or servants of the emperor. The city of Chang'an, capital of the Tang Dynasty, covered an area of 84 sq km and had a population of nearly one million, being the world's biggest international city of the time.

Arabia saw the establishment of the Arab Empire that spanned across Asia, Africa and Europe in the seventh century, but it collapsed in the ninth century. Europe was in the mediaeval times, which featured division and chaos. The

Prosperous Tang Dynasty with Worldwide Reputation

The early Tang of China featured extreme courteousness, advanced culture and far-reaching influence, a sharp contrast with the corruption, chaos and division of the western world.

While the western minds were obsessed with divinity and kept in a state of darkness, the Chinese minds were open, compatible and curious.

—H. G. Wells, *The Outline of History*

prosperous Sui and Tang dynasties, while imposing a far-reaching influence on neighboring countries and regions, extensively absorbed foreign cultures to enrich and develop the Chinese culture and further created enterprising spirits with openness and compatibility. Merchants, scholars, and people of ethnic groups, as well as foreign emissaries and students, gathered in the capital city of Chang'an, and grand feasts filled with singing and dancing were widespread. Women also wore Hu clothes, rode horses, played ball games and joined various sorts of social, sports and entertainment activities. The society was full of vigor and vitality.

Brilliant Culture of the Sui and Tang Dynasties

The Sui and Tang dynasties, integrated in territory, prosperous in economy and liberal in politics, promoted the quick development of culture and education, setting up a complete school education system from the central to the local, involving laws, mathematics and other majors. The social reforms and systematic renovation during the period also gave fresh impetus to the advances in science, technology, literature, and art.

The period saw two great inventions that had a significant impact upon human civilization, namely wood block

Vajra Sutra printed in the 9th year of Xiantong Period of Tang (868).

printing and gunpowder.

Enlightened by the techniques of seal engraving and printing from stone engraving in ancient China, paper printing from wood engraving was created in the early Tang Dynasty. The Zhenguan Period further saw records of engraving and printing. The *Vajra* Sutra, an exquisitely engraved printing work with bright ink in the ninth year of the Xiantong Period of the Tang Dynasty (868), was the earliest wood-block presswork with a definite time record in the world. Invention of wood-block printing that followed the papermaking technique played a significant role in keeping, spreading and developing human culture.

In the early Tang Dynasty, people stumbled upon the formula for gunpowder as they were making medicines. Sun Simiao, a medicine expert in the early Tang Dynasty, recorded in the book *Alchemical Scriptures* the way to make gunpowder. First, put two liang of sulphur and another two liang of saltpeter into an earthen pot, then burn the Chinese

Honeylocust hot and put it inside the pot, which will jointly create raging flames. There are other records of peasants' insurgent troops that applied gunpowder to wars at the end of the Tang Dynasty. In addition, gunpowder was also used in hunting, mountain digging and stone mining.

Ancient Chinese architectural art entered a period of maturity during the Sui and Tang dynasties. Yu Wenkai, an architect of the Sui Dynasty, used drawings and models to design and direct the construction of the spectacular Daxing City, which was expanded as the city of Chang'an in the Tang Dynasty, and Luoyang City, demonstrating the superb techniques in urban construction. The Zhaozhou Bridge, designed and built by Li Chun, a workman of the Sui Dynasty, is a 50-plus-long single-hole stone arch bridge with a span of 37 m wide. It has been well preserved until today and is reputed as "a wonder in world bridge-building history." The Tang Dynasty was the golden age of ancient Chinese poetry, with more than 50,000 poems passed down to the present generations. Prosperity, openness and cultural diversity, as well as the enterprising spirit encouraged by

Zhaozhou Bridge in Hebei, built in the Sui Dynasty, is the earliest single-arch stone bridge well-preserved in the world.

The Drunk Li Bai by Su Liupeng represents Li Bai was supported by two eunuchs after getting drunk in the palace of Emperor Xuanzong.

the fresh official selection system jointly created the brilliance of Tang poetry. Tang poems have orderly rhythm and proper parallel, and represent the feelings and emotions of the poets. Gao Shi, Cen Sen, Wang Changling and other frontier fortress poets sang the praises of soldiers and officers at the frontline with strong, bold and generous words. Poems written by Meng Haoran, Wang Wei and other idyllic poets expressed the peaceful harmony between man and nature. The most notable poets in the Tang Dynasty were Li Bai and Du Fu. Li Bai, called the God of Poetry, wrote poems that were bold and unconstrained, representing the vigorous and personality-oriented spirit in the prosperous period of the Tang Dynasty. His romantic poems contained profound realistic meaning and deep love of fellow human beings.

Du Fu, called the Saint of Poetry, was destitute and homeless and worried about the country and the people all his life. His poems reflected contemporary social reality, especially people's difficult lives amid the chaos caused by war. His poems were heavy and indignant, and called "poetic history."

Paintings of the Tang Dynasty covered more and more fields, with figures, landscapes, flowers and birds separated from each other. Systematic painting techniques were invented and diverse schools of painting emerged, too. Wu Daozi, respected as the Saint of Artists, combined his interest in calligraphy with line drawing, enriching the movement and expressive force of the lines and achieving the artistic effect of "drifting clothes and moving lines."

The reunification in the Sui and Tang dynasties brought about the combination of calligraphic styles of both the South and North, which featured gracefulness and vigorousness respectively. Ouyang Xun, Yan Zhenqing and Liu Gongquan were the representatives of the regular script. Ouyang's scripts were bold and dignified. Yan's calligraphy was round and simple, while Liu had a serious and vigorous style. Zhang Xun and Hui Su were famous for cursive hand, with calligraphic characters smooth, drifting and unrestrained.

Affected by alien cultures, the music and dance in the Sui and Tang dynasties were colorful in styles. Emperor Xuanzong, acquainted with music rhythms, once imparted dancing and singing techniques to 300 musicians in a pear park, and created *The Ancient Dance Music of Imperial Palace* by himself by taking the styles of Western Regions for reference.

Mogao Grottoes, located in Dunhuang, Gansu, a key site along the Silk Road, is the world's biggest and best-preserved Buddhist artistic treasure. There are more than 3,000 colorful sculptures and 45,000-square-meter frescoes preserved at present, most of which are works from the Sui and Tang dynasties. The Buddhist statues with different facial expressions look vivid and lively, and the fres-

Yan Qingli Stele by Yan Zhenqing in the Tang Dynasty.

Ladies of Kingdom Guo on a Spring Outing (part) represents the life of the ladies in the Tang Dynasty, filled with the exoteric atmosphere of the age.

Tang's colored statue in Dunhuan Mogao Grottoes. The Bodhisattva, with a round face, plummy stature, coiled bun and loosely dressed in silk clothes, reflects the aesthetics of the society then.

coes with smooth and drifting lines are splendid and bril-liant, displaying a unique verve and infinite charm.

The heydays of the Tang Dynasty showcased the features of Sino-foreign penetration and Hu-Han permeation in ide-ology and customs, as well as the spirit of grandness, open-ness, robustness and innovation.

Song and Yuan Dynasties: Diverse Cultural Collisions and Great Socio-economic Development

Confrontations between the Northern and Southern Song Dynasties and Liao, Xixia and Jin, and the Merging of Southern and Northern Cultures

The later reign of Emperor Xuanzong was marked by corrupt politics and weakening of power. Eunuchs seized power in the court while the warlords held control over local areas. The empire was rocked by sweeping peasant uprisings at the end of the Tang Dynasty and ended by warlords in 907. In the next 50 years, the Yellow River Valley was under the reign of the Later Liang (907–923), the Later Tang (923–936), the Later Jin (936–947), the Later Han (947–950) and the Later Zhou (951–960), collectively called the Five Dynasties.

The period from 960 to 1368 saw three historical stages of the Northern Song confronting with Liao and Xixia, the Southern Song confronting with Jin, and the unified Yuan.

In 960, General Zhao Kuangyin initiated a mutiny and overturned the Later Zhou to establish the Song Dynasty in Bianjing (today's Kaifeng, Henan), called the Northern Song period. The Northern Song successfully quelled the various rebellions and reunited the central plains and spacious southern areas. Having learned the lessons from usurpation by key ministers and the revolts of warlords, the Northern Song applied a series of measures to "deprive their power, control their finance and grain, and reorganize their forces." In the central government, the prime minister's power was divided into three independent sections for the convenience of the emperor's control. Tongpan (magistrates) were established in local counties to supervise local governors. On the military front, the force dispatching and leading rights were

Portrait of Zhao Kuangyin, Emperor Taizu of the Song Dynasty.

separated. The imperial guard troop was regularly changed but the leader did not shift with the troop to avoid usurpation. The central government also selected the elite of local troops to the imperial guard troop to defend the capital and weaken the local units. All taxation income was submitted to the central government except a small part for local expenses. These measures to reinforce centralization were helpful in maintaining unity and stability and promoting economic development. However, some over-corrective actions resulted in repeating structure organizations, low efficiency, enormous expenditure, indirect military direction and low battle effectiveness and other serious negative influences.

In 916, Khitan's chieftain, Yelu Abaoji, living in the desert and northeastern regions, came to the throne and built the Liao regime in Shangjing (today's Lindong Town, Balin Left Banner, Inner Mongolia). The Khitans, who mainly lived on nomadism, fishing and hunting, gradually learned farming, building for settlement and invented characters based on Chinese character components. The Khitan nobles constantly looted southward and forced the Later Jin to cede Youzhou, Jizhou and 14 other prefectures and then occupied the North China Plain.

In 1004, about 200,000 Liao soldiers attacked the Northern Song and approached Tanzhou from the north side of the Yellow River, near Bianjing, the capital. Prime Minister Kou Zhun advised that Emperor Zhenzong lead the army himself. The Song army had a high morale and defeated the Liao troops. Emperor Zhenzong accepted the peace negotiation under an advantageous condition and signed the Chanyuan Agreement. Under the mutual agreement, the Song would give Liao 100,000 liang silver and 200,000 pi thin silk each year, the Liao would withdraw their army to the boundary, and both parties would become brother countries. The Chanyuan Agreement, a product of the comparable power of

Song and Liao, further increased the Northern Song people's burden. About a century-long peace was achieved after the agreement. Both parties continued to trade, resulting in a flourishing economy and cultural development.

In the early Northern Song Dynasty, the nomad Dangxiang ethnic group gradually sprang up in the northwestern regions. In 1038, Dangxiang Chieftain Yuanhao ascended the throne in Xingqing (today's Yinchuan, Ningxia), known as the Xixia. Xixia often invaded the Northern Song and won frequently. However, the battles destroyed the normal mutual trade. The Northern Song's firm defense caused grain shortage and the financial collapse of Xixia. In 1044, Yuanhao offered a peace agreement to the Northern Song. Both parties agreed that Yuanhao would cancel the title of emperor and submit to the Northern Song. The Northern Song gave silver, silk and tea to Xixia as "annual payment" and reopened border trade. From then on, Song and Xia maintained a generally peaceful trade relation.

In the middle and later Northern Song Dynasty, the Nvzhen ethnic group living on fishing and hunting in the Heilongjiang River Valley steadily rose up in arms against the oppression of the Liao. In 1115, Wanyan Tribe's Chieftain Aguda came to the throne and set up the Jin regime in Huining (today's A'cheng in Heilongjiang). After exterminating Liao in 1125, Jin initiated an invasive war against the Northern Song and captured Bianjing the next year. In 1127, Emperor Huizong and Qinzong were captured, marking the end of the Northern Song.

In 1127, Zhao Gao, a Kang Vassal from the imperial family, ascended to the throne and relocated the capital to Lin'an (today's Hangzhou, Zhejiang), known as the Southern Song. Under the leadership of Yue Fei and other famous generals, the military-civil forces of the Southern Song bravely fought against invasion by the Jin troops and won major victories.

But, vilified by the surrendering forces, Yue Fei was executed by Emperor Gaozong Zhao Gou under a fabricated charge. In 1141, Song and Jin inked an agreement that the Southern Song emperor would submit to the Jin, cede the region in the north of the Huaihe River and pay silver and silk as annual tributes to the Jin. Thus, the Southern Song only stayed in a corner in the southern bank of the Yangtze River, showing a Song-Jin confrontation in the south and north respectively.

The Image of Four Generals in the Resurgence Period describes Liu Guangshi, Han Shizhong, Zhang Jun and Yue Fei, famous generals resisting the Jin troop's attack in the early years of the Southern Song Dynasty.

Liao, Xixia and Jin's successive southward invasions brought widespread calamity to the central plains. The Song people constantly resisted the northern nomad groups' invasions and effectively fought the battles, winning a relatively sustainable peaceful development environment for the central plains and the southern regions.

The northern ethnic groups also absorbed the advanced culture of the central plains during the expansion. Liao, Xixia and Jin successively imitated the political system of the dynasties in the central plains, awarded reclamation and migrated Han people northward, resulting in further economic exchange and ethnic amalgamation.

In 947, the troops of Liao captured Kaifeng and returned to the North after depredating on local properties, which met with strong opposition. Deeply touched by that, Emperor Taizong of the Liao Dynasty drew two major lessons from the war, i.e. "indulging troops in plundering the city" and "robbing people of their private properties." He further shifted to "governing areas based on local customs" and implemented the policy of "dividing officials into two parts, with one part governing Qidan based on the state's systems

and the other governing the Han people based on the Han systems." In the regime of Emperor Shengzong, the two different systems adopted in the North and South were gradually integrated into one, with the Han systems widely applied in the central plains. Encouraged by such measures as awarding the poor with farm cattle and exempting those that reclaimed barren land from tax and duties, the vast expanses of northern bordering areas were developed during this period. In the middle of the 10th century, Liaohai in Northeast China saw a thriving phenomenon described as "hundreds of thousands of registered households and "thousands of miles of reclaimed fields." Meanwhile, great advances were taking place in iron-smelting, silk-weaving, porcelain-making, wood block printing and other handicraft sectors.

Above: A fresco of Liao Dynasty delineates the horses and attendants in a brigade, indicating the permanent nomadic living of Chitan.

Below: Iron Smelting in Xixia.

Xixia in Northwest China implemented two systems, namely the Han system and the Dangxiang system, for its official positions, and intimated the official selection through imperial examinations. The rulers of Xixia attached great importance to the culture of the central plains. They had Xixia characters created based on the Han characters, classic books of the central plains translated and printed by using the movable type printing techniques, and the coins with

Marco Polo Bridge (Lugou Bridge), built after Jin's capital relocation in Beijing as Zhongdu and measured 266.5m in full length, has 501 large and small carved stone lions sitting on rails, vivid and shape-diversified.

Han characters "Tian Shou Tong Bao" molded. With regard to production, Xixia's handicraft sectors like iron-smelting, printing, porcelain-making and wool textile making were in leading positions. The printing works with Xixia characters that have been preserved until today are the world's earliest known movable type printing work. With advanced vertical wind boxes, its iron-smelting could produce extremely sharp weapons that were reputed as the "No.1 in the world." With regard to agriculture, the farming techniques of the central plains were adopted in an all-around way, and irrigation systems were built in the river bends and Hexi Corridor areas, making great contributions to the development of the northeastern regions.

After eliminating the Liao and Northern Song dynasties and occupied areas north of the Huaihe River, Jin implemented a series of reforms to pave the way for its administration in the highly developed farming areas. Wanyan Liang, King Hailing of the Jin Dynasty who was familiar with Han characters and loved reading Han books, often discussed political affairs with Confucian scholars. In 1153, he moved the capital from Shangjing Huining to Yanjing (present-day Beijing), a city of courtesy with vast expanses of fertile land and a population full of vitality. By imitating the Liao and Northern Song dynasties, he implemented all-round reforms in official systems in 1156, restricting the hereditary privileges of the Nvzhen nobles and establishing a new regime characterized by centralization. Jin also encouraged Nvzhen people to move southward to the central plains, promote the shift of productive relations to the land tenancy system and printed notes and molded cooper and silver coins to drive forward the advances in handicraft and commerce. Meanwhile, Nvzhen people were also encouraged to marry Han people, making customs more similar to those of the Han people. According to *the History of Jin*, during the two decades following the capital move, Nvzhen people gradually changed their former customs and practiced those of Han people in daily life, music and many other aspects. Even the descendants of royal families also "practiced the Han customs since their childhood" because they knew little about their own Nvhen culture.

The northern ethnic regimes also paid attention to removing the malpractices of the central plains' dynasties in the course of the full implementation of the Han system. Thus, the Han rangers could live a happy life in the north, too.

Through decades of confrontation, collision and communication, the ethnic groups and cultures of the South and North further mixed together based on the culture of the central plains.

Social Reforms and Highly Developed Civilization of the Song Dynasty

By implementing a series of measures designed to intensify its centralized regime, the Northern and Southern dynasties ended the division since the end of Tang Dynasty and achieved reunification and stability. In the mean time, the troops and people in the central plains bravely fought against attacks from the northern nomad ethnic groups, offering a relatively peaceful environment for the southern areas that saw fast social and economic growth.

The Song Dynasty inherited and further developed the reforms adopted since the Sui and Tang dynasties, pushing forward profound changes in society.

Porcelain Pillow for Child made in the Song Dynasty. The porcelain industry was prosperous in Song. A great deal of porcelain wares, together with silk and tea, were marketed to all over the world through sea routes.

The Song Dynasty "didn't curb land merge" and allowed free sales of land. In the middle Northern Song Dynasty, most of the land had been privately owned by middle and small landlords. Agriculture and handicraft sectors saw the development of contract relationships. Tenant peasants and craftsmen were formally registered by the state. The landlord economy based on land tenancy system and yeoman economy jointly took a major position of social economy, private handicraft workshops enjoyed rapid growth, too. In 1027, Emperor Renzong explicitly ordered that tenant peasants could move freely after the tenancy contracts ended, and the land owners couldn't arbitrarily block their way. Later on, it was further stipulated that landlords couldn't use the tenant peasants' families as servants. In case of death of a tenant peasant, "his wife who gets remarried is allowed to do so and his daughter can marry anybody she likes." Besides, most handicraft workshops also employed craftsmen, paying their wages based on contracts, making craftsmen relatively free and resulting in loose personal dependency.

Adoption of land tenancy systems and employment systems was a landmark reform in production relations, resulting in high enthusiasm in the working people and much more social and economic growth.

The population at the end of the Northern Song Dynasty increased to 100 million, offering vast numbers for the workforce. Large-scale reclamation of terrace and low-lying fields resulted in more farming land—twice the area as before. New types of farm ware, like plowshares with steel blades and seedling horses for paddy rice planting, were widely used for intensive farming. Champa paddy rice, a superior breed from Vietnam, was introduced and popularized, too, greatly increasing grain output. In the Southern Song Dynasty, the proverb known as "When the area around Dongting Lake has a good harvest, the entire country has enough food" had spread across the country, showing that the national economic center has shifted from the Yellow River basins to the Yangtze River basins.

The Song Dynasty saw big progress in its handicraft sector and boasted the world's No.1 coal exploitation yields. The site of a coal mine from the late Northern Song Dynasty, located in Hebi, Henan, has a laneway as long as 500 m that

Block of *Huizi*, a paper currency in the Southern Song Dynasty.

could accommodate hundreds of miners. Its facilities for lighting, ventilation and drainage and exploitation techniques were close to the levels in modern history. Also, smelted metals such as iron and copper also represented the world's highest level of the time either in quality or quantity. During the regime of Emperor Shenzong of the Northern Song Dynasty, up to 100,000 copper-smelting craftsmen worked around Qianshan, Xinzhou alone. It is estimated that the iron output of the Song Dynasty roughly equaled the combined output of all the European countries in the 18th century. At the end of the Southern Song Dynasty, coke was used in iron smelting. As for the textile sector, cotton spinning rose during the Southern Song Dynasty, with new types of tools like spinning wheels, catapults and weaving machines. This was in addition to the development of traditional silk weaving that was characterized by more colorful patterns and more diversified categories. The porcelain-making sector was also taken to a new stage. The black and white porcelains produced in Jingdezhen, Jiangxi, were sold both at home and abroad, which is the origin of China, literally meaning "the country of porcelains."

The signpost of Jinan Liujia Needle Shop.

The Song Dynasty boasted an unprecedented prosperous commodity economy. Commercial activities went beyond the restrictions imposed since the Tang Dynasty, such as designated places and time for transactions. A large number of commodity distribution places emerged around cities and major traffic routes in rural areas, leading to the formation of bazaars and towns of different sizes. In the Northern Song Dynasty, a commercial tax was levied in towns under the county level, resulting in dense commercial tax networks and making the commercial tax one of the major revenues for governments. In the early 11th century, Sichuan saw the presence of the world's earliest paper currency—*Jiaozi*, which was designed to facilitate transactions. In the Southern Song Dynasty, *Huizi* and other types of paper currencies were widely used in circulation. Credit transactions with written deadlines and pledged by the rich emerged, too, as well as other commercial means of payment like *Bianqianwu*, an officially-operated financial organization for exchange, *Didian* for storage and negotiation and *Zhiku* for mortgage. A needle shop in Jinan, Shandong, designed its signpost like this: on the upper side was its name "Jinan Liujia Needle Shop." In the middle was a white rabbit that was accompanied by the words "recognizing the white rabbit in front of the shop as the symbol" on both sides. On the lower part were the messages for advertisement: "the needles made of superior steel bars are thin and easy to use. Any one who buys the needles in large quantities for wholesale can enjoy special offers." That is a proof of the presence of trademarks and advertisements in the Song Dynasty, and the formation of the business mode combining raw material procurement, processing and wholesale. According to *Prosperities and Dreams in the Eastern Capital*, the "transactions of gold, silver and silk" in Bianjing of the Northern Song Dynasty took place in a lane in the southern part, where "buildings were spectacular and shops were spacious," and "every deal involved an amazing sum of money," resembling today's financial street. The city of Bianjing saw densely-distributed shops in more than 400 sectors, including big markets of rice, vegetables, meat, fish and fruits, cloth, scarves, folding fans, belts, combs, needles and ironware, as well as high-grade gold and silver shops and jewelry shops. In addition to these shops, morning and night fairs along the streets took place.

The Song Dynasty also boasted an extremely advanced ship-making sector and ocean navigation techniques. Large-sized ships capable of carrying tens of thousands of *shi* of grains were equipped with sealed cofferdams and drew deep with their pointed bottoms. Compasses were adopted for navigation, making trips more safe and speedy. Encouraged by the governments, foreign trade developed quickly, with trading ships traveling to the West Pacific Ocean, Indian Ocean and Persian Gulf, and trade links with more than 50 countries and regions. In addition, the superintendencies of merchant shipping were established at important ports for administration. "Fanfang" was set up as the places for the foreign merchants to live, where "Fan Markets" and "Fan Schools" were available and Arabian merchants were allowed to build mosques and public tombs as well. In the Southern Song Dynasty, Quanzhou rose to be the world's biggest international trade port. The combined foreign trade tax collected by the superintendencies of merchant shipping in Quanzhou and Guangzhou was as much as 2,000,000 guan, making up a big part of the government's revenue.

With the economic development and social progress, the social structure and social life in the Song Dynasty experienced profound changes.

The Song Dynasty saw the final withdrawal of the scholar-bureaucrats from the historical stage. The commoner-landlords who became officials through imperial examinations took major positions and constituted the backbone of the royal ruling. The "cultivating officials" policy that highlighted preferential treatment

Imperial examinations in the Song Dynasty.

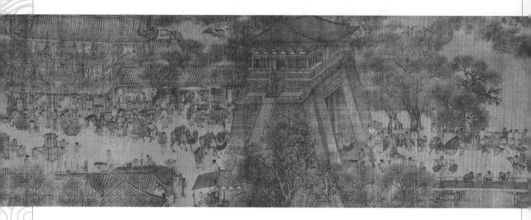

of scholars made "not killing ministers, scholars and advisors" as the "domestic disciplines passed down from ancestors," and offering high salaries and treatment for officials at various levels. That resulted in a loose and rational political atmosphere. According to the history record, Emperor Shenzong of the Song Dynasty once wanted to kill an official guilty of a crime but was stopped by his ministers by citing the "domestic disciplines." He then changed his mind and decided to send the official into exile, to which the ministers responded by saying, "it is better to die when life is a disgrace." Emperor Shenzong sighed, saying, "It's hard to do even one thing that could make him feel good." The ministers said, "He might as well not do such kind of pleasant things."

Since the Tang and Song dynasties, the country had implemented the policy of sharing profits between the government and the businessmen. With this policy, the troublesome operation of the government-run businesses and franchised businesses was contracted to the businessmen and part of the franchised business profits was shared with the businessmen. There were franchise certificates such as salt certificates and tea certificates for monopolized products.

The participation of the businessmen improved efficiency and total profits. The actual income of the government from the franchised products was increased manifold though it was only a share of the total profits. Many businessmen, especially the salt businessmen, cooperated with the government and got rich while serving the country, enjoying a respectable position. The Song Dynasty removed the former restrictions that descendants of those engaged in industrial and commercial businesses couldn't be promoted as officials, and some rich businessmen even had marriages with the royal families and officials of the court. Every time when the results of imperial examination for official selection were released, the rich would hurry to select the successful candidates to be their sons-in-law, which was called "catching sons-in-law upon release of the candidates list."

The yeomen and semi-yeomen in the Song Dynasty accounted for more than 50 percent of the total population, and tenant peasants took up 35 percent. Both the tenant peasants and craftsmen were rendered the status of civilians.

Economic growth and the rise of cities led to the increaseof the urban population in the Song Dynasty. Those non-peasant urban residents constituted the citizen class, which was dominated by businessmen, scholars and intellectuals of the upper class, craftsmen in various fields, as well as mountebanks, fortune-tellers, street artists and coolies. In the city of Bianjing, as shown in *Along the River during the Qingming Festival*, a well-known painting of the Song Dynasty, the people depicted are from all walks of life, including carpenters, blacksmiths, silversmiths, pottery makers, barrel makers, painters, grass shoe weavers, fan makers and mirror makers, as well as those selling oil, salt, paper, porridge, cakes, spices and drugs. They are jostling each other in the crowd and working hard for their own businesses, rendering the city extreme vigor and vitality.

An overwhelming majority of the population in the Song Dynasty lived in rural areas, most of whom could maintain their daily life and enjoyed a better life quality. Villagers would watch opera, listen to story-telling and have other fun during their leisure time, greatly enriching their cultural life.

A thriving commodity economy and the growth of the citizen class gave rise to booming citizen culture. Restaurants, hotels and teahouses were widespread, with the bigger ones boasting a daily guest number of up to 1,000. Just as the description goes, "Flooded with talks and laughter, the places

◗ Data Link

The Highly Developed Civilization in the Song Dynasty

The Song Dynasty of China was so modern that it surprised the whole world with its unique currency economy, paper notes, circulation bills and highly-developed tea and salt workshops...In areas of daily life, including art, entertainment, system and craftsmanship, China was a country that was "second to none" in the world and could be proud enough to call the rest of the world as "unenlightened regions."

—Jacques Gernet, *Daily Life in China on the Eve of the Mongol Invasion, 1250-1276* saw long queues of people and carriages waiting outside every time the dawn falls, and the business wouldn't be much affected in case of poor weather." The recreational places in the cities were called "*washe*," where poetic dramas, acrobatics, history-telling, story-telling, sword-dancing and other popular programs were staged all night long, making those who passed by or spectators have no thought of leaving. The development and booming of such recreational places best demonstrate the interests of the citizens and the thriving vitality of ordinary life.

The profound changes in the production relations and social structure during the Song Dynasty took social civilization to a higher level. Meanwhile, many fresh things that hadn't been seen previously emerged, too, showing the trend of evolution toward modern society.

Yuan Empire Expanded the Unified Multi-ethnic Country

At the end of the 12th century, the Mongol ethnic group, previously under the reign of Liao and Jin, grew stronger. In 1206, Temujin unified the Mongolia prairie and established the state of Mongolia. He took the title of Genghis Khan. Expeditions led by him and his successors led to a rapid conquering of vast areas across Eurasia, bringing severe tribulations to the people. The Mongolian Empire bestrode Europe and Asia, but it was actually an unstable political and military union lacking a common economic base and comprehensive laws and codes. In 1271, Kublai changed the title to Yuan and set up his capital in Yanjing to move the sovereign center toward the central plains. In 1276, Yuan troops captured Lin'an, announcing the end of the Southern Song. In 1279, Yuan unified the whole country.

Kublai, Emperor Shizu of the Yuan Dynasty, was entrusted

to rule over the Han settlements in South Desert in his early years, where he was deeply affected by the culture of the central plains. After ascending the throne, Kublai issued orders that "the state shall put its people first; people put food and clothes first and food and clothes shall rely on agriculture and sericulture." He also opposed massacring the inhabitants of a captured city and making them servants, forbade Mongolian nobles to arbitrarily take peasants' land and barren farming land as pastures. That was why the "bustling city wasn't affected by the war and remained as prosperous as before" when Lin'an, the capital of the Southern Song Dynasty, was attacked by the troops of Yuan.

Establishment of the policy of "agriculture and sericulture of primary importance" marked a significant turning point in the national policies of the Mongolian Empire and accelerated the transformation from a nomad economy to a farming civilization. The court successively set up organizations and legal systems, and attached great importance to the popularization of advanced science and technologies, which proved to be quite fruitful. The *Dasinongsi* was set up at the central level, taking charge of nationwide agricultural and sericultural

Genghis Khan's Mausoleum.

affairs. Such criteria as "growing households," "increasing reclaimed fields" and "affordable tax and duties" were adopted for achievements measurement as well as awards and punishment for local officials. The "system of agriculture and sericulture" implemented nationwide also offered extremely detailed provisions on planting affairs. Many local governments had farming and weaving pictures painted, making "its officials acquainted with basic knowledge when they passed through the paintings." Encouraging and highlighting farming then became the fashion of the time. Kublai further ordered *Daisinongsi* to compile the *Essentials of Agriculture and Sericulture* based on agricultural books both in the past and at present. This book was circulated nationwide and some 10,000 copies were printed in 1332.

While abolishing some backward Mongolian systems like "integration of army and civilians," "dividing and sharing land among people" and hereditary official positions at prefecture and county levels, Kublai imitated the systems of former Tang, Song, Liao and Jin dynasties, "establishing official positions in charge of different affairs" to stabilize political situations and appease the public. Three major systems, namely Zhongshu Ministry, *Shumiyuan* and *Yushitai*, were established at the central level, and *Xuanzhengyuan* was also set up to manage nationwide religious affairs and Tibetan areas. In addition, *Xingzhongshusheng*, or simply called "*xingsheng*," was established as the local branches of the Zhongshu Ministry and administrated by officials directly dispatched by the central government. In some remote areas inhabited by ethnic groups, *Xuanweisi* was set up for administration. To timely convey political orders and strengthen ruling over local areas, *Tongzhengyuan* and posthouse systems were also established nationwide, delivering top-to-bottom or bottom-to-top files and documents and offering traveling emissaries and officials daily necessities and traffic tools. That played a big role in consolidating the reunification.

To maintain the privileges of Mongolian nobles, the Yuan Dynasty classified people of different ethnic groups into four classes, namely Mongolians, Semu people, Han people and South people, which reflected its negative and backward side like racial discrimination and differentiation. On the other hand, the reunification of the Yuan Dynasty facilitated communication and exchange among people from all ethnic groups, resulting in the gradual amalgamation of Qidan and Nvzhen people who moved southward to the central plains. Many Persian and Arabian Islamites immigrated to China and mixed with the Han and Mongolian people, shaping a new community known as the Hui ethnic group.

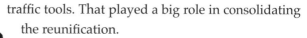

Statue of Kublai Khan, Emperor Shizu of the Yuan Dynasty.

Yuan realized a wider grand unification based on the civilization of the central plains. With vast territories, the empire expanded from areas north of the Yinshan Mountain in the north, to islands in South China Sea in the south, and stretched from present-day Sakhalin Island in the northeast to areas including Xinjiang and Central Asia in the northwest. Yuan officially included Tibet into the Chinese reign, set up an executive secretariat in Yunnan and a patrol inspection administration in Penghu under the jurisdiction of Jinjiang County, Fujian to administrate Penghu and Liuqiu (present-day Taiwan). The effort intensified Yuan's jurisdiction and exploration in these areas. The Semu people, including the ethnic groups in Xinjiang, became part of the top ruling class of the Yuan Dynasty, increasing the contacts between the central plains and Xinjiang areas.

Following the historical retrogression caused by the

changes of dynasties, the Yuan Dynasty witnessed rapid economic recovery and further consolidation of the unified multi-ethnic country. The period also saw smooth domestic traffic and outbound traffic including both land and sea routes as well as frequent Sino-foreign exchanges. Such cities as Dadu (present-day Beijing), Hangzhou and Quanzhou were much more prosperous than in any previous days. Rabban·Sauma from Uihur was once sent to Europe from Dadu, who established ties with Roman Church and wrote the first Chinese records on what he saw and heard in Europe. Marco Polo, an Italian businessman, arrived in Dadu in 1275 through the Silk Road and stayed in China for 17 years, where he was once appointed by Kublai as an official of the Yuan Dynasty. His book, *The Travels of Marco Polo*, dealt with many aspects of the Chinese life like the bustling cities, social situations, folk customs, religious beliefs and unique products, creating a sensation among the European society. The unprecedented expanding of Sino-foreign economic and cultural exchanges in the Yuan Dynasty imposed a significant influence on the world's history.

Diversified Cultures in the Song and Yuan Dynasties

In the Song Dynasty, the previous monopoly of power by military officials was broken and the national policy of "desisting from military activities and encouraging culture and education" was implemented. Against the backdrop of a thriving commodity economy, the rise of the citizen class and a relatively loose political atmosphere, such fields as science and technology, as well as ideology and culture, took on a new look.

The period saw a complete education system with schools at different levels. The institutes of higher learning included

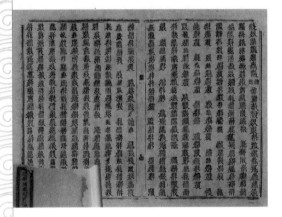

The sutra in Xixia characters printed with movable type.

private academies besides *Guoziji-an* (the Imperial College) and *Taixue* (the highest seat of learning). In 1308, Emperor Renzong of the Song Dynasty issued an order to set up schools in prefectures and counties nationwide. Meanwhile, private primary educational institutes and enlightening academies were widespread both in urban and rural areas. Such elementary textbooks as *The Chinese Family Names* and *The Thousand-Character Classic* were popularized in rural places, too. That resulted in far higher levels of overall education and literacy than in any previous dynasty.

The scientific and technological achievements during the Song and Yuan dynasties were mainly reflected in the improvement and wider application of the printing techniques, compass and gunpowder, as well as the renovation in cotton-spinning techniques.

Bi Sheng, a commoner of the Northern Song Dynasty, invented movable type printing, the earliest of its kind in the world. He engraved individual character models on clay,

The copper gun of the Yuan Dynasty has the inscription "the third year of the Zhishun Period" on its body, indicating it was made in 1332. It is the earliest metal gun with authentic record discovered in the world to date.

◉ Data Link

Influence of Ancient China's Four Great Inventions

The introduction and spread of China's four great inventions in the early European Renaissance period once played a big role in the formation of the modern world. Paper-making and printing techniques replaced religion as a pioneer in the reforms and made the popularization of public education possible. The invention of gunpowder helped remove the feudal systems and set up the national military system. The invention of the compass led to the discovery of America, making the entire world rather than Europe the stage for history.

—Thomas Francis Carter, *The Invention of Printing in China and its Spread Westward*

and then burned the clay. The clay blocks could be disassembled and stored after type setting and printing, and could be reused. The state of Xixia had wood movable type technique. The movable type printing was successively introduced into Korea, Japan and Arab countries. The technique was further disseminated to Europe in the 13th century, and to Persia and Egypt through Xinjiang, making great contributions to world civilization.

The Song Dynasty saw the extensive use of the compass in ocean navigation. Sailors fixed the magnetized steel needle on a compass with carved directions to point north, making all-time navigation possible. In the Southern Song Dynasty, compasses were introduced to Europe through Arabia, offering significant foundations for their global voyage and the discovery of the "New Continent."

In the Song Dynasty, gunpowder-making techniques were improved and gunpowder was widely used in military wars. In the Northern Song Dynasty, *Guangbei Gongchengzuo*, a state-owned

The cotton spinning wheel (an illustration from *The Agricultural Book* written by Wang Zhen of the Yuan Dynasty).

Portrait of Zhu Xi.

arm shop, was specially set up, which successively invented combustible and explosive firearms, as well as "toxic smoke ball" and pipe-shaped guns used to shoot bullets. In the middle 13th century, gunpowder was introduced to Arabian and later to Europe, arousing a sensation in European society.

While talking about the Europe before the presence of textile machines in the 18th century in his book *Capital*, Marx said, "It isn't easier to find a spinner who can spin two threads simultaneously than to find a double-headed man." But in the early 14th century, Huang Daopo, a working woman in the Yuan Dynasty, could spin three threads at the same time. Based on the principle of how a hemp spinner worked, she restructured the one-thread spinner powered by hand into a three-thread spinner powered by feet. Huang further created a set of systematic advanced techniques used in every part of textile-making, from cotton seed grinding, cotton fluffing, and spinning, to crossing threads and color matching in cloth weaving, which led to fundamental changes in the cotton textile sector in Songjiang area and helped it become an important part of the handicraft sector. In the Yuan Dynasty, cotton gradually replaced silk and hemp, becoming a kind of widely adopted raw material for clothes.

Guo Shoujing, an astronomer in the Yuan Dynasty, invented a new type of armillary sphere—equatorial torquetum, which was easy to use and compact. It was created 300 years earlier than similar devices invented in Europe.

Brush Talks from the Dream Brook, written by Shen Kuo of the Northern Song Dynasty, covers the latest achievements in a wide range of fields, including astronomy, geography, mathematics, chemistry and medical science. It was reputed as "a milestone in Chinese history of science."

The Chinese philosophy underwent great changes in the Song Dynasty. Cheng Hao and Cheng Yi of the Northern Song Dynasty and Zhu Xi of the Southern Song Dynasty abstracted the concepts of the three cardinal guides and five ethical norms to "law," and set up Neo-Confucianism, jointly called "Cheng-Zhu Neo-Confucianism." It argued the validity of despotism and class orders between the ruler and the subjects and father and son from the height of philosophy. They insisted on deepening experience to pre-existing "law" on the basis of experiencing knowledge by means of investigation of things and finally understanding the law. Lu Jiuyuan, a scholar of the Southern Song Dynasty, proclaimed that "the universe is my mind and vice versa" and one should conduct self-examination. His philosophy is called the School of Mind.

Cheng-Zhu Neo-Confucianism emphasized the immu-tability of the three cardinal guides and five ethical norms to maintain the rule of despotism and compress the natu-ral appeal of the people and generated adverse influence. However, Neo-Confucianism attaches importance to will, moral integrity, moral character, self-discipline and working energetically, and emphasizes one's social responsibility and historical mission, highlighting the dignity of human beings.

Cheng-Zhu Neo-Confucianism set up an exquisite and rigid theoretical system and became the mainstream of Con-fucianism, having a far-reaching impact on political life, cul-tural education and social cultivation.

In the Song Dynasty, the emerging Ci was the mainstream in Chinese literature. Ci, also known as the "long and short sentences," made it easy to express one's ideas flexibly and could be sung accompanied by music. After Tang Dynasty poetry, Ci poetry was another peak in ancient Chinese literature. Su Shi and Xin Qiji were representatives of the Heroic School of Ci poetry. Su Shi's Ci poetry was open and vast, elegant and unconstrained. The Ci poetry of Xin Qiji, who lived in the chaos caused by war in the Southern Song Dynasty, were generous, fevered and sorrowful. In the Song Dynasty, urban life was rich, so the Gracious School of Ci poetry emerged. Liu Yong was a representative. His poems were periphrastic and implicit, and were so popular that there was a saying that "where there was a well, there were people singing Liu Yong's Ci poetry." Li Qingzhao was the most noticeable woman Ci poet in the Song Dynasty. The style of her poems was distinct. In the early stage, her poems were happy and joyful, while in the later stage after the destruction of the state and the death of her husband, her poems conveyed feelings of homelessness and regret at the country's rise and fall.

Portrait of Guan Hanqing.

Zaju opera of the Yuan Dynasty is a kind of opera art that combines multiple performing forms, including poetry and Ci poetry, music, dancing, role-playing, singing and dialogue, to tell a complete story. Zaju as a popular form of art got unprecedented development in the period, showing that popular literature that is close to commoners' life and highlights story-telling began to rise as the mainstream of the literature. Guan Hanqing was the most famous of all the playwrights in the Yuan Dynasty. His representative work *The Injustice Suffered by Dou E* complained about the official corruption through the injustice done to Dou E, who was grief-stricken and crying "Earth! How can you be the Earth since you can't tell right from wrong? Heaven! How can you be the Heaven since you mistake the good for the guilty?" *The Romance of the Western Chamber*, created by Wang Shifu, another playwright of the Yuan Dynasty, told the love story of Zhang Sheng and Cui Yingying, conveying the common aspiration of young couples to oppose traditional restraint and struggle for free love.

The rise of the Neo-Confucianism made scholars pay more attention to self-cultivation. As for calligraphy, there were four great calligraphy artists in the Song Dynasty, namely Su Shi, Huang Tingjian, Mi Fu and Cai Xiang. They admired the calligraphic style of the Wei and Jin Dynasties, stressed personality, ignored rules, and advocated "with verve and without rules." The landscape paintings of the time focused more on the impressionistic style and expressions of temperament and highlighted verve and spirit. Among the realistic paintings that showed ordinary life, *Along the River during the Qingming* Festival by Zhang Zeduan of the Northern Song Dynasty, was the most famous of all. By adopting the "scattered dot" perspective painting technique, the painter vividly reproduced the prosperous scenes in Bianjing and along the Bianke River at the end of the Northern Song Dynasty on a five-meter-long scrolling paper, making those who watch it feel like "being personally in the bustling crowds in the city of Bianjing."

From the 10th to the 13th century,

The mural paint of Guangsheng Temple in Hongdong, Shanxi shows the theater performance scene in the Yuan Dynasty.

Europe was oppressed by feudal land ownership. The serfs were humble in position and ideology was still fettered by theological obscuration. On the other hand, the great inventions and their application, as well as the boom in urban economy and overseas trade in the Song Dynasty of the same period, marked a new height of Chinese social economy and technology, giving it a leading position in the world at the time.

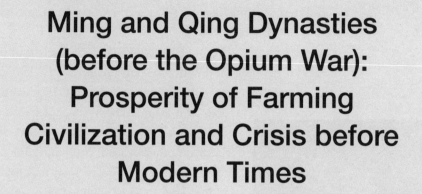

Ming and Qing Dynasties (before the Opium War): Prosperity of Farming Civilization and Crisis before Modern Times

Changes of Ming and Qing Empires and Measures Aimed to Intensify Imperial Power

The period from 1368 to 1840 was the Ming and Qing dynasties in Chinese history.

At the end of the Yuan Dynasty (1279–1368), the situation of class differences and national contradictions was deteriorating, which triggered large-scale peasant insurgence. In 1368, Zhu Yuanzhang headed a peasant army to pull down Yuan rule, defeat the leaders of other peasant uprisings and establish the Ming Dynasty with its capital in Yingtian (Nanjing, Jiangsu Province).

Portrait of Zhu Yuanzhang, Emperor Taizu of the Ming Dynasty.

Emperor Taizu Zhu Yuanzhang and Emperor Chengzu Zhu Di of the Ming Dynasty enforced imperial power by abolishing the prime minister, creating the system of Grand Secretariat and setting up secret services to enforce control over grassroots thinking and cultural circles. They moved the capital to Beijing during their reign, formulating the basic structure of the Ming Dynasty system of centralized monarchic despotism. At the same time, the rulers of the early Ming Dynasty implemented economic policies to encourage cultivation of wastelands, reduce corvee and taxes, reward those who planted cash crops and lift the social status of the craftsmen, which helped recover and develop the economy. The Yongle Period (1403–1424) of Emperor Zhu Di saw social stability and strong national strength and was another prosperous time in Chinese history.

In the early days of the Wanli Period (1573–1620), Premier Zhang Juzheng reformed the taxation and corvee systems and implemented the Single-Whip Reform to combine the

Thirteen Ming Tombs. Thirteen emperors of the Ming Dynasty were buried there.

original land taxes, corvee and incidental taxes into one and levy taxes based on land area. The reform stimulated development of the commodity economy and more than 30 industrial and commercial cities emerged south of the lower reaches of the Yangtze River. New changes similar to capitalism in western countries emerged in the production relationship and labor combination in the handicraft workshops, indicating the early emergence of capitalist relationships.

In the late Ming Dynasty, land mergers deteriorated and the peasants were forced out of their homeland, leading to the abandonment of vast lands, which became wasteland. The ruling class was greedy, cruel and corrupt and dispatched a large number of eunuchs to act as mine supervisors and tax levy officers to rob people arbitrarily, seriously damaging folk industry and commerce. At the end of the Ming Dynasty, the invasion of the Late Jin and natural disasters over several consecutive years finally triggered large-scale peasant uprisings that lasted nearly 20 years and involved several millions of people. In March 1644, the insurgent peasant army headed by Li Zicheng occupied Beijing and Emperor Chongzhen committed suicide. The Ming Dynasty came to its end. In April of the same year, the Qing army, which had arrived at Shanhaiguan Pass, summoned Wu Sangui, commander of Ningyuan of the Ming Dynasty, to surrender and beat the insurgent army and moved the capital from Shengjing (Shenyang, Liaoning) to Beijing in September, seizing the supreme dominion of the country.

The Manchu, who established the Ming Dynasty, were a new federation of ethnic groups formed after Nurhachi unified the tribes of Nuzhen during the late Ming Dynasty. Nurhachi proclaimed himself as Khan and established a kingdom named Late Jin. His son Huangtaiji ascended the throne and proclaimed himself emperor in Shengjing and changed the title to Qing. After entering Shanhaiguan Pass,

The Military Affairs Division.

the Qing army seized land on a large scale, forced the poor as their servants and compelled the residents in southeastern coastal areas to move inward for 30–50 *li*. They also forced the Han people to shave their hair and comb plait with the threat of "if you want to live, you must cut your hair; if you keep your hair, you will be killed" to follow the system of the Qing, making it a symbol of the reign of Manchu nobility. The policies of ethnic group oppression and the backwardness of the production relationship implemented in the early Qing Dynasty worsened the social economy, which had been seriously damaged by years of civil war and the trend of evolving into a modern society was interrupted.

Portrait of Emperor Kangxi.

The cruel policies implemented in the early Qing Dynasty aroused fierce resistance and the campaigns against the Qing rulers speeded up the conquering of the savage conquerors by advanced civilization. The basic crisis of the separation between the land and the laborers at the end of the Ming Dynasty was removed with the peasant warfare. A favorable condition was created for policy adjustment for the recovery of economic development in the early Qing Dynasty. During the reigns of Emperor Kangxi, Emperor Yongzheng and Emperor Qianlong, the social economy developed rapidly and reached a new height in the history of China.

The Ming and Qing dynasties saw further strengthened centralism and highly swelling imperial power.

The Six-Department System from

The History of China

the Sui and Tang dynasties remained basically unchanged during the Ming and Qing dynasties, while the Three-Ministry System was adjusted and reformed to further reduce the power of the prime ministers and enforce the power of the emperor.

During the period of Hongwu (1368–1398) of the early Ming Dynasty, the Zhongshu Ministry was cancelled and the post of prime minister was removed too. The emperor was in direct charge of the six departments and handled state affairs in person. Zhu Yuanzhang set up Diange Daxueshi to help him handle state affairs and documents and offer consultation. The cabinet system was developed during the Yongle Period (1403–1424). In the early Ming Dynasty, the cabinet had no power in deciding any state affairs independently and was only the assistant of the emperor. But the power of Daxueshi became increasingly strong and the cabinet head was actually like the prime minister of earlier times.

Wooden seal of Jinyiwei (imperial guards agency) of the Ming Dynasty.

Emperor Yongzheng of the Qing Dynasty set up the Military Affairs Division. Including military affairs, the Military Affairs Division also took part in discussions on all critical state affairs such as the military and administrative programs, civil and diplomatic affairs, including official promotions, removals and assignments and important case hearings, and drafted orders for the emperor. It was a hub for the emperor to issue orders and handle state affairs. However, the ministers of the Military Affair Division were of lower ranks without dedicated government office or subordinates and were forbidden from contacting officials without authorization. All the reports submitted by the officials would be presented directly to the Emperor and then forwarded to the Military Affairs Division to handle after being read by the emperor so as to ensure that the will of the emperor was followed without any obstacle. The decision-making and administration system centered on the emperor was efficient and confidential, enabling the emperor to maximize his control over the political situation and state affairs.

The control of the central government over local areas was beefed up during the Ming and Qing dynasties. In the Ming Dynasty, the Buzhengshi Division was set up to manage the administrative affairs of a province as a representative from the central government. Tixing Anchasi Division and Duzhihui Division were set up to manage criminal law, and military and administrative affairs. The three divisions, as representative offices of the central government in the provinces, were independent from each other, and discussed all critical issues before reporting to the central government, facilitating vertical leadership of the central government. In the Qing Dynasty, in addition to the viceroy who governed one or several provinces, Xunfu (governor) was set up in the province to take charge of administrative affairs of the province. The viceroy and Xunfu were favorites of the emperor and had the right to send confidential reports to the emperor. Sometimes the viceroy and Xunfu would be stationed in the same city and would be responsible for different affairs. They contained each other and their tenure was not long, facilitating the control of the emperor. The Ming and Qing dynasties also promoted reform in the southwestern areas and dismissed the hereditary Tusi and appointed Liuguan (appointed official) to manage local administration and exercised a similar system in the remote areas as the system in the central plain. The Qing Dynasty set up a "general" in the northwestern and northeastern areas to handle military and administrative affairs and enforce control on frontier areas.

In the Ming and Qing dynasties, the supervision system was even more rigid. Duchayuan was set up in the central government, which was responsible for inspecting and delating the officials. Duchayuan was in charge of Supervision Censors, which supervised the local officials respectively. Corresponding to the six departments, Six Division Jishizhong was set up to inspect and correct mistakes and violations of the six departments. The supervision system played an active role in cracking down on separatist forces, rectifying the official administration, punishing corruption, improving administrative efficiency and consolidating centralist rule. However, the supervision system in the Ming and Qing dynasties emphasized assessment of the loyalty of officials, but neglected supervision of duty fulfillment, especially lack of constraining and supervision of the important decision-making of the emperor. While enforcing their supervision and control over officials both inside and outside the capital city, the rulers of the Qing Dynasty also removed the right of Jishizhong to return orders of the emperors.

In the Ming and Qing dynasties, the country once again integrated the kin-based clan organizations in rural areas and controlled the grassroots people relying on these organizations. The huge control net formed by Baojia (neighborhood administrative system) and clan could be found even in remote areas and became a powerful tool for the rulers of the Ming and Qing dynasties to control the grassroots.

In the early Ming Dynasty, the emperors established *Jinyi Wei* (Brocade-Clad Guard) and *"Dong Chang"* (an espionage agency) under their direct control, which were collectively called *"Chang Wei."* They were endowed with privileges like detection and crime investigation, and inquisition by torture and killing. They constituted a compactly-organized military espionage institution and reliable support for the autocratic imperial power. To establish the absolute authority of the imperial power, the Ming Dynasty also built the *"Tingzhang* System," which allowed the emperors to arbitrarily flog any ministers who they found unsatisfactory at

the imperial court. Zhu Yuanzhang once made a guilty censor review cases at court with his feet fettered, which was called "handling public affairs in fetters." Grand ministers of state in the Qing Dynasty were kept on duty by turns in small and miserable houses near the Palace of Heavenly Purity day and night, and were asked to kneel to present written records when called in by emperors. The relationship between the king and his ministers totally became one of a master and his servants or slaves.

The centralist regime of the ancient China was highly centralized but orderly and well organized, and exercised efficient management over the vast territory and a large population with the professional bureaucrats selected via the imperial examination system. The regime was of great significance in promoting the formation and development of a multi-ethnic country and boosting economic and cultural prosperity for a long time. But the separation of power in ancient China was merely a form of work division and balancing under imperial power and could not veto the emperor, even with the expostulation system. It was a supplement to the rule of absolute monarchy. In the Ming and Qing dynasties, the monarchic regime came to a

The Palace Museum in Beijing is the imperial palace of the Ming and Qing dynasties. In the picture is the Taihe Palace, a grand palace with the uppermost hierarchy in the Palace Museum for holding the court ceremonies by emperors.

● Data Link

The Political System of Ancient China

The political system of ancient China featured precise specialization and functional division, and was managed by professional bureaucrats based on highly rationalized and verifiable established rules and precedents. In many aspects, China was extremely equipped with conditions for its transformation to a modern one… (but such ideal choice that could extensively satisfy the social need) precisely gave rise to its indolence to resist flexibility and almost excluded any possibility of changing.
　—Gilbert Rozman, *The Modernization of China*

peak and the officials were reduced to being servants of the emperor. With complete abandonment of the expostulation system in the Qing Dynasty, the possibility of correcting mistakes was systematically blocked out. Finally, the fate of the country was tied to one person, which caused serious consequences that hindered China from undergoing modern transformation.

Consolidation and Development of the Unified Multi-ethnic Country

The Ming and Qing dynasties (before the Opium War) witnessed unprecedented consolidation and development of China as a unified multi-ethnic country.

In the early 16th century, the western colonial forces rapidly expanded into the eastern world following successful opening up of the navigation routes by Portugal and Spain. In 1548, troops of the Ming Dynasty heavily defeated the invading Portuguese fleet in Shuangyu near Ningbo, Zhejiang, burning 77 battleships of different sizes. After that, the Portuguese employed means of fraud and bribery by saying their commercial ships had suffered windstorm, and were thus permitted to set up sheds in Macao for rest and clothes drying. They further built ramparts, barbettes and official mansions on the pretext of defending the invasion of the Dutch. In 1621, the Ming government destroyed the Qing-zhou city built by the Portuguese, and levied an annual silver tax of 20,000 liang upon the Portuguese in Macao. That paved the way for Macao's later development into a colonial site, though the Ming Dynasty still had sovereignty over Macao.

In the middle Ming Dynasty, Japanese warriors, merchants and pirates often harassed the southeastern coastal areas, who were called "Japanese pirates" by the Chinese people. They even once attacked Shanghai and Suizhou and finally reached Nanjing. In 1555, Qi Jiguang was entrusted to resist the Japanese pirates in East Zhejiang, succeeding in nine battles in Taizhou and basically driving away the Japanese pirates in 1565.

In 1598, the Spanish attacked Guangdong, building houses and clustering at Hutiaomen. But their houses were later burnt by the Ming troops and they were chased off the Chinese territory.

Statue of Zheng Chenggong stands in the Gulangyu Islet.

The Ming's Great Wall, starting from Yalu River in the east and extending to Jiayu Pass in the west, is 6,350km in full length.

In 1642, Dutch colonists invaded and occupied Taiwan, where they cruelly milked the Taiwanese. In 1661, Zheng Chenggong, who insisted on the wars against the Qing Dynasty in southeastern coastal areas, led a troop of 25,000 soldiers and hundreds of battleships to cross the straits eastward from Jinmen, successfully capturing Chiqian City, the strategic site of the Dutch troops. After another eight months of besiegement, he launched a fierce attack and finally forced Frederick Coyett, the Dutch Governor, to sign a surrender. Zheng's successful reoccupation of Taiwan checked the further eastward expansion of the western colonists, ensured the stability of China's southeastern provinces and played an indirect role in protecting other Asian countries.

In the 1640s, Russian troops launched large-scale invasions by taking the chance of the Qing troop's entry into the mainland of China, occupying such northeastern areas as Yakesa and Nerchinsk. They brazenly plundered the areas, severely infringing upon the sovereignty of the Qing Dynasty and endangering the safety of both life and property. The troops of Qing waged two counterattacks in Yakesa successively in 1685 and 1686, heavily defeating the Russian troops, who were forced to agree to a peace talk with only dozens of remaining soldiers. In 1689, both parties signed The Treaty of Nerchinsk, finalizing the sovereignty over the drainage areas of the Heilong River and Wusuli River, including Kuyedao (Sakhalin Island). The treaty also provided that traveling businessmen of both countries could cross the borders for trade by holding their passports. After the signing of The Treaty of Nerchinsk, the eastern part of the bordering areas between China and Russia enjoyed a relatively peaceful and stable situation that greatly facilitated bilateral trade.

The period from the Ming Dynasty to the early Qing Dynasty saw effective counterattacks for safeguarding sovereignty, as well as zigzag but generally upward development

Imperial Summer Resort and its Outlying Temples,Chengde imitates the Potala Palace, Tibet in pattern.

in bordering areas where ethnic groups lived.

In the early Ming Dynasty, the remaining forces of the Yuan Dynasty that retreated to the Mongolia pasture launched constant military attacks to the southern areas. In the middle of the Ming Dynasty, Wala unified all the Mongolian tribes, defeating a 500,000-soldier troop of the Ming Dynasty at Tumubao, capturing Emperor Yingzong alive and threatening the capital city of Beijing. In the early Jiajing Period of the Ming Dynasty, the Andahan Tribe of Tatar grew particularly strong. Between the Longqing and Wanli periods, the Grand Secretary Zhang Juzheng initiated new reforms in the bordering areas, highlighting "increasing the exchanges between the Han and Mongolians externally and reinforcing defensive systems internally." Then vigorous effort were made to amend and cement the Great Wall and consolidate the defense along the northern borders, with major participation of Qi Jiguang and other famous generals, which greatly improved the overall defense capability. Andahan had to beg for imperial conferment and peace talks because he couldn't break through the borders and urgently needed to exchange the products produced in the farming areas. The court of the Ming Dynasty accepted his request, conferring the title of King of Shunyi upon Andahan and agreed to open 11 markets for exchange. From then on, the northern border areas saw a growing population, increasing reclaimed land and frequent commodity exchange. Some key border towns developed into the "pearls at the frontiers" that had little difference from the central plains. The Mongolian areas boasted not only a booming stockbreeding sector, but also fast-developing agriculture and the rise of Guihua City (present-day huhhot) with vast reclaimed land and numerous villages. The Mongolians and Han people gradually merged with each other in many aspects like ideology, culture and folk customs. According to historical records, the Han people "living in bordering areas somewhat looked like the alien people," and this was why they were called "Han aliens" (*Han Yi*) during the Wanli Period. The Mongolian leaders also practiced the customs of Han, and even "prayed to be a member of Han in his afterlife."

After coming into power in the middle 17th century, Galdan from Mongolia's Janggar Tribe in the West Desert constantly launched attacks on its neighboring tribes. He later occupied areas both south and north of the Tianshan Mountain and colluded with the Russians to wage a large-scale rebellion. In 1690, Galdan attacked Inner Mongolia, threatening to jointly attack Beijing. To maintain national integrity, Emperor Kangxi of the Qing Dynasty personally led his army in the war and defeated the rebel forces in Uklark Poktu. Since then, the troops of Qing carried out wars against Galdan and his successors for another 70 years, and eventually destroyed the aristocratic forces of Janggar in 1571 and unified the areas north of the Tianshan Mountain. The Qing Dynasty established the post of general in Uliastai (present-day Dzhavkhlant, Mongolia) and counselor minister in Hovd (present-day Hovd in Mongolia). It also extensively set up military sentries "Kalun" along the northern borders, with densely-distributed posthouses and smooth post roads, intensifying its direct control over the northern border areas. In the meantime, the Qing Dynasty paid great attention to cultivating its popularity among the top leaders of ethnic groups by implementing the policy of "retaining their own customs based on religious beliefs," retaining their jurisdiction over their respective tribes, reducing taxes and tributes and awarding ranks of nobility and high salaries. The royal family of the Qing Dynasty even made marriages with the Mongolian nobles. In addition, 11 spectacular Lama temples were built outside the Chengde Imperial Summer Resort, where the royal members of Mongolia, who were designated to visit the emperors of the Qing Dynasty, would accompany the emperors to practice Wushu and go hunting. That helped coordinate and develop Qing's relations with all tribes of Mongolia, and helped the Qing Dynasty "rally people of all ethnic groups to consolidate his power."

In the early Ming Dynasty, the court set up seven garrisons with Hami as the center to beef up its control over the northwestern borders. In the early Qing Dynasty, Uygur ethnic group, the Islamic converts distributed in areas south of the Tianshan Mountain, were called "*Huibu*." In 1757, Burhan al-Din and Khwaja Jinan, nobles of Huibu, launched rebellions. But their tyranny and despotism made them quickly loose the popularity among the people and led to their defeat by the troops of the Qing Dynasty. After suppressing the rebellion, the Qing Dynasty established the post of general in Yili in 1762, who was in charge of all the military and civil affairs in the areas both south and north of the Tianshan Mountain. The whole Xinjiang area, including the Balkhash Lake, enjoyed unprecedented peace and stability.

During the Yongle Period of the Ming Dynasty, the court set up Nu'er Gandu Si in Telin, the estuary of the Heilongjiang River, having jurisdiction over the drainage areas of the Heilongjiang River and Wusulijiang River. In 1433, the imperial inspector minister of the Ming Dynasty had the stone tablet "Reconstruction of the Yongning Temple" erected, recording all the details about the court's administration over Nu'er Gandu Si. The inscriptions were written in Han, Mongolian, Nvzhe and Tibetan characters, serving as witness to the joint efforts of all ethnic groups in developing the northeastern areas. That was also the place where the Manchu people rose, who later replaced the Ming Dynasty with the Qing Dynasty. In the early Qing Dynasty, posts of generals respectively in Fengtian, Jilin and Heilongjiang were established to strengthen its patrol and defense along the Sino-Russian borders and check Russian invasions. That ensured the stability and safety in bordering areas and led to the unprecedented development in Northeast China.

Tibet accepted the jurisdiction of the Ming Dynasty after the Yuan Dynasty ended. The court sent troops on several occasions to put down the rebellions plotted by Janggar nobles and defeated the invasion of Gurkha. Emperor Shunzhi of the Qing Dynasty formally conferred the title of "Dalai Lama" upon the Fifth Dalai. Emperor Kangxi later conferred

Gold seal granted to Dalai Lama by the Qing court.

the title of "Panchen Erdini" upon the Fifth Panchen. In 1727, the Ming court set up the post of Minister to Tibet. In 1793, *The Tibet Statutes Published by the Imperial Order* was promulgated, stipulating that the rights of official appointments and the removal, administrative, financial, military and foreign affairs of Tibet was under the Minister to Tibet. Emperor Qianlong further formulated the "Golden Vase Lottery" system, providing that the candidates for the reincarnated Living Buddha of Lamaism must be supervised by the Minister to Tibet and determined by drawing lots in the golden vase awarded by the court. Those measures helped stabilize the political situation in Tibet, push forward the local economy and further make Tibet an inalienable part of China.

The Ming and Qing dynasties adopted the policy of "changing tribal authorities to regular officials" in southwestern areas, abolishing the post of Tusi and implementing the regime system that was the same as those in the inland areas. Furthermore, efforts were made to register households and population, measure land and reclaim barren fields, sort coins and grains, exempt Tusi's miscellaneous taxes and duties, build roads and set up schools, which changed the backward production relations. Advanced production techniques were also introduced from the inland areas, promoting local economic growth.

The gold cup inlaid with treasures indicating the stable Qing Empire, collected in the Palace Museum in Beijing.

After a century-long struggle against invasions from outside and the rebel forces from inside, the Qing Dynasty finally founded an unprecedented unified and consolidated country. It boasted vast expanses of territory that stretched from Balkhash Lake and Congling in the west, to the Sea of Okhotsk and Sakhalin Island in the east, and extended from Siberia in the north, to the Paracel Islands and Spratly Islands in the south and Taiwan and other islands in the southeast. That basically laid a foundation for the scope of today's Chinese territory. Besides, there were some other neighboring countries that were subject to, or tributary states of, the Qing Dynasty.

There were great advancements in the development of the bordering areas during the first half of the Qing Dynasty. In the reign of Emperor Qianlong, the agricultural produce in Northeast China were not only supplied for local needs, but also transported to the inland areas. The four cities, namely Qiqi Ha'er, Mo'ergen, Hulan and Heilongjiang, boasted a grain storage as much as 450,000 *shi*. Since the late Ming Dynasty, some key towns in the bordering areas between Han and Mongolia, such as Zhangjiakou, had seen the emergence of various shops, including those of silk, cloth, wool and groceries, extending for 4–5 *li*. Areas north of the Tianshan Mountain boasted up to 560,000 mu of military agricultural colonies during the middle reign of Emperor Qianlong alone. In particular, Yili was a place "where there were vast numbers of immigrants from inland areas, densely distributed villages, herds of sheep and horses and crowds of merchants. Even the wine of Shaoxing and Kunqu Opera could be seen here."

The formation and development of China as a unified multi-ethnic country was not only reflected in definite political attachment, consolidated military defenses in borders and mutual economic dependency between inland and bordering areas, but also in harmonious relations among ethnic groups as well as close cultural exchanges and psychological identity of customs. At the critical time during the resistance of the Russian invasion, Kerk Mongolia was completely defeated due to the sudden attack from Galdan of the Janggar Tribe. When discussing the solution, the Mongolian top leaders said, "Russians never embrace Buddhism and have customs, languages and clothes different from ours, so mixing with the

Russians is not a strategy for long-term stability. If we immigrate to the inland areas and be submitted to the Emperor of the Qing Dynasty, we could enjoy a happy life for thousands of years." In the third year of the reign of Emperor Congzhen of the Ming Dynasty (1630), the Turehot Tribe that was forced by Janggar to move to the areas around Volga River, began their journey in 1770 (the 35th year of the reign of Emperor Qianlong) and finally returned to motherland after experiencing all sorts of hardships and difficulties. All the above showed that only when the nomadic economy at the frontiers was combined with the commodity economy typical of the central plains and areas south of the Yangtze, and when all ethnic groups merged with one another based on mutual identity, can the vast expanses of the border areas become an inalienable part of the unified multi-ethnic country.

Prosperity of Farming Civilization and Early Emergence of Elements Typical of Modern Times

The period from the 13th to 18th century, the heyday of the Ming and Qing dynasties, witnessed great advances in farming civilization and all-around development in both social and economic fields.

In the second half of the Ming Dynasty, the Single-Whip Reform was implemented, integrating the original land taxes, corvee and incidental taxes into one. Taxes were levied based on land area. The reform stimulated development of the commodity economy and some rich people even abandoned their land properties and engaged in commercial business. In the early Qing Dynasty, the reform of Substitution of Farming Land Tax for Poll Tax adopted to levy taxes only according to land area, completely canceling the poll tax and weakening the personal bondage. That marks the maturity of the ancient tax system and shows the significant renovation in production relations.

There were obvious progressions in production techniques and managerial levels. *The Exploitation of the Work of Nature*, written at the end of the Ming Dynasty, covered about 30 techniques in both industrial and agricultural production, gaining leading position in the world. Two-season rice was promoted and unit production was increased significantly. The introduction and enlargement of the planting area of high-yield plants such as corn and sweet potato, in addition to the wide planting of cotton, significantly changed the food and clothing structure of the people. The big increase in grain output not only satisfied the needs of the growing population, but also facilitated the cultivation of economic crops, paving the way for the flow of people from the agricultural sector to the handicraft sector, and breaking the traditional agricultural structure.

During the Ming and Qing dynasties, the private handicraft

Sceneries of the Imperial Capital (part) delineates the scenery of Beijing in the mid-Ming Dynasty.

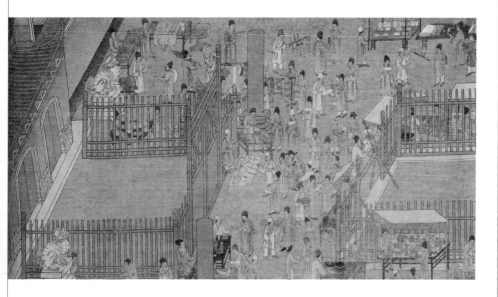

sector grew rapidly, replacing officially-operated workshops to take a dominant position. Closely linked with the market, the private handicraft sector constantly improved operations and effectively drove forward the development of the handicraft business.

Since the middle Ming Dynasty, commodity circulation expanded, with silver being the major currency in the market and commercial capital becoming increasingly active. Businessmen with huge sums of money traded and transported bulk commodities across the country, and further got involved into the production fields.

In the middle and late Ming Dynasty, some distribution centers for handiworks and raw materials appeared in areas along the Grand Canal and south of the Yangzte, and further developed into industrial and commercial cities. Clusters of numerous merchants and *Yahang*, who were intermediary businessmen that introduced deals for both sellers and buyers and appraised commodity quality and prices, proliferated there. In Suzhou, Songjiang, Hangzhou, Jiaxing and Huzhou alone, there were more than 30 cities and towns in the middle Ming Dynasty, and the number increased to more than 200 in the early Qing Dynasty.

The powerful national strength of the Ming and Qing dynasties was particularly reflected in its expanding farm land and growing population. The farming fields rose from 850 million *mu* in the Ming Dynasty to around one billion *mu* in the Qing Dynasty. The registered population surged from 66 million in early Ming Dynasty to more than 100 million at the end of the Ming Dynasty and 410 million in 1840, the 20th year of the reign of Emperor Daoguang of the Qing Dynasty.

During 1720 to 1820, the proportion of China's GDP to the world's total increased at a rate that was far higher than that of all of Europe. At the beginning of the 19th century, six out of the 10 cities with 500,000 residents and more were in

China. From the middle and late Ming Dynasty to the early Qing Dynasty, half of the world's total silver output flew into China. China was one of the centers for world economy and trade. The Ming and Qing dynasties in their heydays had obviously improved comprehensive national strength than their previous dynasties and took a leading position in the world.

A new form of business operation known as workshop handicraft had emerged in some economically developed areas since the middle Ming Dynasty.

Historical records show that in the Wanli Period of the Ming Dynasty, most of the households of Suzhou lived on silk weaving, and "most of the households in the northeast city are workshop owners." Detailed work divisions, such as the weaver, damask worker, yarn worker, dyer and cartwright, indicated that production had reached a certain size and relative high technique. The record that "the workshop owners provide the fund while the workers labor over the work" indicates that there was a pure employment relationship.

The Prosperity of the Southern Capital (part) describes the serried stores and prosperity in Nanjing in the mid-Ming Dynasty.

The workshop owners bought the laborer with the fund and production materials while the laborer enjoyed personal freedom. The employers and the employees were in a currency relationship "paying by day or hour." The records about employees "being common people who earn their own livings" and "asking others who haven't been employed to substitute them in case of absence due to particular reasons" show that employees had their personal freedom. In Suzhou, there were also temporary craftsmen in addition to the weaving craftsmen with fixed employers. The temporary craftsmen came to different sites according to their strength and waited for employment from the big employers. This record indicates that a job market was formed at that time.

This private form of operation that combined scattered employees featured a division of labor, a high degree of socialization and working efficiency. It offered qualitative changes when compared to traditional officially-operated workshops and small civil workshops. With commodity production that gets added profits from labor being its form of business operation, it highlighted free employment of labors and shows the early emergence of capitalism. The *Tongsheng Well Contract* (1779) in the reign of Emperor Qianlong of the Qing Dynasty, and *Tianyuan Well Contract* (1796) in the reign of Emperor Jiaqing, reflects that the operation forms like joint partnership, "sharing responsibilities and profits based on respective shares" were already adopted in the salt production in Zigong, Sichuan, and this kind of labor combination shows some traits of the modern stock system.

The changes that largely differentiated the late Ming and Qing dynasties from traditional economic modes indicate that the over-mature farming civilization didn't remain unchanged all along. Growth of the new elements had paved the way for the formation of a modern world and incorporated the trend of evolution towards the industrial civilization.

Culture of the Ming and Qing Dynasties with Both Old and New Forces

The Ming and Qing dynasties saw drastic changes in the Chinese society and were a turning point of great historical significance. Extraordinarily sharp contradictions and conflicts between the old and new forces resulted in a pattern in the scientific and ideological fields that was characterized by intertwining new and old elements.

The development of a commodity economy since the middle Ming Dynasty triggered the demand for renovated techniques, promoted scientific and technological growth and gave rise to a number of scientists who made certain breakthroughs in some traditional scientific fields.

An Outline Treatise of Medical Herbs, written by Li Shizhen of the late Ming Dynasty, covered an extensive range of areas including medicine, pharmacy, biology, chemistry, mineralogy, geology and phenology. He initiated the classification methods for Chinese medicines, breaking down the medicines in the inorganic sphere, plant sphere and animal sphere based on the principle of "from small to big" and "from humble to noble," which obviously incorporates the ideas of biological evolution. Li also pointed out the similarities between apes and human beings. The parts of the book that dwelt on the seven species of chicks and the domestication of goldfish were once cited by Darwin in his argument for "the differentiation occurring in the

The book photograph of Li Shizhen's *An Outline Treatise of Medical Herbs.*

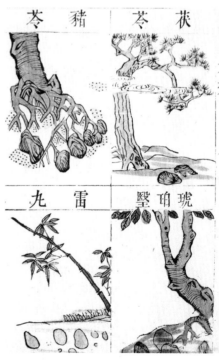

The History of China

The book photograph of *The Exploitation of the Work of Nature*.

domestication of animals and plants." Li was the first to bring forward the idea of "brain being the house of original spirit," saying human thoughts were the function and product of brains, which is of great significance.

The Exploitation of the Work of Nature, the representative of Song Yingxing at the end of the Ming Dynasty, was an encyclopedia about Chinese science in the 17th century. With a scientific attitude, he offered lots of precise data. Song's descriptions about the proportions of gold, silver and copper, and statistics about the oil yields ratio both employed specific quantitative and proportional concepts. *The Exploitation of the Work of Nature* was successively translated into Japanese, English, Germany, French, Italian, Russian and other languages and had a far-reaching influence in the world.

Zhu Zaiyu, a descendant of the royal family of the late Ming Dynasty, once submitted written statements to resign his office on seven occasions, with a view to committing himself to scientific research. He proposed the thought of "principles reflected by numbers and numbers from principles" and created the Twelve-tone Equal Temperament and the musical theory Xinfamilü, solving the theoretic problem of achieving tone changing in musical instruments that puzzled people for more than 2,000 years. Joseph Needham (1900–1995), therefore, called him "a man from the times of Renaissance although he is far away from Europe."

An Agricultural Encyclopedia, written by Xu Guangqi in the Ming Dynasty, not only summarized the previous and latest achievements, but also absorbed ideas and methods in western agricultural science and technologies based on long-term experiments, thus ensuring the agricultural book to be a scientific, pioneering and advanced one. As "the first to introduce the western science," Xu has been reputed as an epoch-making Chinese scientific pioneer in modern history because of his spotlight on mathematical research and persistence in investigation, experiment, observation and summary as trends for modern scientific research.

Xu Xiake's Travel Diaries, finished by Xu Hongzu at the end of the reign of Emperor Congzhen of the Ming Dynasty, is distinctive from common travel notes or those describing sporadic segments on superficies. In many aspects, like the descriptions about igneous rock, terrestrial heat and springs, the erosion of flowing water on rocks and the dependency of plants on climate, the book boasted the highest level of the time. His scientific investigation paved the way for research of natural science featuring precise description, in-depth analysis and revealing laws. In 1953, the Chinese Academy of Science re-investigated the 15 water-eroded caves that he once explored and drew roughly similar data. Joseph Needham appraised his traveling dairies as "having amazing capability in analyzing various sorts of landforms and employing a wide range of jargons in a very systematic way," and added that the book "reads more like investigation records finished by a field explorer in the 20th century than something written by a scholar in the 17th century."

Swarms of scientists who emerged in the late Ming Dynasty paid greater attention to experiments and mathematic methods, showing features typical of modern scientific research. But generally speaking, the science and technology in the Ming and Qing dynasties lagged far behind those of the western world. In particular, the period since the Qing Dynasty no longer saw the short-term brilliance of the late Ming Dynasty due to the suppression from the cultural autocracy and stereotyped writing system, as well as the consistent implementation of some significant achievements made previously. That led to increasingly bigger gap between China and the western world in the scientific and technological fields.

The Ming and Qing dynasties imposed tight control over the ideological and cultural fields, and the literary inquisitions, in particular, were frequently implemented in the early Qing Dynasty to crack down on any opponents and keep thoughts under control. Once careless, people would be questioned, condemned and sent to jail for reasons of boldly discussing political affairs and encroaching upon the dignity of emperors. For instance, Wang Xihou, an official candidate in the imperial examination from Jiangxi, was beheaded for his book, which was regarded as not literarily dodging the names and posthumous titles of the three emperors including Kangxi. All of his seven descendants were beheaded. Hai Chengyin, the provincial governor of Jiangxi, was sentenced to death on a probation for weak supervision, and another two officials were also suspended from duty for not pointing out the "false" parts. The cruel literary inquisitions forced the intellectuals to be divorced from real life and they engaged in obsolete books to protect themselves from misfortunes.

In the Ming and Qing dynasties, Neo-Confucianism had occupied a dominant position in official ruling thoughts. The examinations focused on the Four Books and Five Classics. The Four Books refer to *The Great Learning*, *The Doctrine of the Mean*, *The Confucian Analects*, and *The Works of Mencius*. The Five Classics include *The Book of Odes*, *The Book of History*, *The Book of Changes*, *The book of Rites*, and *The Spring and Autumn annals*. All are classic books of Confucians. The answers had to be based on the notes and commentaries of Zhu Xi and personal views couldn't be aired. The style of writing was rigidly provided to be composed of eight parts and was called "Eight-part Essay" or "Stereotyped Writing." The imperial examinations, to a great extent, evolved into a tool of the court to bring the people's thoughts under strict control. Xie Jishi, a censor during the reign of Emperor Yongzheng, was condemned as "unscrupulous" and exiled to bordering areas because he made notes to the books of Neo-Confucianism in a way different from that of Cheng and Zhu. Such cultural despotic ruling led to a depressing situation among intellectuals and seriously hindered scientific and cultural growth.

The Ming and Qing dynasties was a period that witnessed intertwining contradictions of all sorts and huge changes and renovations. On one hand, the despotism swelled and ritual norms became increasingly rigid. On the other hand, the ruling class grew extremely corrupt. Both political and religious situations went beyond control and position of the dominant ritualism was seriously threatened. The peasants' war at the end of the Ming Dynasty increased public suspicion of and criticism against the despotism and established rules. The early emergence of new economy and introduction of modern science of the west since the middle Ming Dynasty also offered a fresh impetus to the cultural renovation. Some enlightened intellectuals at the turn of the Ming and Qing dynasties, catering for the trend of commodity economy, initiated a wave of early enlightenment in the ideological field that called for personal liberation, equality and democracy.

Xu Guangqi and Italian missionary Matteo Ricci.

Li Zhi of the Ming Dynasty was famous for his heterodoxy. He lashed out with his criticism of Cheng-Zhu Neo-Confucianism, which was greatly promoted by the ruling class, and denied the claim that the doctrines of Confucianism and

Mencius were the best. In his philosophy, Confucius was not a saint, but "a common person" and the Four Books and Five Classics should not be the only thinking standards. Li said every person had selfish motives and "individual habits in dressing and eating reflect the relations among people." It is a natural gift to seek material pleasure and every one can follow one's nature to emancipate one's personality.

During the turn of the Ming and Qing dynasties, great thinkers included Wang Fuzhi, Huang Zongxi and Gu Yanwu. Wang Fuzhi emphasized that laws of things are embodied in the material world and these laws could be correctly understood with observation. His philosophy toppled the theoretic foundation of apriorism of Cheng-Zhu Neo-Confucianism. He also confirmed the rationality of emotional desire and selfish desire as natural instincts of human beings. Huang Zongxi alleged in public that, "the emperor

The Grand View Garden (part) drawn by Qing artists according to *A Dream of Red Mansions*.

is the biggest bane of the world." In his philosophy, the ruler and the subject were not master and servant, but equal teacher and friend, denying obsolete ethical norms completely. He also advocated replacing "the laws of the world enabling every person to get their own share" with "the single law of a family" to constrain the rule of the emperor. With reference to the fact that scholars addicted to reading the annotations of Cheng (Cheng Hao and Cheng Yi) and Zhu (Zhu Xi) were seriously removed from reality, Gu Yanwu exclaimed that "every person is responsible for the rise and fall of the world." He insisted on being pragmatic and caring about the national economy and people's livelihoods, and being dedicated to social reform.

Orchids and Bamboos by Zheng Banqiao in the Qing Dynasty.

The thinkers during the Ming and Qing dynasties also put forward diverse theories and assumptions about restricting the imperial power. The most prominent concept was to advocate freedom of speech, establish bottom-to-top supervision mechanisms to ensure clean politics, proper decisions and social stability.

The progressive thinkers passed criticism on the Neo-Confucianism with an unprecedented incisive style of writing, initiating a wave of progressive thoughts characterized by profound and novel philosophical concepts, political insight and a practical, critical spirit, and launching fierce attacks to the despotic ruling. Their thoughts had a tremendous enlightening influence that have lasted for centuries and gave great inspiration to the later generations.

In the Ming and Qing dynasties, industrial and commercial

towns and citizen class emerged and promoted literature development. Chapter-style novels, developed from play scripts in the Song and Yuan Dynasties, focused on narration and were close to people's lives and social reality, so novels became the mainstream of literature.

Among the "four great books" that gained nationwide popularity during the Ming Dynasty, *The Romance of the Three Kingdoms*, written by Luo Guanzhong, was the first long historical novel in Chinese history. *The Water Margin*, written by Shi Nai'an, was the first heroic and martial art novel. *The Journey to the West* written by Wu Cheng'en, was a representative of immortal being novels. *The Golden Lotus* written by Xiaoxiaosheng from Lanling, was an exemplary novel that described the ways of life and the changes in social customs. The popular short stories that featured ordinary citizens during the late Ming Dynasty vividly described the life experiences and pursuit of common people and reflected the social reality of the time.

The picture of *Thirteen Top Performers during the Tongzhi and Guangxu Periods* delineates 13 famous Peking Opera actors/actresses during the Tongzhi and Guangxu periods.

The Qing Dynasty saw the emergence of a number of literature works that put forward criticism on reality. *A Dream of Red Mansions*, written by Cao Xueqin, was the most of all. It focused on the tragic love story of Jia Baoyu and Lin Daiyu, and presented the general condition of society through the rise and fall of a noble family. The plots in the novel are complicated, but the narrative line is explicit. The language is concise and vivid, and the figures are lively and full of personality. The book is recognized by all as the pinnacle of classic novels. In addition, *The Strange Stories from a Chinese Studio*, written by Pu Songling, is "a book of indignation" aimed to express the author's dissatisfaction with the social darkness. *The Scholars*, written by Wu Jingzi, reveals and satirizes the ugly side of society and was the first long ironic novel in China.

The novels of the Ming and Qing dynasties were taken to a higher peak either ideologically or artistically, being the brilliant treasures in classic Chinese literature.

Some painters of unique styles emerged in the Ming and Qing dynasties, too. Bold and unconstrained, their artworks were a sharp contrast to the paintings of traditional style. Among the representative painters, the eight famous reclusive artists and Shi Tao were clansmen of the Ming Emperor, and became monks after the Ming Dynasty was destroyed. Through calligraphy and painting, they expressed their experience of life and their sorrow at the destruction of the country. In the mid-Qing Dynasty, eight artists, known as the Eight Eccentrics of Yangzhou, broke conventional rules in painting and manifested sharply defined personalities. Most of their works focused on flowers and birds and were in the impressionistic manner. Zheng Xie, one of the eight eccentrics, was good at painting orchids and bamboo, singing praises of lofty and unyielding character based on poetry and painting.

In the middle and late period of the Ming Dynasty, Kunqu Opera that combines poetry, music, singing, dance and drama prevailed on both sides of the Yangtze River and further developed into an opera performed nationwide. It is thus called "the origin of all kinds of opera." Kunqu Opera had elegant lyrics and dulcet aria accompanied by pauses. Performers sang and danced, and soft dance and gentle arias were combined to amuse the ears and eyes of the audience.

Anhui Opera took a dominant role during the reign of Emperor Qianlong of the Qing Dynasty by absorbing arias and performing manners from Hubei Han Tune, Kunqu Opera, Qinqiang melody and Bangzi melody. On such a basis, a new form of opera—Peking Opera—came into shape in Beijing. Peking Opera is integrated with essences of ancient opera art and presents an almost perfect artistic pattern. By comprehensively using artistic means of singing, speaking, performing and beating, performers are able to represent everything in the big world on the limited stage.

Peking Opera took the distinctive Chinese opera to a new level and is always shining in the hall of human culture.

Crisis before Modern Times

During the Ming and Qing dynasties in China, the historical development of the world experienced significant changes. One after another, the main European countries completed the leap from early capitalism to realization of capitalist class revolution and industrial revolution and embarked on the road to modern industrial civilization. The Chinese empire reached a new height in agricultural civilization and some changes from the traditional mode emerged in the social economy, and intellectual and cultural circles, with a tendency toward industrial civilization. However, when the British capitalist revolution happened, China was mired in peasant wars at the end of the Ming Dynasty before the Qing entered the Shanhaiguan Pass. Since then, the Ming Dynasty entered a track completely different from that of the western countries. In western countries, commercial economy replaced the natural economy, the industrial production replaced handicrafts workshops, state power marked by law replaced the privilege of kings and nobles, reasoning broke the hold of divinity over human minds that had continued since the Middle Ages, and science overcame ignorance. The industrial revolution helped the western bourgeoisie "create more massive and more colossal productive forces than those created by all preceding generations together." But the Qing monarchs, even during the prosperous era of emperors Kangxi and Qianlong, knew nothing about the historic transformation caused by the spread of industrial civilization, causing the country to go to the brink of its deepest crisis. The period was the watershed moment when China changed from being a leading world power to a backward country.

During the Ming and Qing dynasties, the economic structure characterized by a combination of farming and weaving
and self-sufficiency still took a dominant role throughout the
country, but civil handicraft and commercial sectors gained
a strong momentum. Since the late Ming Dynasty, the social
values and morality have changed to be money-and benefit-
oriented. The businessmen who had been despised previously were granted a very high social status and claimed
"ordinary citizens were the group of people with the mor-
alist conduct." Even Emperor Yongzheng also sighed by
saying that, "I feel it ridiculous that businessmen top all the
professionals and the scholars, on the contrary, were located
in the lowest position." Correspondingly, the proposals like
"handicraft and commerce jointly constitute the foundation
of society" and "the rich are those the whole state depends
upon" were put forward in the civil society. However, the
rulers of the Qing Dynasty believed that "one more person
engaged in commercial business would reduce one peasant
working in the farmland," and thus insisted on implementing the policies of "encouraging all the peasants to commit
themselves to farming" and "making both labor and land
exhausted." That kind of highly-intensive operation mode,
which confined vast numbers of excessive labor to limited
farm land, significantly dampened the impetus of scientific
innovation. Long-term existence of the family production
structure featuring "man tills and women weaves" also hindered the expansion of handicraft development, froze and
consolidated the natural agricultural economy.

The rulers of the Qing Dynasty considered that "mining
is bound to result in the gathering of people, which would
further lead to turbulence." Therefore, they issued orders
forbidding mining on multiple occasions, and imposed re-
dundant and heavy commercial taxes on the activities of

businessmen and owners of workshops. Under the policy, the businessmen and workshop owners could not
enlarge production by capital accumulation and forced some commercial
capital to land exploitation. That constrained the new production relationship effect and reform of large-scale
industrialization.

While practical study prevailed
and the western learning gradually
flowed into the east, the court of the
Qing Dynasty still kept the pragmatic
knowledge about science and technology outside, continued its system of
official selection through stereotyped
writing, constrained the public minds
with Neo-Confucianism and vigorously launched the literary inquisitions.
This made it difficult for modern
elements in political and ideological
fields to develop. Instead of using uniform, standardized and efficient edu-

cational selection mechanisms to push for industrialization
and social transformation, the Qing Dynasty went against
the social trend, stubbornly replicating old bureaucratic and
legal systems and seriously hindering the process of modernization.

*Farming and
Weaving Painting*
vividly reflects
ancient China's
production mode
of men for farming
and women for
weaving.

Constraint from the intensive farming mode and control
by the system of stereotyped-writing education and official
selection were also deadly stings to the science and technologies of the Qing Dynasty. There were little advances in
the scientific innovation during the period, leading to the
absence of powerful impetus for industrial revolution and

social renovation.

Before the 16th century, China's ocean navigation and ship-making techniques took a leading position in the world. From 1405 to 1433, the Ming Dynasty successively sent Zheng He to the Western Oceans on seven separate occasions. Zheng led hundreds of huge ships and thousands of sailors, reaching more than 30 countries in Asia and Africa and increasing friendly exchanges and economic communication. However, the Ming Dynasty highlighted "giving more but getting less" and seldom took economic benefits into account, making production of most goods for export supervised or forced by the official governments. That further led to the fleeing of a vast number of craftsmen and the end of the feat of ocean navigation, which was later considered as a "bad policy." The Qing court posed as a Celestial Empire, believing that it "has abundant resources and products and doesn't need to exchange goods with alien nations." Meanwhile, it closed its doors to the outside world by prohibiting sea trade and foreign trade, in a bid to prevent "alien" invasion and the anti-Qing forces in coastal areas. It closed all the trade ports except the port of Guangzhou, and only allowed "*Shisan Hang*," an officially-franchised organization, to manage foreign trade. Though the closed-door policy played a certain role in defending the nation against western colonists, it did not narrow the gap between the west and China. Instead, the policy curbed the development of foreign trade and navigation, and made the Qing Dynasty lose the opportunity to tap overseas markets, stimulate capital expansion and promote industrialization through foreign trade. It further caused a deepening obstruction and stagnancy and took China far away from the developmental tide sweeping the world.

Since the Ming Dynasty, the western Jesuits came to China in succession. They helped the spread of advanced western science and technologies while preaching, making the western learning gradually flow into the eastern world. This offered China rare opportunities to broaden its horizons and merge into the tide of industrial civilization. Xu Guangqi at the end of the Ming Dynasty timely put forward the proposal of "overtaking the western counterparts by learning wildly from other's strong points and combining them with local features based on assimilation of knowledge." But the rulers of Qing stuck to the idea that China was different from alien nations and all the western knowledge originated from the Chinese culture. The communication between the east and west came to a halt following the exile of the Jesuits during the reign of Emperor Yongzheng.

The rapid growth of capitalism put the entire world into the torrential ride of commodity circulation. The western powers swarmed into other land across the ocean, plundering

Shisan Hang, Guangzhou in charge of foreign trade in the Qing Dynasty.

valuable things, trading slaves and establishing respective colonial rulings. That resulted in a swift change in the comparison between the western power and the Qing Empire, who had always been enthusiastic about Neo-Confucianism and went all out to defend its farming-based ruling. During the reign of Emperor Qianlong, George Lord McCartney (1737–1806), an emissary from Britain, once claimed that only several three-mast battleships would be enough to destroy the whole coastal fleet of the Qing Dynasty if China forbad Sino-British trade or caused severe loss to them. The seemingly ridiculous prediction did come true, and this was why Emperor Daoguang sighed and said, "what a shame it is not to repel the attack of two alien ships! It is no wonder we are despised by the alien nations given our poor military strength."

The Opium War in 1840 finally broke the natural process of China's society and the Chinese people faced the arduous, solemn and inspiring war of gaining national independence and embarked slowly on an arduous, complex and unique road to modernization.

● Data Link

Doomed Fate of the Qing Empire

A great empire that made up almost two thirds of the world's population ignored the changes in the outside world and felt content with things as they were. It was isolated from the rest of the world by itself and had consequently attempted to self-deceive by the illusion that the empire was an extremely perfect one. Such an empire was doomed to be a loser in the final deadly duel.

—Karl Marx, *History of the Opium Trade*

Fall and Struggle
of Modern China

Western Powers Invade China and Chinese People Rise in Resistance

In the 16th century, western colonial powers came to the remote eastern land to seek destinations for markets and overseas colonies. In 1514, the Portuguese landed on Chinese land. Afterwards, the Spanish, Dutch and British came to China in succession. In 1793, a British delegation led by McCartney required the Qing imperial courts to open trading ports, establish firms, and even provide Zhoushan Islands for "dry goods." The Qing imperial court determinedly refused.

Britain, which was in a deficit in trade with China, started to smuggle opium and seduced Chinese civilians and soldiers to get addicted to opium in order to overturn the condition of trade deficit. The quantity of opium imported had reached more than 40,000 boxes per year by 1840.

The Chinese people suffered a lot from imported opium. If the import had continued without any restriction, China would "have no troops to resist invasion and have no money to afford the army." Lin Zexu, the government inspector, organized the destruction of captured opium in Humen,

Relief: Destroying Opium at Humen.

Guangzhou, in June 1839. Britain outrageously invaded China in June 1840, launching the Opium War. China had backward military equipment and was weak in military operations. Moreover, the Emperor of the Qing Dynasty was anxious to win at the beginning and quickly turned to compromise and surrender after failing to win within a short time. Therefore, China lost the war. In August 1842, the imperial court of the Qing Dynasty *signed The Sino-UK Treaty of Nanking*, remising land and paying silver to Britain. The treaty humiliated the nation and forfeited its sovereignty.

On Aug. 29, 1842, Chinese and British representatives inked *The Sino-UK Treaty of Nanking* in British vessel Cornwallis.

In the six decades between the Opium War and the early 1900s, China was invaded and humiliated by superpowers several times. The Second Opium War, Sino-French War, Sino-Japanese War and the invasion of the Eight-Power Allied Forces, forced the imperial court of the Qing Dynasty to sign a series of unequal treaties, which affected Chinese political, economic and cultural fields and infringed Chinese sovereignty of territory, jurisdiction and administration. Since then, China ceased the approach of independent development and was involved in the western capitalist system,

and gradually reduced to being a colony or semi-colony.

When western powers invaded China, they violently destroyed China's situation of remaining separated from the outside world, and destroyed the country's traditional economy of natural self-sufficiency. They directly established factories and built railways in China to exploit the cheap labor, dump commodities and plunder resources. At the same time, they spread new social factors, acted as an unconscious historical tool and initiated China's modernization to some extent. As western powers attacked China, national bourgeoisie and the proletariat came into being in the country. With the bankruptcy of a large quantity of farmers, a semi-proletariat class was created.

After World War I, Japan consolidated its power in

Remnants of the Yuanmingyuan Garden. The imperial garden of the Qing Dynasty was burned by the combined armies of English and French and Eight-Power Allied Forces.

On Sept. 9, 1945, the official surrender ceremony of Japanese troops in Chinese Theater was held in Nanjing. Okamura Yasuji, commander-in-chief of the Japanese invasion army, is signing on the Instrument of Surrender.

China. In 1931, Japan instigated the Mukden Incident and invaded Northeast China, and instigated the Marco Polo Bridge Incident in 1937, extending its invasion scope to northern China and even the whole Chinese territory. During the 14 years while Japan invaded China, it turned occupied areas into military and industrial bases to raven economic resources in "military management" and "consignment operation" manners. Japanese invaders made the extremely cruel Nanking Massacre, and carried out brutal germ wars and chemical wars. According to statistics, the number of people killed by Japanese invaders was 35 million, the direct economic loss was $100 billion, and indirect economic loss reached $500 billion.

Over the 100 years since the Opium War, the Chinese

◔ Data Link

Gradual Collapse of the Natural Economy

On the eve of the Opium War, the early emergence of capitalism cultivated in the Chinese feudal society somewhat grew through centuries of development, but the growth was slow and the feudal natural economy featuring self-sufficiency still played a dominant role in China.

In the wake of the Opium War, treaty ports were opened in succession, resulting in a huge influx of foreign goods into the Chinese market. Foreign cotton and cloth replaced local cotton and cloth because of their high quality and low price, making "weaving" separated from "farming" in China. Songjiang and Taicang in Jiangsu were previously China's center for the cotton textile sector and enjoyed the reputation of clothing and quilting the world. But "the cloth markets in Songjiang and Taicang shrank significantly" after the Opium War due to the sales increase of foreign cloth. The textile-dominated rural areas in southeastern coastal regions suffered a huge attack, too, and no cotton was available for spinning and no cloth for weaving. Though such phenomena occurred locally, they were the omen of the collapse of China's natural economy.

Foreign businessmen also bought large quantities of agricultural produce, byproducts and local specialties from China, with silk and tea as the bulk goods. The foreigners controlled China's export trade in silk and tea, making the production increasingly commercialized and objectively eroding the base of the former natural economy of China.

people shared the same hatred to invading powers and rose to fight. Guan Tianpei and Chen Huacheng strictly guarded cannon stands in the Opium War. Zuo Zongtang heavily beat Russian invaders and took back Xinjiang. Feng Zicai led his army to victory in the important battle in Zhennanguan, defending state sovereignty and national dignity. Deng Shichang sacrificed on Zhiyuan Warship in fighting against the Japanese army in the Yellow Sea. Solders and civilians in Taiwan continued fighting after the Qing imperial court had to remise the land. These heroes represent the brave, utterly fearless fighting spirit of the Chinese.

In August 1945, the Chinese people won the Anti-Japanese War after eight years of fierce fighting, with the support of international anti-Fascist forces.

Dr. Sun Yat-sen and his wife Soong Ching Ling.

Democratic Revolutions in Modern China

Since the Opium War, Chinese people fought against foreign enemies on the one hand, and on the other hand struggled to overthrow the Qing imperial court and establish a democratic political system.

The Taiping Heavenly Kingdom farmers' uprising, which broke out in 1851 and lasted 14 years, shook the domination of the Qing Empire. When Hong Renxuan, one of the leaders of the rebel army, directed the regime, he imitated western countries and proposed *A New Treatise on Political Counsel*, the first social reform scheme with capitalist features in modern China. The policy advanced the democratic process to some extent in modern China.

Between the 19th and 20th centuries, national

capitalism was in its initial stages, and the national bourgeoisie launched a campaign for democratic revolution.

In 1898, the advocates of reform, led by Kang Youwei and Liang Qichao, persuaded Emperor Guangxu of the Qing Dynasty to carry out comprehensive reform. The reform required the setting up of newspaper offices and translation bureaus, freedom of speech, training a new type of navy, transforming the old imperial examination system, establishing new types of schools, transforming the financial system, and planning the national budget and final settlement. However, the reform lasted only 103 days, as the conservatives, led by Empress Cixi, put an end to the process.

Sun Yat-sen, a pioneer of democratic revolution, established the China Revival Society with more than 20 patriotic overseas Chinese in 1894. The organization was the first bourgeoisie revolutionary group in China. Since then, China began the bourgeoisie democratic revolution. In 1905, the Chinese Revolutionary League was formally founded, and the revolutionary guiding principle was to "repel foreign invaders, revitalize China, establish a republic and average

Abdication of the Emperor of the Qing. On Feb. 12, 1912, Emperor Puyi announced to abdicate.

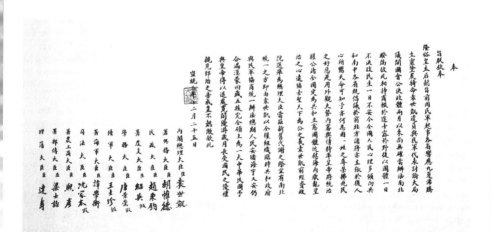

land," which was proposed by Sun Yat-sen. He subsequently simplified the guiding principle into the Three People's
Principles, namely nationalism, democracy and the people's
livelihood.

On October 10, 1911, the Wuchang Uprising broke out, firing the first shot at the Qing imperial court. In the following
months, rebellions flared in all provinces. The Qing Empire
disintegrated. Individual independent provinces negotiated
and approved the *Organization Outlines of the Provisional
Government of the Republic of China,* confirming that the provisional government had implemented a presidential republic system.

On January 1, 1912, Sun Yat-sen was sworn in as the inter-
im President of the Republic of China in Nanjing, marking
the founding of the Republic of China. The provisional government in Nanjing promulgated *the Provisional Constitution
of the Republic of China,* stipulating that the sovereignty of the
Republic of China belonged to all nationals, and citizens had
the right to personal freedom, election, participation in political activities, habitation, free speech, publishing, assembly,
communication, and freedom of religion. The provisional
government issued decrees to announce that the Republic of
China would conduct friendly communications with other
countries, be subject to international laws, abolish various
taxes, protect national industries, reward overseas Chinese
people for domestic investments, advocate moral education
for citizens under the tenets of "freedom, equality and affection," and oppose the old ethical education.

On February 12, 1912, Emperor Puyi of the Qing Dynasty
announced his abdication, marking the end of the Xinhai
Revolution. The revolution had several historical signifi-
cances, including overthrowing the Qing Empire that ruled
China for more than 200 years, overturning the autocratic
monarchy that lasted for two millenniums, establishing

a democratic republic, and achieving a breakthrough in the progress of Chinese political civilization. The revolution put the concept of democracy and republic deep into everyone's heart, laid an ideological foundation for subsequent bourgeoisie revolution, and paved the way for keeping up with international development trends and realizing the modernization of the Chinese nation's political system.

The site of the First National Congress of the CPC in Shanghai. On July 23, 1921, the First National Congress of the Communist Party of China was held in the place.

After the Xinhai Revolution, Chinese political fortunes turned. Widespread skirmishes among warlords led to disasters to both the people and the state.

After the victory of the October Revolution in Russia in 1917, a number of pioneering Chinese intellectuals began to accept Marxism and Leninism. The May Fourth Movement, aimed at striking against imperialism and feudalism, was also a new cultural movement that disseminated democracy and science. The movement further helped combine Marxism and the Chinese labor movement. The Communist Party of China was founded in Shanghai in 1921, which was a milestone of new democratic revolution led by the proletarian class. The Communist Party of China merged Marxism and Chinese practices and finally accomplished the victories of the Anti-Japanese War, the Liberation War and the new democratic revolution, overcoming many difficulties along the way.

The People's Republic of China was founded On October 1, 1949, which brought the Chinese nation to a brand new historical stage.

National Capitalist Development

From the very beginning, China's national industry had two kinds of government-run industries predominated by the state and private capital enterprises.

The Anqing Interior Arsenal, the result of the Westernization Movement of the Qing imperial court, was established in 1861, indicating the start of government-run industry of national capitalism. Prior to the 1870s, the Westernization Movement called for "self-renewal." A number of military factories were set up, and large factories included Kiangnan Arsenel, Fuzhou Ship-Building Bureau and Tianjin Manufacturing Bureau. After the 1870s, the Westernization Movement called on "wealth," and a number of civilian-use factories were built, such as the Shanghai Merchants Steamship Bureau, Kaiping Mining Bureau, Shanghai Weaving Bureau and Hanyang Iron Factory. These factories utilized advanced technologies and equipment, and their products were for both military and civilian use. They somewhat resisted the expansion of the economic strength of foreign capitalism.

Government-run industry initiated by the Westernization Movement marked the takeoff of Chinese industrialization and left a precious legacy for Chinese industrial, military and educational departments.

Private enterprises emerged in the 1870s. Outstanding private companies were Shanghai Fachang Machinery Factory, Guangdong Jichanglong Filature Factory and Tianjin Yilaimou Machinery Mill. After the Sino-Japanese War in 1894, the Qing imperial court loosened its restrictions on private factories and set up the ministry of commerce in 1903 to encourage industrial and commercial development. At that time, an upsurge in the spirit of saving the country through industry emerged in China, and a number of industrialists made contributions to the nation.

However, there were extreme difficulties on the way to the development of a modern national capitalism in China. Western powers suppressed national industrial development depending on rich capital, technological advantages and priorities snatched in China. The high tax rate of the Qing Dynasty and extortion by governments at all levels increased the cost of products, thus reducing their competitive edge. Private enterprises had to rely on foreign capitalism to a certain extent or seek protection from the domestic government in order to survive.

The foundation of the Republic of China in 1912 raised the political status of the national bourgeoisie and evoked the aspiration among national capitalists to revitalize industry.

During World War I, major capitalist countries in Europe were busy with the war, so capital and commodity exports to China were reduced, and Chinese national industry developed rapidly. From 1903 to 1908, the number of registered factories in China was 21 per year. The number increased to 41 between 1913 and 1915 and 124 between 1916 and 1919. Soon after the end of World War I, foreign capital staged a comeback, putting Chinese national industry under heavy

Left: Jiang Nan Machinery Manufacture Arsenal founded during the Westernization Movement.

Right: China Cement Works in Nanjing, built in the period of the Republic of China, is one of the representatives of China's early national industry.

pressure through its great strength and competitive edge.

In the 1930s, bureaucratic capital emerged prior to the Anti-Japanese War, and the four largest families were its representatives. They implemented "economic ruling" policies by making use of their political rights, and obtained a great deal of resources and income by unified purchase and unified sale, monopoly sale, price restriction and bargain measures. The four families took up a dominant position in national industry.

Since the Opium War, Chinese people suffered from the chaos caused by war and their living standards were

A workshop of a spinning mill in the period of the Republic of China.

also lowered. During the period of the Republic of China, the limited social and economical development could not shake off the shackles of poverty for the people. The purchasing power of the legal tender issued by the government of the Republic of China is a good example. Before the Anti-Japanese War, 100 yuan was worth two bulls, two eggs in 1945, two pieces of coal ball in 1947, and only 0.0001gm of rice in 1949. In the same year, China had 20,000 km of railways, of which roughly just half could be used. The length of useable highway was less than 80,000 km, and most of the roads were located in developed southeastern coastal areas. Highways were not available in mountainous regions and in the border areas inhabited by ethnic groups, which made up more than two-thirds of the gross land area in the state. As foreign commentators said, China was a country that needed to import even an iron nail.

Exploration Progress of the People's Republic of China for Socialist Modernization

On October 1, 1949, the People's Republic of China was founded, indicating that the Chinese nation was liberated and independent and had begun a historical approach to socialist modernization. The New China has been exploring its route to socialist modernization through the construction of democracy and legal systems in the political field, economic system reform, participation in international competition and cooperation, and maintenance of world peace and stability.

October 1, 1949 witnessed the establishment of the People's Republic of China. Chairman Mao Zedong declares the Announcement of the Central People's Government on the Tian'anmen Rostrum.

Political Construction of New China

Since its foundation, New China has dedicated itself to building a political system that is suitable for practical conditions. The political system is comprised of the people's congress system with the principle of democratic centralism, multi-party cooperation and political consultation under the

leadership of the Communist Party of China (CPC), and the system of regional autonomy of ethnic minorities with ethnic groups as their own administrators.

The people's congress system is the fundamental political system of China. According to the *Constitution of the People's Republic of China*, the power of the nation belongs to the people. The National People's Congress and the local people's congresses at various levels are the organs through which people exercise state power. Local people's congresses at various levels are constituted through democratic elections. They are responsible to the people and subject to their supervision. The National People's Congress is the supreme organ of state power. It is entitled to amend the Constitution, enact laws, elect national leaders, approve national economic development plans and determine war and peace.

The Monument to the People's Heroes stands in the Tian'anmen Square, Beijing.

The system of multi-party cooperation and political negotiation under the leadership of the CPC is characteristic of modern China. The first constitution of New China formulated in 1954 stipulated the ruling party status of the CPC and the right of participation in the management of state affairs. In 1982, the CPC once again proposed its principle on democratic parties, namely "long-term coexistence, mutual supervision, sincere treatment of each other and the sharing of weal or woe." The system of multi-party cooperation and political negotiation was further enhanced.

The system of regional autonomy of ethnic minorities is adapted to the basic national conditions of a unified multi-ethnic country. China has 56 ethnic groups, and Han people

October 1, 2009, the 60th anniversary of the establishment of the People's Republic of China.

account for more than 90 percent of the gross population. Over the years, people from various ethnic groups have come to inhabit some areas together, and some ethnic groups are centralized in some areas. Regional autonomy of ethnic groups is under the unified leadership of the state

○ Data Link

Hong Kong and Macao's Returns to Motherland

Hong Kong and Macao have long been part of the Chinese territory since ancient times. Hong Kong was occupied by the United Kingdom after the Opium War; Macao was occupied by Portugal step by step after the mid 16th century.

The Chinese government put forward the policy of "One Country, Two Systems" to solve the Hong Kong and Macao issues left over by history. In December 1984, the Chinese and British governments signed *The Joint Declaration on the Future of Hong Kong*. In April 1987, the Chinese and Portuguese governments signed *The Sino-Portuguese Joint Declaration on the Question of Macao*.

The Chinese government resumed its exercise of sovereignty over Hong Kong on July 1, 1997, and Macao on December 20, 1999. On the days when Hong Kong and Macao returned, special administrative regions were established, respectively, and the policies of "Hong Kong people administering Hong Kong," "Macao people administering Macao" and "a high degree of autonomy" have been implemented since then.

and aims at equality of each ethnic group and national unity. Regional autonomy is implemented in some areas inhabited by ethnic people, and autonomous governments are established to exercise the right to autonomy. At present, China has five provincial-level autonomous regions and more than 100 autonomous prefectures and counties.

Since the 1980s, China has intensified its policy of political reform and the reform of democracy and legal system. In 1999, the tenet of "governing the country according to law" was added to the Constitution, which was a milestone marking China's entry into a new historical stage of building a law-based society.

Socialist Economic Development

When the People's Republic of China was founded, it possessed nothing. In 1953, the CPC determined the "general line during the transition period," planning to realize socialist industrialization and complete socialist rebuilding of the national agriculture, handicraft industry, and capitalist industry and commerce in the long term.

In 1953, China began implementation of the first five-year national economic development plan. The goals of the First Five-year Plan were reached in advance in 1957. China built up aircraft manufacturing, motor manufacturing, electricity generation equipment manufacturing, metallurgical equipment manufacturing, high-level smelting and other industries. Basic industries took an initial shape. Iron and steel, coal and power facilities were built in the central and western areas. A reasonable industrial layout took shape and the process of socialist industrialization had begun.

At the end of 1956, the socialist rebuilding of agriculture, handicraft industry, and industry and commerce was completed, and a planned economic system was established in

China. The system paved the way for the development of Chinese socialist industrialization and also exposed various defects of the system, foreshadowing later difficulties in economic development.

Due to the underestimation of the arduous, complex and long-term socialist construction process, Chinese economic construction stressed one-sided high speed in 1958. Movements of "smelting iron and steel," "people's commune" and "great leap forward" emerged in China, upsetting the balance of national economy proportion, destroying the ecological environment and discouraging people's initiative for production.

Farmers are filled with joy of harvest through the implementation of the household contract responsibility system.

Between 1956 and 1966, Chinese modernization experienced a tortuous path, but great achievements were still made. An independent industrial system of a certain size and technical level was established. Power, mining and machinery industries largely thrived. Electronic, atomic power and space industries emerged and grew. The construction of

the Daqing, Shengli and Dagang oil fields deleted China's reputation of being poor in oil. Apart from Tibet, the railway linked all provinces, municipalities and autonomous regions.

From 1966 to 1976, China suffered the unprecedented calamity of the Cultural Revolution. Pinko mistakes in economic development permeated, badly interrupted and destroyed the national economy, and hindered the progress of Chinese industrial modernization. According to estimations, the national economic loss during the Cultural Revolution

A street in
Shenzhen in 1981.

Today's Shenzhen.

Pudong, Shanghai
has evolved into a
base of hi-tech and
modern industries
from a rural area.

was worth about 500 billion yuan.

The Third Plenary Session of the Eleventh Central Committee of CPC was convened in 1978. The session decided to carry out reform and opening-up and transfer the key point of CPC's work to economic development, initiating economic reform in China.

The reform began in rural areas. The household contract responsibility system, characterized by fixing of farm output quotas for each household, provided farmers with autonomy in production and management, which dramatically encouraged farmers. Township enterprises emerged and flourished, promoting economic development in rural areas and improving the living standard of farmers.

The reform in rural areas drove the economic system reform in urban areas. In 1992, the 14th Central Committee of the CPC put forward the goal of Chinese restructuring of the economic system, which was to establish a socialist market economy by deepening the reform of state-owned enterprises, establishing a modern enterprise system, and encouraging enterprises to become legal entities and competitors.

The reform of state-owned enterprises promoted competitiveness of enterprises and forged a number of powerful and thriving large-scale enterprise groups. State-owned assets increased sharply. Some enterprise groups entered the global market.

During the reform of state-owned enterprises, some problems occurred, such as an increase in the number of laid-off workers and economic difficulties of some employees. As the social security system is gradually perfected, the situation is also being improved.

While carrying through domestic reform of the economic system, the Chinese government implemented opening-up as well. Since 1980, China has set up five special economic zones along its coastline, opened a host of coastal port cities, promoted foreign investment and energetically developed export-oriented industries. In 1990, the central government decided to open and develop Pudong, Shanghai. In the 1990s, China created an all-dimensional, multi-tiered and wide-ranging opening pattern from the coastal area to inland, and from the eastern to the central and western regions.

China entered the WTO in 2001, indicating that its opening up had reached a new stage. China's access to the WTO is a necessary means for the country to go global and is an opportunity for China to integrate with the international economic system.

Over the past three decades, reform and opening-up have advanced each other and prompted China's fast economic growth. From 1979 to 2008, the growth rate of GDP was 9.8 percent per year, which is rare in world economic records.

◗ Data Link

Process of China's Opening Up to the Outside World

Since 1978, China's opening up has undergone six phases: (i) trial establishment of special economic zones; (ii) opening of coastal port cities; (iii) further expanding coastal areas for opening up; (iv) opening and developing Pudong New Area of Shanghai; (v) all-around opening of cities in bordering areas, along the Yangtze and interior provincial capital cities; (vi) China's entry into WTO, marking a brand-new phase for its opening-up.

Over the past 30 years since its opening up, China has successively set up five special economic zones, opened 14 coastal port cities and Pudong New Area of Shanghai, establish 15 bonded areas, 32 economic and technological development zones, 52 high-tech development zones and 38 export processing zones, and opened 13 border cities, six cities along the Yangtze and 18 provincial capital cities. That helps formation of an all-dimensional and multi-tiered pattern for China's opening up.

According to World Bank statistics, the GDP per capita in China was merely \$230 in 1978, ranking 104th among the 126 countries and regions listed. At that time, many Chinese people did not have sufficient food or clothing. In 2008, the GDP reached \$4.32 trillion, and China's economic aggregate was at the third place in the world, with GDP per capita hitting \$3,266.

In 2002, the 16th Central Committee of the CPC called for the building of a well-off society in an all-around way, proposing the ambitious objective of reaching a GDP in 2020 that would be four times that of 2000, on the basis of optimized structure and increased profits.

Foreign Relations of Modern China

After World War II, the western world and the eastern world faced off. As soon as the People's Republic of China was founded, the Chinese government started frequent diplomatic activities.

In terms of relations with neighboring and friendly countries, China proposed the Five Principles of Peaceful Coexistence, namely mutual respect for each other's sovereignty and territorial integrity, non-aggression, non-interference in each other's internal affairs, equality and mutual benefit, and peaceful coexistence. These magnanimous and open principles, which were

not bound by ideology and social system, were gradually recognized by the international community, and became basic principles for conducting international relations. At the Bandung Conference of 1955, China insisted on the guideline of "seeking common ground while reserving differences." The participants reached an agreement of Ten Principles under the Five Principles of Peaceful Coexistence, promoting unity and cooperation among Asian and African countries.

In 1971, the 26th General Assembly of the United Nations (UN) approved the proposal overwhelmingly, recovering all

The 26th General Assembly of United Nations resumed the legal seat of the People's Republic of China in October 1971. Members of Chinese delegate laugh heartily.

In February 1972, US President Nixon visits China upon invitation.

legal rights of the People's Republic of China in the UN.

The Ping Pong Diplomacy and the secret visit of Kissinger to China in 1971 revived Sino-US relations. US President Richard Nixon visited China in 1972, and both sides signed the *Sino-US Joint Communique*, emphasizing the conduction of Sino-US relations under the Five Principles of Peaceful Coexistence. In 1979, China and the United States established formal diplomatic relations.

Japanese Prime Minister Tanaka Kakuei visited China in 1972, and signed the Agreement of Relation Normalization between China and Japan, marking a new era in Sino-Japanese relations.

As relations between China and the US and Japan improved, many western countries established diplomatic relations with China.

In August 1978, China-Japan Peace and Friendship Treaty is inked in Beijing.

Since the 1980s, China has continued to insist on the Five Principles of Peaceful Coexistence. China did not ally with any big country or big groups of countries. Rather China developed friendly and cooperative relations with all counties.

In December 2001, China enters WTO, marking China's position as an important part in the global economic system.

China's independent and peaceful diplomatic policies have been enriched and improved, and a new full-range diplomatic pattern was formed in the 21st century.

China has also contributed to regional peace and stability. China joined APEC (Asia-Pacific Economic Cooperation) in 1991 and played an important role in the APEC cooperation progress. China signed the *Foundation Declaration of Shanghai Cooperation Organization* with Russia, Kazakhstan, Kyrgyzstan, Tajikistan and Uzbekistan in Shanghai, to establish the Shanghai Cooperation Organization. In addition, trade cooperation between China and ASEAN developed in an all-around way, with the China-ASEAN free trade zone being established in 2001.

Since China recovered its lawful seat in the UN, the country has carried out activities in accordance with the objectives and principles of the UN Charter and is trusted and recognized by the international community. As a permanent member of the UN Security Council, China actively takes part in peacekeeping actions and promotes the UN

In 2008, China successfully held the 29th Olympic Games.

disarmament plan, making positive contributions to moderating the international situation and maintaining world peace.

By the end of 2009, China had established diplomatic relations with 171 countries in the world, joined more than 100 inter-governmental organizations, and signed almost 300 international treaties. Today's China insists on peace, development and cooperative principles, an independent foreign policy of peace, a peaceful development approach, and an opening-up strategy of mutual benefit, and continues to endeavor to play a constructive role in international affairs and urge the international order to develop in a more reasonable and just direction.

Appendix:
Chronological Table of the Chinese Dynasties

The Paleolithic Period	Approx. 1,700,000–10,000 years ago
The Neolithic Age	Approx. 10,000–4,000 years ago
Xia Dynasty	2070–1600 BC
Shang Dynasty	1600–1046 BC
Western Zhou Dynasty	1046–771 BC
Spring and Autumn Period	770–476 BC
Warring States Period	475–221 BC
Qin Dynasty	221–206 BC
Western Han Dynasty	206 BC–AD 8
Eastern Han Dynasty	25–220
Three Kingdoms	220–280
Western Jin Dynasty	266–316
Eastern Jin Dynasty	317–420
Northern and Southern Dynasties	420–589
Sui Dynasty	581–618
Tang Dynasty	618–907
Five Dynasties	907–960
Northern Song Dynasty	960–1127
Southern Song Dynasty	1127–1276
Yuan Dynasty	1271–1368
Ming Dynasty	1368–1644
Qing Dynasty	1636–1911
Republic of China	1912–1949
People's Republic of China	Founded in 1949

Struggle and Suffrage
in
Windsor

Struggle and Suffrage in Windsor

Women's Lives and the Fight for Equality

By Katharine Johnson

PEN & SWORD
HISTORY

AN IMPRINT OF PEN & SWORD BOOKS LTD.
YORKSHIRE · PHILADELPHIA

First published in Great Britain in 2019 by
Pen & Sword History
An imprint of
Pen & Sword Books Limited
Yorkshire - Philadelphia

ISBN 978 1 52671 925 6

A CIP catalogue record for this book is available from the British Library

Typeset in 11.5/14 point Times New Roman
by Aura Technology and Software Services, India

Printed and bound in England
by TJ International, Padstow, Cornwall

Pen & Sword Books Limited incorporates the imprints of Atlas,
Archaeology, Aviation, Discovery, Family History, Fiction, History, Maritime,
Military, Military Classics, Politics, Select, Transport, True Crime, Air World,
Frontline Publishing, Leo Cooper, Remember When, Seaforth Publishing,
The Praetorian Press, Wharncliffe Local History, Wharncliffe Transport,
Wharncliffe True Crime and White Owl.

For a complete list of Pen & Sword titles please contact
PEN & SWORD BOOKS LIMITED
47 Church Street, Barnsley, South Yorkshire S70 2AS, United Kingdom
E-mail: enquiries@pen-and-sword.co.uk
Website: www.pen-and-sword.co.uk

Or
PEN AND SWORD BOOKS
1950 Lawrence Rd, Havertown, PA 19083, USA
E-mail: Uspen-and-sword@casematepublishers.com
Website: www.penandswordbooks.com

Contents

Introduction

The first question you might ask is why Windsor? In some ways this book is about social change from the mid-nineteenth to mid-twentieth centuries and so could have been written about any British town. Well, yes – except that Windsor during this period was not any town. It had the distinction of being the primary residence of the royal family – and also of having some of the worst squalor and pollution in Britain, making it a unique microcosm of the country.

The struggle for women's equality didn't begin as a campaign for women's votes. It had its roots in social injustices found in so many areas of women's lives: the home, schools, health and the workplace – and during two world wars. The effects of these injustices can clearly be seen in Windsor where, in the shadow of the castle, the town was riddled with poverty, violence, alcoholism and prostitution.

The birth of the women's suffrage movement went hand in hand with the demand for change. Women weren't campaigning for the right to be able to mark a cross on a piece of paper – they wanted the vote in order to have a voice.

Women in the nineteenth and early twentieth century had very few legal rights and in many ways were treated as second-class citizens. As visiting speaker Alice Abadam put it at a drawing room women's suffrage meeting in Frances Road in 1909, 'All women are lower class.'[1]

A wealthy female landowner was not allowed to vote, while her male staff were. Well-informed, well-educated women were not allowed to vote, but a male drunkard was. Without the vote, women had no say in how their lives were governed and no opportunity to help bring about changes.

A common misconception about the suffrage movement is that it was one or two organisations, whereas it was in fact a collection of different groups and societies that certainly didn't agree about everything, but shared a common cause.

In Windsor alone suffragists and anti-suffragists belonged to several different religious and political societies, including men's groups. And yet most people have never heard of them or the main characters in the town's suffrage story.

Neither did votes for women come about because of one or two events. At school I vaguely remember learning about the suffragettes chaining themselves to railings and one of them throwing herself in front of the king's horse, but of course the truth is quite different. Women weren't 'given' the vote in 1918 – they won it after a very long series of battles and setbacks.

Windsor's story is a little different from that of some of the more industrial towns. The Windsor suffragists were predominantly middle-class, middle-aged, educated people and were suffragists as opposed to suffragettes – which is to say they belonged to the NUWSS (National Union of Women's Suffrage Societies) as opposed to the militant WSPU (Women's Social and Political Union) – although suffragettes did come to Windsor.

The Windsor suffragists' aim was to win the vote through peaceful means – but this didn't mean they were meek. They were passionate about their beliefs and tireless in their efforts to get their message across and correct misunderstandings or false accusations from the other side.

But Windsor also had its anti-suffragists. It became known as the town in which suffragettes were most hated. Women's suffrage supporters had to put up with belittling, ridicule and rage.

But the issues surrounding women's suffrage weren't all black and white, and many characters in this story don't fall conveniently into 'good' or 'bad' camps. Some people who had no interest in women's suffrage or were vehemently opposed to it nevertheless contributed in other ways to improve women's lives through charitable acts, fundraising or donations.

Because of the town's small physical size, ardent supporters and opposers of women's suffrage were often neighbours in the same street. During the First World War staunch suffragists and anti-suffragists found themselves working together for the war effort.

While the contribution of men towards the town's transformation is well-documented, the role women played has been much less talked about. Very little has been written specifically about women in Windsor showing how their lives interconnected.

Following the centenary anniversary in 2018 of the first votes for women, this book aims to redress the balance and explore the lives of women in Windsor above and below stairs, looking at ways in which their lives were affected by a century of enormous social and political change and ways they contributed to that change.

As I've learned more about the Windsor suffragists in researching this book however, I've also learned so much about the town. Windsor today is probably most often associated with picture-postcard prettiness, State visits and celebrations. The castle, the pageantry, the historic buildings and lovely Thameside setting give it a coffee-table-book appeal and make it one of the most desirable and expensive towns in which to live.

Between the start of Queen Victoria's reign and the reign of Queen Elizabeth that bookend this story however, Windsor was transformed from a poverty-stricken, sewage-ridden army town whose streets, according to the *Windsor Express* in 1836, 'swarmed with prostitutes and beggars', into a genteel place that people would come to visit on daytrips.

I've lived on the doorstep of Windsor for twenty years and my children have grown up here so for me the town will always be associated with memories of watching the Changing of the Guard, feeding the ducks along the river, walking the dog in the Great Park, and going to the shops and cafes.

But it's only during the past year-and-a-half that I feel I've really come to know the town. Now when I'm in the Windsor Royal Shopping centre in the old Windsor Royal Station I like to do a bit of mental time-travelling and find myself amid the jumble of slums, brothels and boarding houses that were there when Queen Victoria came to the throne. The streets were cramped, noisy and smelly, full of urchin children, soldiers and prostitutes, drunken brawls and pickpockets.

If we fast-forward a few years the slums have been replaced by the new station, bringing with it, for those who could afford a ticket, the chance of discovery and adventure and also bringing people into the town, eager to see the castle or buy one of Madame Caley's hats.

Fast-forward again and we see ladies in long skirts, one or two on bicycles, making their way up to the castle to join a women's suffrage rally where a visiting speaker addresses the crowd through a loudspeaker from her motorcar.

In 1850 when our story begins, Britain was on the verge of an extraordinary period of social and economic change. Queen Victoria was 31 years old. She had been monarch for thirteen years, married for ten years and had seven children (with two more to follow in the next decade). The prime minister was Sir Robert Peel, in his third administration.

During the first years of Victoria's reign, leading up to 1850, the Chartist movement for 'one man, one vote' had gained substantial support with three national petitions being presented in 1839, 1842 and 1849.

The invention of the telegraph in 1837 and penny post in 1840, had made communication quicker and less expensive. Slavery had been abolished in the British Empire in 1838 and in the same year the London–Birmingham railway opened, starting the railway boom.

Income tax had been introduced in 1840. The Factory Act in 1844 had improved conditions for women and children working in factories and restricted their hours. There had been a four-year potato famine in Ireland from 1845. The repeal of the Corn Laws in 1846 lifted the restrictions on imported grain which had kept food prices in Britain punishingly high.

Charles Dickens had written eight novels including *Oliver Twist, Dombey & Son* and *A Christmas Carol*. Mrs Gaskell had written *Mary Barton*. And the Pre-Raphaelite movement had just been born.

The Industrial Revolution was already leading to a marked increase in female and child labour, and a resultant surge of people from the country into towns for work. The population of Windsor in 1851 had almost doubled in fifty years although the town's main industry was its breweries rather than factories.

Over the century from 1850, the country would see remarkable advances in science, industry, health and communications, starting with the Great Exhibition of 1851, Prince Albert's showcase for the world's most exciting inventions and works of art, which attracted nearly 6 million visitors, many of them travelling to London for the first time by train.

The building of the railways in Windsor from December 1849 would change the lives of many women in Windsor – although not immediately for the better, as houses were pulled down and the town was flooded with railway workers and their families.

But among better-off, well-read women, due partly to church mission work and partly to the novels they were reading, a new social consciousness was dawning.

From the woman who founded Windsor's home for fallen women, the Sisters who formed a convent, the first female war correspondent, and the suffragettes who threatened to invade the castle, to the women who worked for the armed services or took in evacuees during the Second World War, women throughout Windsor helped shape its future. That future has become our history.

CHAPTER ONE

Queen Victoria and Princess Elizabeth

Key dates:
1819 – 24 May: birth of Alexandrina Victoria.
1837 – 27 June: Victoria becomes queen on the death of William IV.
1838 – 28 June: Coronation of Queen Victoria.
1839 – A difficult political year: the Hastings Affair and the Bedchamber Crisis.
1840 – 10 February: marriage of Victoria and Albert.
1901 – 22 January: death of Queen Victoria.

Although this is a story about ordinary women, it wouldn't be complete without mentioning the two most famous female Windsor residents whose reigns mark the start and finish of the period covered by this book, 1850–1950, and their huge influence on ordinary women in Windsor – Queen Victoria and Princess Elizabeth.

Queen Victoria was the first Windsor queen, choosing the town as her home, while Princess Elizabeth would be given the surname Windsor and spend the war years at the castle, giving local people encouragement and reinforcing the monarchy's link with the town.

As well as being one of history's most iconic queens, Victoria in many ways put Windsor on the map. If she hadn't decided to make Windsor her primary royal residence instead of London, it would be a very different town today and the lives of many women within would also have been different. Having a monarch in residence brought the town employment opportunities, better transport, festivities and tourism. It also gave this once most disreputable town a sense of pride.

Victoria's sixty-three-year reign, which covers half the period explored by this book, was an era of enormous political, industrial, cultural and scientific change. It saw the invention of the radio, telephone, 'bone shaker' bicycle, gramophone, electric light and camera. Railways and the London Underground were built. Darwin published his Origin of Species, votes were extended to most men following the Reform Acts, compulsory free education was made available to children and the suffragette movement was born. By the end of her reign, she was ruler not just of Great Britain but of the largest empire in the history of the world.

But it was no easy ride. This diminutive (4ft 11in) 18-year-old girl who few had expected to become queen had to battle to establish and maintain her authority and independence, deal with thirteen prime ministers and tread a difficult line between maintaining political neutrality and showing concern for social welfare.

In 1839, the young queen's handling of two situations made her unpopular. Public opinion turned against her when she believed false allegations that Flora Hastings, a popular lady-in-waiting, was pregnant when Flora in fact turned out to be dying. As a result stones were thrown at the queen's carriage at the funeral.

Victoria was also booed and called Mrs Melbourne at Ascot races following the Bedchamber Crisis. As a condition of accepting the role of prime minister, Robert Peel had requested she replace some of her Whig ladies-in-waiting with Tories. She refused, so Lord Melbourne was reappointed prime minister but this was seen by many as unconstitutional.

She faced a considerable amount of public opposition during her reign and had to cope with at least seven assassination attempts, including one in Windsor when she was an elderly widow. A pistol was fired at her from close range as her coach left Windsor central station.

One of the things she is best remembered for is the way she redefined the British monarchy, restoring its reputation, which had been tarnished by the licentious behaviour of her uncles, and ensuring its survival for future generations. At a time of great political turmoil when other European countries faced revolutions, Queen Victoria presented the royal household as a loving, stable, close-knit family and a model of respectability and stability.

Victoria and Windsor

Windsor suited Victoria partly because she was in some respects an outsider. At her birth on 24 May 1819 few people expected her to become queen. She was only fifth in line to the throne, the daughter of Prince Edward, Duke of Kent (the fourth son of George III) and Princess Victoria of Saxe-Coburg. Both the Duke of Kent and his father George III died in 1820 when she was a baby. It was assumed George IV's daughter Charlotte would inherit the throne but in 1817 Charlotte died following a stillbirth.

Victoria had just turned 18 when her uncle, William IV, died on 27 June 1837 without an heir. One of the first decisions she took as queen was to assert her independence by refusing to continue sharing rooms with her mother, and to move away from the controlling influence of her mother's comptroller John Conway.

So it's no surprise that Windsor appealed to Victoria. It gave her freedom and independence away from the bustle and scrutiny of London but was within a reasonable carriage ride for conducting her regal duties.

The Coronation celebrations in Windsor

The day after her coronation in Westminster Abbey, London, on 28 June 1838, Victoria returned to Windsor. Despite terrible weather she was greeted by tumultuous crowds as her coach drove through the streets decorated with triumphal arches, flowers and lighting. Long tables were set out in the Long Walk and 4,000 poor and old people of the borough sat down to dinner in the pouring rain.

As well as the arrival of the queen, the crowds were treated to the sight of a solo flight by the first female aeronaut Margaret Graham in The Royal Victoria hot air balloon. Mrs Graham's husband had hoped to accompany her on the flight but due to the appalling weather the balloon wouldn't take off with the couple's combined weight so Mr Graham had to get out and watch as his wife took off into the clouds, waving a handkerchief in triumph.

So the ordinary women of Windsor were given two examples that day of bold, independent females, proving that women could be something more than just decorative.

The coronation festivities set a precedent for celebrating royal events in Windsor. Throughout the next century Windsor residents would turn out to celebrate state visits, the birth of the Prince of Wales, the marriage of Prince Edward to Princess Alexandra of Denmark and the queen's Jubilees.

The huge crowds these occasions brought provided the taverns and shops, seamstresses, bonnet makers and street traders with business and made Windsor into a tourist destination.

Victoria and Albert

It was at Windsor Castle in 1839 that Victoria proposed to Albert. The Royal Wedding took place in London on 10 February 1840, but after the ceremony the couple made the three-hour carriage journey to Windsor to spend their honeymoon. Shortly before 7 p.m. the newlyweds passed through the triumphal arch at Eton where they were met by a fairy-tale scene of gas and oil illuminations and the walls of the houses lit up with crowns and stars. Wealthy Windsor residents enjoyed public dinners and a ball at the town hall while thousands of poor people were given free food and drink.

The backwater market town was a welcome retreat for the royal couple, giving them peace and space in which to bring up their children. Albert also preferred Windsor to London society where he initially struggled to be accepted. Coming from the little-known state of Saxe-Coburg, he was dismissed by some of the aristocracy as being a pauper prince. His reserved manner and lack of enthusiasm for the traditional aristocratic pursuits of gaming, drinking and hunting, did nothing to endear him to them or vice versa.

At Windsor, Victoria and Albert could walk, paint, play the piano, enjoy recitals, play shuttlecock and battledore in the long corridor, and have picnics on the shores of Virginia Water Lake. In winter Albert used to drive the children around the Great Park in a sleigh and they skated on the pond at Frogmore House by the castle when it was frozen.

Model Family

But despite her power and prestige, Queen Victoria represented the model of femininity and respectability. Portraits of the couple in a homely setting with their nine children presented a picture of domestic bliss and Victoria was known as the 'mother of the nation'. It was also hoped that the children would help to bring harmony and lasting peace to Europe by being married into ruling families.

An illustration of the Royal Family sitting around a decorated tree in Windsor Castle published in the *Illustrated London News* in 1848 inspired ordinary families to introduce similar celebrations in their homes.

Queen Victoria and the Train

A huge change to women's lives in Windsor was brought about by Queen Victoria's decision to grant approval for the building of a railway in the town. In 1842, Victoria had become the first monarch to travel to London by train. The royal party had travelled by horse and carriage to Slough where they boarded the royal saloon carriage, with its padded silk ceiling, blue velvet sofas and silk curtains. A device was fitted to the top of the carriage so they could signal to the driver if they felt they were going too fast and Albert asked them to slow to 30mph because the queen had found the top speed of over 40mph alarming.

Despite her initial misgivings, the queen wrote to her Uncle Leopold afterwards that she was 'quite charmed' by this new way of travelling and became a regular train traveller.

The decision to extend the branch line to Windsor was taken only after much deliberation. For one thing, Queen Victoria was afraid the vibrations of the track might cause structural damage to the castle.

Other people in the town objected for different reasons. Dr Hawtrey, the headmaster at Eton, feared that being given such easy access to London might be too much of a temptation for his boys. But the queen finally agreed and in doing so she changed the future of the town.

The faster speed of travelling by train enabled the royal couple to spend more time in Windsor. But it also improved travel and trade for the ordinary townsfolk, giving birth to a tourist industry as Windsor became a destination for days out.

It would also mean in the next century that Windsor women could more easily access the suffrage meetings and marches in London, while visiting speakers from London suffrage societies could come to address meetings in Windsor.

The Widow of Windsor

After Albert's death Victoria became known as The Widow of Windsor. For several years she retreated from public life, to such an extent that ironic placards were tied to the gates of Buckingham Palace declaring the property for sale or rent. There was talk that she had inherited George III's madness and growing anger at her apparent disinterest in poverty, hunger and political unrest.

In Windsor, when her son Bertie (the future Edward VII) married Princess Alexandra of Denmark in 1863, the queen had a raised walkway built between the east end of the castle and St George's Chapel so that she could attend the wedding without being seen.

But Windsor residents regularly saw a small, plump figure driving around the town in her donkey cart, dressed in her widow's weeds. She was often accompanied by John Brown, her favourite servant with whom she had a very close relationship.

During this period she focused on her family, securing marriages for her children across the continent, as she and Albert had planned, and earning herself the nickname 'grandmother of Europe' because of the alliances formed.

However, things didn't turn out as hoped. After her death, her dream of a united Europe would come to an end when in 1914 three of her grandchildren – King George V, Kaiser Wilhelm II and Tsar Nicholas II – found themselves at war with each other.

With her children, the queen continued Albert's support of the arts and social welfare. In Windsor in 1880 the Royal Albert Institute was opened in his memory to promote the study of science, literature and the arts which would benefit many women. Plays and concerts would be performed there including in the twentieth century suffragist plays. The Institute has been demolished but the statue of Albert still stands on an office block where it used to be.

The queen was finally coaxed back into public life in 1877 when Prime Minister Disraeli agreed to make her Empress of India as a unifying figurehead. Politics during the 1880s was dominated by the Reform bills and the Irish Question. The rise in Fenian activity targeting the House of Commons, Scotland Yard and the Home Office made the queen nervous of driving around London, especially after a plot to blow up Westminster Abbey was uncovered during the Golden Jubilee.

But at the same time another movement was gaining prominence – women's suffrage.

Queen Victoria and the suffragists

Windsor women on both sides of the suffrage argument would in due course name Queen Victoria as an example in their campaign for or against women's rights.

In response to anti-suffrage claims that women shouldn't be involved in politics because they lacked the intellectual capacity to understand law and were too delicate for the political arena, suffragists often pointed to Windsor's most famous resident: the queen. Did she not govern as well as any man? Did she not say she wished she had Florence Nightingale in the War Office?[1]

In many ways the queen provided a role model for ordinary women in Windsor, showing that it was perfectly possible for a woman to not only succeed, but to excel in a traditionally male-dominated arena.

Queen Victoria was no supporter of the suffrage cause however, and was vehemently opposed to women being given the vote. Despite being the richest and most powerful woman in the world, raising her daughters to be strong, highly educated rulers and recognising her eldest daughter's superior intellect over her eldest son and heir's, Victoria's attitude to women's suffrage seems at first puzzling. She famously described women's rights as 'mad, wicked folly', and on hearing that Lady Amberley was a supporter of women's suffrage Victoria said the lady deserved 'a good whipping'.

Reflecting the views of many people at the time, she maintained that men and women were different and should occupy their own spheres: men, the world of business and politics, and women the home. Otherwise, women would lose their femininity and become 'hateful, heartless and disgusting' human beings.

This was a few decades before the women's suffrage movement became militant, and Lady Amberley's aims were hardly outrageous by modern standards: at a lecture in Slough in 1870 she called for the restoration of privileges for girls under educational endowments; said girls should have the same educational opportunities as boys; all professions should be open to women; married women should have property rights; a widow should be recognised as the legal guardian of her children; women should have the vote; they should not be subordinate in marriage and should be entitled to the same wages as men for doing the same work.

And yet Queen Victoria wouldn't have seen any contradiction between her experience and her views on women's rights – she was royal and royals were an exception. As the monarch she wasn't supposed to get involved in politics – but if she had approved of women's suffrage, and had expressed that approval, it's arguable that women might have gained the vote much earlier, without the police brutality, hunger strikes and deaths that occurred in the twentieth century.

But as it was, the queen's comments in a letter asking people to join with her in opposing women's suffrage were seized by anti-suffragists and used for their propaganda by the Men's League for Opposing Woman Suffrage in a pamphlet in 1908.

Queen Victoria would no doubt have been horrified, had she lived longer, to have witnessed her goddaughter Sophia Duleep Singh turn from socialite to suffragette in the twentieth century, addressing crowds, leading the Black Friday demonstration and getting arrested for not paying her taxes as a member of the Women's Tax Resistance League, with their slogan *No Vote, No Tax.*

The queen's daughters, on the other hand, showed much more sympathy with women's rights, and a strong interest in improving ordinary women's lives. Princess Alice was concerned with reducing the mortality rate for mothers in childbirth, and in 1864 helped establish a home for pregnant women in Germany where she lived.

Princess Helena, who was a great admirer of Florence Nightingale (as was the queen), helped establish nursing as a career for women, becoming president of the British Nurses Association and a founder member of the Red Cross.

Victoria's fourth daughter, the unconventional, artistic Princess Louise[2], was very sympathetic to the suffrage movement, perhaps influenced by her sister-in-law, Lady Frances Balfour. Lady Frances was president of the London Central Association for Women's Suffrage and helped lead the Mud March in London in 1907, which was the first large procession for women's suffrage and got its name from the poor weather conditions with heavy rain and muddy streets but nevertheless attracted around 3,000 participants.

Louise played a part in improving education for women, helping to set up the Girls' Day School Trust for girls whose parents couldn't afford to pay for their education, and founded The Ladies' Work Society for ladies who needed to improve their practical skills.

She also met and wrote to Josephine Butler and Elizabeth Garrett and gave tacit support to the move to repeal the Contagious Diseases Act which affected Windsor badly (see the chapter on Health) although she was prevented from doing so publicly as being associated with such a cause was considered unseemly for a royal.

The Jubilees

After the London celebration of the Golden Jubilee in 1887 marking Queen Victoria's fifty years on the throne, crowds lined the streets to welcome her back as she was driven through Eton to the castle. The town was illuminated and a lunch for 6,000 children was provided by the queen. The 15ft-high statue of the monarch was unveiled in front of the castle and has become a famous landmark.

Similar celebrations marked the Diamond Jubilee in 1897, with street parties, parades, fireworks and cricket games throughout the country. Victoria arrived in Slough on 24 June, a day after the celebrations in London and was driven by coach to Windsor through streets decorated with arches and floral tributes. This time the statue in front of the castle was dressed with a special canopy. The celebrations continued with bonfires, fireworks and torchlit processions. The queen is said to have been so overwhelmed by the tumultuous welcome that she cried.

The Final Years

In March 1883, the queen fell down some stairs in Windsor Castle and as a result had difficulty walking. Later that same month she was devastated by the death of John Brown, her beloved Scottish manservant. During her later years she increasingly used a wheelchair 'for the smallest movement' according to *The Times* on 22 January 1901.

Although she had expressed a wish to die at Windsor, she in fact died at Osborne House, Isle of Wight, on 22 January 1901 after a series of strokes. She was buried with Albert in the royal mausoleum. In line with her instructions, her wedding veil, Albert's dressing gown and a plaster cast of his hand were placed in her coffin.

Despite Queen Victoria's reactionary views on votes for women, her reign introduced many people to the concept of a strong female authority figure and inspired them to reassess what women were and what they were capable of.

Princess Elizabeth

Key dates:
1926 – 21 April: born Princess Elizabeth Alexandra Mary.
1947 – 20 November: married Philip Mountbatten, Duke of Edinburgh.
1952 – 6 February: became queen.
1953 – 2 June: coronation.

Our century of change that starts with Queen Victoria's reign ends with Princess Elizabeth on the brink of becoming queen. Elizabeth II is the country's longest-serving monarch and during her reign many improvements would be made to women's lives.

In a similar way to Queen Victoria, Elizabeth wasn't thought very likely to inherit the throne when she was born, being only third in line. But when her Uncle David (Edward VIII) abdicated in order to marry Wallis Simpson, her father became King George VI and Elizabeth the heiress presumptive.

The princess, who loved horses and dogs, regularly spent weekends and her birthdays at Windsor Castle. On her twelfth birthday she celebrated with a tea party at the castle in which she played hostess to the king and queen and poured the tea herself. She also took on her first appointment, becoming president of the Children's League of the Princess Elizabeth of York Hospital for Children in London.

When she was 13 and her father had been king for only three years, war broke out. For their safety, the two princesses stayed in Windsor with their governess Marion Crawford ('Crawfie'), and saw their parents at weekends.

Although they were away from London they weren't completely out of danger – 300 bombs fell in Windsor Great Park during the war, including one on the Royal Lodge, killing the lodgekeeper and his wife. The Lodge itself was undamaged apart from smashed windows but was closed until the end of the war and the royal household members that had been staying there were accommodated in the castle. The princesses did their bit to support the war effort and keep up the spirits of other children.

Princess Elizabeth's radio address during the war to other evacuee children captured people's hearts and boosted morale in the midst of the Battle of Britain. Speaking on the BBC's *Children's Hour* in October 1940, the 14-year-old princess sounded very young but composed as she expressed her sympathy for children living away from their homes, and gratitude to the families that had taken them in. The fact that she and Margaret were also children living away from their parents meant she could come across with empathy.

They also helped raise money for the war effort. The castle's valuable paintings had been taken down and put into storage for the duration of the war so they wouldn't get damaged. To cheer themselves up and take their minds off the war, the princesses put on a pantomime of *Cinderella* in 1941, with Margaret who was 11 years old playing Cinderella and 15-year-old Elizabeth, playing Prince Florizel for a private audience at Windsor Castle. It was such a success they staged other pantomimes over the next three years, raising money for the Royal Household Wool Fund.

Princess Elizabeth's first public engagement was inspecting the Grenadier Guards on her sixteenth birthday in 1943. In the war she became the only female member of the royal family to have entered the armed forces, joining the ATS when she was 18.

During the period of austerity that followed the war, the princess provided a bright spot of glamour in people's lives. In 1947 she made her first official foreign trip, going with her parents to South Africa where she made a speech from Cape Town on her twenty-first birthday pledging lifelong service to her people.

Like Victoria, she was determined to marry the man she loved regardless of people's reservations so soon after the war about Philip being 'too German'. She had first met Philip in 1939 when she was 13 and the two princesses had been given a tour of the Royal Naval College.

Philip had to give up his naval career, his Danish and Greek royal titles and his Germanic surname and became a British subject in order to become a member of the British royal family. He took the surname Mountbatten and was given the title Duke of Edinburgh. Princess Elizabeth adopted her husband's title, becoming Princess Elizabeth, Duchess of Edinburgh.

The wedding, which took place in Westminster Abbey on 20 November 1947, two years after the war ended, was called an austerity wedding and the queen had to save up clothing coupons to buy her dress. Members of the public sent her their own coupons but as it was against the law to transfer coupons these had to be returned. The dress was a stunning design in silk with embroidered stars and a 15ft train with flowers inspired by Botticelli's painting Primavera to symbolise rebirth in Britain after the war.

A year later their first child, Charles, was born, followed in 1950 by Anne. Two more children would follow in the next decade – Andrew in 1960 and Edward in 1963. Between 1949 and 1951 the royal couple spent much of their time in Malta where Prince Philip was stationed while in the Royal Navy and the couple were able to live a normal life.

But in 1950, the end of our century of change, Princess Elizabeth had no way of knowing that within two years, at only 25 years old, she would become queen.

In 1951 however, the king's health was failing and Elizabeth stood in for him at a number of events. Then, the following February while on a visit to Kenya, she received the sad news that her father had died.

The Coronation in 1953 was ground-breaking because it was broadcast on television, and watched by millions around the world and Elizabeth's monarchy would be the first in Britain to be so open to public scrutiny. Afterwards, the queen made her state entry into Windsor and a week of celebrations followed, including parties, balls, banquets and carnival processions.

Her long reign would see the Empire become a Commonwealth, the Cold War, the landing on the moon, the first female prime minister, the pulling down of the Berlin Wall, terrorism, and the invention of social media.

On a personal level there would be an assassination attempt, her children's divorces, Princess Diana's death, press intrusion and the fire at Windsor Castle but there would also be the arrival of grandchildren and great-grandchildren.

The fact that Queen Elizabeth had fixed cars, driven trucks and sheltered from bombs earned her respect at the start of her reign but she has since had to navigate the monarchy through some difficult periods.

In a subtle way her reign has been inspirational to women. She inherited the throne as a young woman of 25 in a world still dominated by men in top positions of power, and has remained in control, providing stability and continuity in some turbulent times, bringing the monarchy up to date while upholding some of its most prized traditions.

She's modernised the monarchy in many ways including opening up Buckingham Palace to the public, allowing television cameras into her home and volunteering to pay tax. And perhaps most importantly she oversaw the royal rule of succession so that in future generations the first-born child will succeed to the throne regardless of gender.

In the twenty-first century Queen Elizabeth has made the monarchy less aloof, even appearing in a cameo performance with James Bond at the Olympics in 2012. The younger generation of the royal family have shown a commitment to keeping the monarchy relevant and engaged with ordinary people, and Kate and Meghan, the new royal Windsor women, have shown support for women's rights including the #metoo campaign in 2018.

Meghan, Duchess of Sussex gave a powerful speech during a visit to New Zealand in October 2018, recognising the 125th anniversary of New Zealand granting votes to women in 1893 – the first country in the world to do so. She expressed her admiration for the women who had campaigned for women's suffrage, saying,

'Yes, women's suffrage is about feminism but feminism is about fairness.'

CHAPTER TWO

Home

Key dates:
1834 – The Poor Law Amendment Act.
1848 – Public Health Act.
1857 – Divorce and Matrimonial Causes Act.
1870 and 1882 – The Married Women's Property Acts.
1886 – The Children's Act.
1919 – The Sex and Disqualifications Removal Act
1923 – Matrimonial Causes Act
1949 – Formation of National Health Service

A woman's place, as the anti-suffragists frequently argued, was in the home. But for many women the home was far from a haven. During the nineteenth and early twentieth centuries, many people in Windsor lived in squalid slums – if they were lucky enough to have a home at all.

Neither was the home free of politics. As Harriet Cockle said at a suffrage meeting in Windsor in 1908[1], whether people liked it or not, politics was part of the home. Women were affected by laws concerning marriage and motherhood that they couldn't hope to change unless they had the vote.

Although women had the responsibility of giving birth to and raising the next generation and having to keep them clean, healthy and safe – often in squalid surroundings with no labour-saving devices and while working long hours with no childcare options – mothers had very few legal rights.

Until the Guardianship of Infants Act in 1886 a woman's children weren't legally hers at all. The father was regarded as the sole parent of a child born within marriage. In his will he could bequeath his children to someone else if he wanted and his wife would have no say in the matter. Even if he didn't do this, his relations could apply to the court to appoint a guardian in place of the mother. The Act made the father sole parent only for his lifetime; after his death, if an application was made to the court by a husband's relatives, his wife would have joint custody with the appointed guardian rather than lose custody altogether.

The mother of Windsor resident Lady Florence Dixie had to take her children abroad when her husband died to stop the authorities removing them from her care as they disapproved of her conversion to Catholicism and unconventional lifestyle. She only returned to England when it was eventually agreed she could retain custody.

But joint custody, said Lady Florence when the Act was passed, simply wasn't good enough. This was the reason women needed the vote – so that they could obtain justice by destroying such laws which were 'a disgrace to civilised man'.[2]

Miss Cockle, the visiting speaker from the London Society of Women's Suffrage, addressed an audience of thirty people at 'Bothley' in Frances Road, Windsor, in 1908 and brought up the subject of the Children's Act, which was about to come before Parliament and would rule on whether a woman should be allowed to sleep with her baby beside her in the bed, or whether the child must be put in the cradle. Why shouldn't the women themselves have a say in matters like this that concerned them, asked Miss Cockle? Without representation, women had no voice.

The contrast between wealthy and poor people's housing and lifestyles in Windsor was shocking, especially during the first half of the nineteenth century, with the most wretched slums standing just opposite the regal splendour of the castle. From George Street (now the entrance to the Windsor Royal Shopping centre) down to the Goswells and Bier Street (now River Street) was a labyrinth of filthy, densely populated homes, brothels and lodging houses. Women living in some of these houses would have seen the royal carriages pass by their front doors.

The demolition of the George Street slums in 1849 to make way for the central station removed an embarrassing eyesore from the view of the castle and of State visitors – but also exacerbated the town's problems of homelessness and overcrowding.

Drunkenness and violence

Crowded and poor housing conditions elsewhere in the town sometimes led to anti-social behaviour and violence between neighbours.

Ann Hill was charged with attacking her neighbour Jane Wallis in Bier Lane, where they lived in 1851. Mrs Hill said she was tired of the constant insults from Jane Wallis whose liaisons with Grenadier Guards brought shame on the road. As both women spoke quickly and each had witnesses to back their side of the story, magistrates were unable to decide who was at fault and ordered them each to pay their own costs.

The same solution was reached when Martha Burtonshaw was charged with assaulting her landlady Elizabeth Hall in her home in Prospect Place in 1857. Their fight broke out over whose day it was to use the washhouse and ended up with Mrs Hall claiming she was thrown down and crockery smashed on her head. But Martha Burtonshaw, who was pregnant, argued that Mrs Hall had assaulted her and pinned her against the wall.

On many occasions alcohol was to blame and sometimes had very serious consequences. Maria Shill, a charwoman who worked for a butcher in Eton, had had a difficult marriage. While living in Egham in 1883, her husband Joseph had broken her collarbone when he threw her out of bed. She hadn't reported the incident because he had promised to stop drinking, but on several other occasions she had had to flee the house in fear of her life. In October 1884, when they were living in Bridgewater Place, Maria sent for the police when Joseph threatened to burn the house down; he was sent to Reading jail.

While Joseph was in prison Maria took a room in Victoria Cottages with her three children, a property belonging to Mr Grimsdale.

After his release Joseph joined his family and several complaints were made to the police about his behaviour towards his wife.

On the night Maria Shill disappeared, Mrs Holt (mother of Mr Grimsdale) called the police. She had heard quarrelling and feared something bad had happened to Mrs Shill but couldn't get anyone to answer when she knocked on their door, although she could hear the baby crying. On looking through the window, the police could see Joseph Shill lying on the bed apparently in a drunken stupor with the baby at his side, and a pile of clothes lying on the floor by the fire.

Unable to get his attention, the policeman managed to open the window enough to post in one of the couple's children, who brought the baby out, giving her to Mrs Holt to look after. Assuming the heap of clothes on the floor to be discarded clothing, the policeman left. For the next few nights the children slept in the room with their father. When asked if he'd heard from his wife, or knew where she might be, he said he didn't.

A few days later Mrs Holt sent her granddaughter in to clean the room for Mrs Shill so it would be nice for her when she came back; 9-year-old Annie was sweeping under the bed when her broom hit something hard. Looking under the bed she spotted the shawl Maria was said to have been wearing when she left, and suspected there was something under it. She fetched her father, who uncovered the body.

A large quantity of blood was found on the fireplace, table and chair, and one of the victim's shoes. More blood and some hair was found on an iron in a cupboard. Maria had a head wound consistent with being hit with the iron. Joseph Shill was hanged for the murder. His three children were sent to the workhouse.

Being abandoned

Although drunkenness, violence and disease could afflict homes of any type, such tightly packed housing and poverty, combined with the availability of cheap beer, soldiers and railway navvies made the slum areas in Windsor especially vulnerable. Without the modern safety nets of income protection, pensions, unemployment benefit or a national health service, people's circumstances could change very quickly and it was often women who were left in need through death, divorce or desertion.

A lot of desertion cases are only known about because the wife ended up in the workhouse and the man was then charged with leaving his wife 'chargeable to the parish'.

In one such case in 1851, John Dobson was charged with leaving his wife the previous year and making her chargeable to the parish of New Windsor. He argued that his wife had deserted him rather than the other way round and that he had offered her three shillings a week but she had refused it. Mrs Dobson explained that this was because the sum wasn't enough. The magistrates were told that Mrs Dobson had kept hidden from them the fact that she knew where her husband was at the time the parish had been giving her a shilling and two loaves per week. For that reason John Dobson was excused prison but ordered to pay the parish 1s 6d per week for his wife's keep.

The Poor Law Amendment Act

The help available to destitute people had changed dramatically with the Poor Law Amendment Act of 1834. The original Poor Law in 1815 had made each parish responsible for its poor. Those who were unable to work were given assistance from their local parish which was paid for by taxes.

But resentment among some taxpayers at having to support people they felt didn't deserve help led to distinctions being made between the 'deserving' and 'undeserving' poor whose situation they believed was due to feckless behaviour or stupidity.

Some complained that the Poor Law kept wages low because employers knew that low pay would be supplemented by Poor Law money, while others felt that the availability of parish handouts for illegitimate children was encouraging immoral behaviour.

The New Poor Law in 1834 was brought in to reduce the cost of looking after the poor, take beggars off the streets and encourage 'idlers' to support themselves. Instead of receiving help from the parish poor houses and almshouses, poor people must now get help only from the workhouse. Groups of parishes came together to form Poor Law unions responsible for union workhouses. The Poor Law Union in Windsor formed in 1834 and included Windsor, Clewer, Egham, Thorpe and Sunninghill.

But for many women and children this new law was disastrous. It included Bastardy Clauses which removed all legal rights and help for unmarried mothers, while making them rather than the father (as would be the case with a married couple), responsible for their offspring, the intention being to stop immoral behaviour.

A married woman still couldn't be the legal guardian of her children or keep her property after marriage. This led to unscrupulous men marrying rich heiresses to get their hands on their fortune, and poor women losing their children through no fault of their own.

Divorce

Until the Divorce and Matrimonial Causes Act in 1857, a husband who deserted his wife still had the right to her earnings. The new law gave her the right to keep her property although it was still a long way from perfect. If a man wanted a divorce he had to prove his wife's adultery. But if it was the woman who wanted the divorce, she had to prove not just adultery but cruelty, desertion, incest or bigamy. A blind eye would normally be turned to domestic violence, and rape within marriage wasn't even a concept.

Harriet Ruddock of Spring Gardens, Windsor, successfully applied for her property to be protected from any future claim by her husband under the Divorce and Matrimonial Causes Act in 1858. Her husband John Ruddock, who she had married in 1839, had mistreated her, thrown her out of the house and was living with another woman. Although he had agreed to pay her a weekly sum of 1s 6d for their child, she had received nothing since 1850 when he had left for Australia.

If it hadn't been for the Act, Elizabeth Blackburn of Eton could have had her possessions seized by the parish authorities in 1867 to pay for her absent husband's keep in a workhouse in a different town. She had married Mark Blackburn, a bricklayer, in 1820 in Leeds, but he had abandoned her in 1847 after they moved to Brocas Street in Eton. He had never given her any money to support her or their five children, and only ever visited when he wanted money from her. Elizabeth got herself a job at Eton college and worked hard for everything she owned; without the Act she could have had it all taken away.

The Married Women's Property Acts, drafted by Richard Pankhurst, Emmeline's husband, were significant milestones on the path to women's emancipation in Britain. Until these were introduced, the legal position of a married woman was similar to a slave, as John Stuart Mill pointed out in his book *The Subjection of Women* 1869.

Women who married ceased to exist as legal individuals and became one person with their husband in the eyes of the law. On marriage a woman gave up her property, and the only way she could reclaim it was as a widow. Without her husband's consent she was unable to dispose of any property or make a will.

Her husband could, having deserted her, come back years later and claim her earnings. She had to bring up her children according to her husband's wishes and religion, regardless of her own beliefs and if the marriage broke down she had no right to custody, which must have effectively forced many women to stay in unhappy and violent marriages.

A case at the Windsor petty sessions bench in 1858 shows how little control women had over their lives. Mrs Sevenoakes's husband had been imprisoned for his violent behaviour and since his release had gone back to his old ways. She applied to the petty sessions bench for a divorce because of his ill treatment. But the bench told her they had no power to grant a divorce and were unable to make an order for the protection of her property as she had left her husband, rather than the other way round.

The Married Women's Property Act of 1870 went some way to improve women's rights, recognising married women as individuals and allowing a wife to keep her earnings and property acquired after marriage and to inherit and keep up to £200. This still didn't make the wife equal to her husband but did make her responsible for her own debts and able to sue and be sued (although she couldn't sue her husband.)

Another Married Women's Property Act in 1882 went further, giving married women the same rights over their property as unmarried women but there were still many issues to be resolved. Rhoda Garrett, cousin of Millicent Fawcett and Elizabeth Garrett, in 1872, said there had been several cases in which men had received much harsher sentences for killing other men than killing a woman.

Workhouses

Since the Poor Law Amendment Act in 1834 poor people had been given accommodation, food and clothes by the workhouse, and their children received some education. But it was very much a last resort. Able-bodied residents were forced to do hard, manual work in return for their board and lodging. Their homes and belongings were sold and families were split up, which would have put a lot of women off entering the workhouse.

The new workhouses were designed to deter people so that only the genuinely desperate would choose to live in them. Instead of being a refuge, they were, according to political campaigner Richard Oastler, more akin to 'prisons for the poor'.

Consequently, most people would do anything to avoid being sent there. In the workhouse the roughest and hardest people often lived alongside the most vulnerable – orphans, unmarried mothers, disabled and elderly people, and people with a mental illness. In addition, the workhouses used to double as hospitals for the sickest people who had been refused admission by the charity hospitals.

It wasn't until 1867 that children's homes were set up by Dr Barnardo as an alternative to children living in the workhouse, although orphanages were established by charities. St John's Home for Orphan Girls was founded in Windsor, 1858 by the Community of St John the Baptist but was only for 'children of respectable parents', i.e. those born inside marriage.

The Windsor Workhouse

The first workhouse in Windsor[3] had been set up in 1731 in Sheet Street on the site of the old poor house. In 1840, new premises had been found in Crimp Hill, Old Windsor, in a relatively attractive, Elizabethan-style building; inside however, conditions were bleak. The central portion included the Master and Matron's living quarters. To one side of this was the men's accommodation and on the other side, the women's.

Men's work included gardening and chopping wood, while women's included domestic chores. On each side there was a schoolroom for young children who were later sent to the free school. An infirmary was built at the back and there was another building for tramps which included a cell where they had to break stones for their living.

An article in *Penny Magazine* 1841 described the food to be of fair quality but scant portions. Rooms were 'cheerful, light and airy'. Prince Albert visited the workhouse shortly after it opened and declared himself delighted. Queen Victoria visited in 1864.

Although a report published in *The Lancet* in September 1867 described the inmates of the Windsor workhouse as 'well, and kindly treated', it found the rooms cheerless and highlighted some shocking hygiene faults, including lack of ventilation, poor sanitation and lack of indoor toilets.

Dr Smith, who produced the report, also noted that some women were wrongly judged to be able-bodied when they were in fact heavily pregnant, disabled or mentally ill. There were only three women there who were capable of working, so it was difficult to keep the place clean.

When the National Health Service was created in 1948, workhouses were often merged with hospitals as was the case in Windsor where the Union Workhouse was taken over by the King Edward VII Hospital and used for some time as a maternity ward.

But what were the alternatives to living in the workhouse?

Below Stairs

Many women and girls had domestic service posts and most of these would have been residential. In Windsor some live-in jobs were available at the castle (see chapter on Employment). The accommodation for staff was much improved by Prince Albert as part of his restoration project. The royal couple also had cottages built for estate workers.

Life in the Garrisons

With a high proportion of soldiers in the town (988 out of a population of 11,217 according to the 1851 census), many widows and orphans would have been created by conflicts including the Crimean and Boer wars and found their housing situation altered.

Some lived with their soldier husbands and families inside the garrisons but living conditions were cramped and unhygienic. Until 1860, when separate accommodation for married couples was provided in the Windsor barracks, families had to sleep in the barrack rooms with other soldiers. Queen Victoria was appalled by the sanitary conditions at Clewer Barracks on one of her visits and asked for improvements to be made. As a result they were rebuilt as Combermere Barracks.

Boarding Houses and Brothels

According to Rev. Hawtrey, rector of Holy Trinity church, the combination of two garrisons with a large number of beer houses was largely responsible for prostitution in Windsor. A contributing factor in the growth of brothels and drunkenness may well have been due to the changes in beer and boarding-house laws – the Beer House Act 1830 had abolished beer tax, relaxed the regulations over the brewing and sale of beer and extended the opening hours of public houses from fifteen to eighteen hours a day. Before the Act, licences had to be granted at an annual town meeting but now anyone could brew or sell beer providing they paid an annual fee of two guineas.

The aim of the legislation was to foster competition in order to bring down prices, and encourage people to buy beer rather than ruinous gin. But the reduction of one problem created another: lots of new beer houses, now exempt from magistrate control, opened up all over the country.

The streets around Windsor Castle in the oldest part of the town were packed with taverns and beer houses. Some of the beer houses doubled as boarding houses and some boarding houses doubled as brothels as Mary Ford, who joined the House of Mercy, found when she stayed in one in Peascod Street, saying there was 'not one modest woman in there[4]'.

More brothels lined George Street because of its proximity to the barracks, and there were also some in Eton to keep the boys away from the prostitutes in George Street who were likely to be infected with sexually transmitted diseases by the soldiers.

The Black Horse Inn[5] which used to be next to the Two Brewers in Park Street was closed down after a report that it was frequented by prostitutes and run in 'the most disgraceful manner'.

Some measure of control over the boarding houses had been restored by the Public Health Act of 1848, which gave the local board of health the power to make by-laws to regulate common lodging houses to improve the health of the community and reduce the danger of disease spreading. This included imposing a maximum number of lodgers, segregating the sexes and inspecting the property and prescribing sanitary arrangements but it was hard to enforce.

By 1851, these powers had been extended to local authorities under the Lodging House Registration Act, making it obligatory to keep a register of boarding houses and their owners. Owners had to notify the authority if any of their lodgers were found to have a contagious or infectious disease. But it wasn't until 1869, with the Wine and Beer Act, that it became obligatory for records of licences to be held.

Drunkenness was a nuisance and contributed to much anti-social behaviour and violence among women as well as men. In 1854, Mary Cook, Elizabeth Hedges and Elizabeth Gibbs were sentenced to twenty-one days in Reading jail with hard labour for annoying the public, following them around Sheet Street, the Barracks and the Long Walk and using such obscene language that no respectable woman dared pass them.

Prostitute Ann King of Bier Lane, who was well known to the police and had several previous convictions, was charged in 1864 with being drunk and riotous in Thames Street, making a lot of noise and using foul language. The police officer who arrested her was bitten and scratched and said she was the worst prostitute he'd had to deal with. She was sent to Reading jail for six weeks hard labour.

As Queen Victoria and the royal cortege travelled up Castle Hill to Windsor Castle after Victoria's visit to Germany in 1890, a woman called Julia Walker ran after the procession and clung onto one of the carriages, demanding to see the queen. The policeman who arrested her said her language was the worst he'd heard from a woman. She was charged with being drunk and disorderly and sentenced to fourteen days' imprisonment.

But sometimes it must have been hard for the magistrates to know who was to blame. In 1864, a row broke out between Charlotte Grant and Elizabeth Farmer who lived in Model Cottages. Elizabeth was in North's Lane when Charlotte swore at her, spat and threw horse dung at her. Charlotte, however, maintained she was throwing it back at Elizabeth who was very drunk. The magistrates decided the women should settle the costs between them but as Charlotte refused she was fined 1s and costs of 11s.

Drink also led to domestic violence. Abraham Johnson was brought before magistrates in 1878 for assaulting his wife Jane Johnson. He said he had been out at work all day and when he came back to their house in Victoria Cottages, he found her in bed refusing to get him anything to eat.

Jane argued that Abraham hadn't come in for dinner and she had eventually gone to bed feeling unwell. He came back late at night and asked where his dinner was. When she replied it was on the sideboard he told her to get out of bed and give it to him. She refused and he started hitting her and threatening to 'beat her brains out'. Jane ran downstairs to the landlady for protection. Abraham had assaulted her many times in the past and broken her nose. He was bound over to keep the peace.

Sometimes drunken violence had fatal consequences. Emily O'Shea, a laundress whose soldier husband was away in India, was living with Charles Scott, a glassblower. They had a tempestuous relationship and neighbours were used to hearing them argue. Emily's sister said that when Charles had been drinking he was 'most violent and cruel' and on one occasion had broken Emily's nose. During a final explosive row Emily threw his work tools in the fire. Later Charles appeared in the pub with a bandaged hand and calmly told everyone he'd killed his wife by stabbing her and cutting her throat with a razor saying, 'she defied me to do it'. He was hanged.

Another Windsor murder became famous for inspiring Oscar Wilde's *Ballad of Reading Gaol*. Laura Ellen Glendale, called Nell, had married a soldier, Charles Wooldridge of the Royal Horse Guards after his regiment was posted to Windsor. Because Charles had not been given permission by his commanding officer to marry, Nell wasn't allowed to share his soldiers' accommodation, so when Charles's regiment moved to London she stayed behind in Windsor, lodging in Clewer near the post office where she worked. The distance put a strain on their relationship.

Charles was jealous of the attention paid to Nell by other men and suspected her of having an affair with another soldier. When he visited her on 16 March 1896, he accused her of being unfaithful, and beat her up. A couple of weeks later he returned full of remorse saying he would never do it again, but another fight broke out.

Hearing shouting, neighbours rushed out into the street and found Nell lying in the road with her throat slashed. Wooldridge handed himself in to the police. Many people saw the murder as a crime of passion and felt that the charge should be reduced to manslaughter because of Nell's unfaithfulness. However, the judge said that by taking a razor with him to Windsor, Charles had shown that he had planned to kill his wife. He was hanged.

Oscar Wilde, who was a prisoner in Reading Gaol at the time Wooldridge was executed, later wrote about it in his ballad which features the line 'Yet each man kills the thing he loves.'

Fallen Women

To help ease the overcrowding in the town after the George Street slums had been pulled down in 1849, the two rival railway companies jointly invested in a Mission tent for railway workers' families. Installed on the site where the royal waiting room would later stand at Windsor Riverside station, it accommodated around 300 of these newcomers. Clergy visiting the area were appalled by the poverty and neglect around the tent and appealed to the people of Windsor for help. A Spanish lady called Mariquita Tennant came forward with the offer of temporary shelter for a girl in need. Mrs Tennant, who had been married to an Anglican vicar, had until recently been living in Florence but was now in a house called The Limes in Mill Lane by St Andrew's church. At 37 she had already been bereaved twice and was looking for a new focus in her life.

In 1849, she agreed to take in a troubled 24-year-old vagrant woman by the name of Marianne George, who had just given birth to her fifth child by her stepfather. The original intention was to give Marianne moral guidance and some training in domestic skills in order to help her secure a post somewhere as a domestic servant and get a second chance at life. But fearing Marianne would return to her dysfunctional family and risk falling into a life of prostitution, Mrs Tennant allowed her to stay.

As word got round, other young women in difficult circumstances began turning up on Mrs Tennant's doorstep and were also taken in. The house became known as the Clewer House of Mercy for 'fallen women'. For many of these women, prostitution had been the only means of survival, although others joined who weren't prostitutes but were vulnerable for other reasons such as alcoholism, abandonment or mental illness.

A comprehensive study of Mariquita Tennant and the work of the Clewer House of Mercy can be found in Valerie Bonham's fascinating books: *A Joyous Service: Clewer Sisters and Their Work*; *A Place in Life*; and *Sisters of the Raj: The Clewer Sisters in India.*

To cope with the growing number of residents, the House of Mercy moved into new premises in Hatch Lane in 1851. The house was subsequently run by the Community of St John the Baptist. Women who joined the house were provided with food, clothes, shelter and most importantly safety. Life there was far from luxury however. The women were called 'penitents' and wore a domestic service uniform. Between 6 a.m. and 8.30 p.m. they had to follow a strict regime of prayers, religious teaching, chapel services, Bible reading and chores such as housework, laundry and needlework or nursing the sick of the house. Many of the women had led a vagrant lifestyle before joining the house and hadn't been to school so adapting to the routine must have been especially hard.

The food was basic – soup and bread for the main meal on one day, stew and potatoes another, although this was probably more food than many of the women were used to. Discipline was strict – there are references in the house's records to Mrs Tennant giving the girls 'knocks', although this wasn't unusual for the time.

Some of the women ran away or were dismissed, usually for violent behaviour. But for others the House of Mercy gave them the opportunity they needed to find employment and turn their lives around, and some of the women chose to stay on and become Magdalens, part of the Community of St John the Baptist. Some graves of the Magdalens can be seen in St Andrew's churchyard.

The Development of the Town

Until the mid-nineteenth century, Hog Common was a piece of rough land strewn with old huts, and pigs that strayed out onto the road. In 1841, a squabble broke out between washer-woman Mrs Manley, who was married to a labourer, and her neighbour Mrs Morgan. As a result Mrs Morgan and her sons played loud music outside Mrs Manley's house at night and burned an effigy of her, posting bits of lighted material into her house and threatening to burn it down with her in it.

In late 1849, the humble dwellings on Hog Common were pulled down as part of the improvement scheme for Windsor and replaced with the fine mansions of Osborne Road. But the demolition of these houses led to an urgent need for more small homes to be built for working people.

Prince Albert's vision for improving living conditions for working people and furthering educational and scientific progress led to many improvements in the town as well as the country as a whole.

One of the exhibits at the Great Exhibition in London in 1851, which he masterminded, was the Prince Albert Model Cottage, intended to inspire better quality homes for poorer people. The Model Cottage was designed by Henry Roberts, honorary architect of the Society for Improving the Condition of the Labouring Classes, established in 1844, of which Albert was president.

The same architect, in consultation with Albert, designed the gabled, red-brick Prince Consort cottages in Alexandra Road, Windsor in 1855. Prince Albert followed their construction closely, paying regular visits to check on their progress.

In the second half of the nineteenth century as Windsor developed, largely due to increase in trade and tourism as a result of the castle and railways, more houses were built for the middle classes which form the bulk of the Victorian houses in Windsor today, and in the 1930s many new homes were built in Dedworth.

Middle-class professionals

The professional classes lived in areas such as Claremont Road, Frances Road and Clarence Crescent. One of the most prolific Victorian novelists, Margaret Oliphant (1828–1897), moved into 6 Clarence Crescent with her two sons in 1865, choosing Windsor because of its beauty and cheerfulness. She's an example of a Victorian woman who was successful in her own right without needing to depend on a man for her home or income.

A remarkably resilient woman who spent most of her life caring for feckless men, Margaret Oliphant moved to Windsor after a series of tragedies. After losing two daughters, she and her artist husband moved to Rome because of his poor health but he died there of TB, leaving her with two small children, pregnant and with debts of £1,000. Her third daughter's death followed shortly after and she hadn't been in Windsor long when her brother Frank, a widower with three children, lost all his money and turned to her for help.

Margaret found herself supporting her brother's family as well as her own, and in 1872 she bought 8-9 Clarence Crescent to house the larger family. She wrote over ninety novels – largely to pay for her sons' school fees at Eton, her nephew's training as an engineer and family holidays – but all three died before she did. Perhaps unsurprisingly, given her own experiences, she had low regard for books with happy endings and her heroines were strong, capable women who survived in spite of the ineffectual men around them.

The queen admired Margaret's writing and on several occasions invited her to tea in the castle.

Another road that became fashionable in the later nineteenth century was Park Street adjoining The Long Walk by Cambridge Gate. Originally this road had continued through to Old Windsor, but when the roads were reorganised in 1850 the route was closed at the park and wealthy residents moved into the elegant Georgian houses. Due to the pubs and boarding houses in the area, however, it wasn't wholly genteel. On one occasion in 1861, five women were arrested for fighting in the road and using disgusting language. One of them tore a feather off another's hat and pushed her into the road. Ellen Foley, Sarah Toms and Mary Ann Toms were prostitutes well known to the police and were given three days' hard labour. Rachel and Louisa Wise were not prostitutes but said to be 'heading that way' and fined £5 each to keep the peace.

Lodgers

Taking in lodgers provided essential income for some women, but also left households vulnerable to crime. When Mrs Butler and her fishmonger husband took her cousin William Saunders (31), a brewer's labourer at Nevile Read and Co, into their three-bedroom home in Cranbourne Terrace, Oxford Road, they had no idea of the danger he posed. Their only daughter, 13-year-old Unity, was a bright, popular pupil at St Stephen's School, Clewer.

When Mr Butler came home on 16 July 1907 there was no sign of Unity or the lodger. Mr Butler assumed his daughter had gone with her mother to visit her aunt who was ill. When Mrs Butler returned at 11 p.m. and said she hadn't seen Unity, they realised something was wrong. They searched the house and found her partially dressed body under the lodger's bed with cord tied round her throat and wrists.

The police searched for Saunders and arrested him at Fifield Cross. He told them he had killed Unity because she had sneered at him. He implied in a letter to her parents that he had abused her beforehand.

When the case came to court in October, the judge advised the women in the public gallery to leave because some contents of the case were not fit for their ears. Saunders was found guilty and sentenced to death.

Grand houses

Some fine homes for better-off Windsor residents were built or remodelled during the second half of the nineteenth century. As lifestyles changed after the First World War, some of these houses changed function or were pulled down.

One very impressive house was Queensmead. The site had originally been earmarked for Prince Leopold, but after he chose a different location the house was built in 1880 for his friend, the owner of the Windsor Tapestry Manufactory. It was later (1898–1940) owned by the Spencer Churchill family. Lady Augusta Spencer Churchill, an aristocratic socialite and Conservative suffragist was also founder of the Red Cross Windsor.

When Lady Augusta died in a car accident in 1941 the house passed to her daughter, Augusta Ruby Spencer-Churchill Bathurst, but she found the house too large for just her and her husband so invited the Joint War Organisation to use a portion of the house as a convalescent home for civil defence workers. From 1945–46 the house was used by the Red Cross to look after repatriated Commonwealth prisoners of war. After Mrs Bathurst's husband died, the house was sold to the Brigidine nuns and she moved to a smaller house nearby.

On the edge of the Thames near Boveney Lock, The Willows, built in 1850, belonged to Mary, the Duchess of Sutherland and her husband Sir Albert Rollit. Mary had caused a scandal by conducting an affair with the Duke of Sutherland in full view of his wife Anne (a friend of Queen Victoria) before Anne's death enabled them to marry.

Mary was sent to prison in 1868 for destroying potential evidence in a dispute over her husband's will and as a result was shunned by high society; she subsequently spent a reclusive life in the Windsor home and died in 1912. In June 1914, The Willows, which had been left empty, was set ablaze in an arson attack by suffragettes.

The house was later owned by Sir and Lady Dhunjibhoy Bomanji. Sir Dhunjibhoy Bomanji was a wealthy Bombay businessman who gave generously to support the hospital and war effort and entertained disabled ex-servicemen and the widows and orphans of soldiers at the house. It was described by the *Sketch* in 1927 as the most expensive house in Britain. Built in the Tudor style it had marble statuary and a miniature railway and pony-racing track in the grounds. During the war, Lady Bomanji moved to Harrogate and lent her house for use by evacuee families. She also donated two Rolls Royces to the ARP.

Close to The Willows was The Fishery, home in the 1870s and 1880s of the women's rights writer and campaigner Lady Florence Dixie and her husband Beau (see chapter on Activists).

Oakley Court, a castellated gothic mansion in Water Oakley, Windsor, was built in 1859 for Sir Richard Hall Say and later bought by Lord and Lady Otho Fitzgerald. It became the HQ for the French resistance during the Second World War and was frequently visited by General de Gaulle. Bray Studios was set up next door in the 1950s and Oakley Court has appeared in a number of films.

St Leonard's Hill, built in 1700 as a royal hunting lodge, was once the home of Lady Waldegrave who caused a scandal in the eighteenth century by secretly marrying the brother of George III; when the marriage was discovered, she was banished from court. The house was later sold to Sir Francis Tress Barry, a millionaire who had made his money from a copper mine in Portugal and who later became a Conservative MP; he had the house converted in 1892 into a French chateau.

Sir Francis and his wife Sarah were generous supporters of the King Edward VII Hospital and also helped finance the development of Alexandra Gardens but were opposed to women's suffrage. When Francis died in 1907 Sarah remained in the house, but after the First World War she couldn't find enough staff to run it. After her death in 1926 her son, unable to sell the house, had it demolished.

Housing for the poor in Windsor continued to be a problem in the twentieth century. At the turn of the century a report by Dr H. Timbrell Bulstrode on the sanitary conditions of the borough declared 100 houses in the Goswells unfit for habitation. It wasn't until 1926 that the slums in River Street (formerly Bier Street) behind the theatre were pulled down and replaced by a car park, while new houses were built to replace them in Dedworth. With the post-war building of council and private houses, the town was better able to accommodate its residents.

Changes in law

Changes in law in the early twentieth century made home life fairer and safer for women, although there was still work to be done: with the Sex Disqualifications Removal Act in 1919, women were finally allowed to sit on juries, but male-only juries were still allowed in cases where it was deemed appropriate, which meant that women would often be excluded from taking part in, for example, rape cases, where their opinion might have been most valuable. This didn't change until 1972.

It wasn't until the Matrimonial Causes Act of 1923 that women were able to divorce on the same grounds as men, and a woman still couldn't get a mortgage without a male guarantor until the 1960s. It wasn't until 1994 that rape within marriage was legally recognised.

In Windsor today there are still women who have no home. In the run-up to Prince Harry's wedding to Meghan Markle in 2018, the council announced its proposal to fine rough sleepers up to £100 for leaving their sleeping bags unattended on the street, rising to £1,000 if not paid on time.

CHAPTER THREE

Education

Key dates:
1833 – Factory Act.
1870 – Forster Education Act.
1871 – National Union for improvement of Education for Women of All Classes.
1872 – Girls' Public Day School Company.
1902 – Balfour Education Act.
1944 – Butler Education Act.

The fight for equal education was a major part of the struggle for women's rights and another factor that contributed to the birth of the suffragette movement. In the 1850s, a group of privileged ladies in London formed The Langham Place Group to campaign against a variety of social injustices facing women including the inequality in education, especially the lack of higher education.

The problem was that in the nineteenth century, education was primarily seen as a tool for making women better wives and mothers rather than equipping them with academic knowledge so that they could excel in a chosen field.

A common anti-suffragist view was that women hadn't had enough education to grasp politics. But this argument punished women for not being given the same opportunity as men and created a vicious circle – as long as women were given an inferior education they had no hope of achieving the same level of academic success as men.

Because of the way society was structured it was often thought that educating young women would be a waste of money. Not only were girls less intellectual, went the thinking, they were also less in need of education.

It was widely believed that because of women's hormonal cycle their minds were actually different from men's. Women were emotional and intuitive rather than rational beings, and were incapacitated for around a quarter of the month for reasons nobody would even mention in polite society, so they couldn't dream of taking up a profession. Besides, their future lay in being a dutiful wife, bringing up their husband's children and looking after the home.

There was even a belief that burdening a woman with too much education might have an effect on her reproductive ability – to which Elizabeth Garrett Anderson retorted that the real enemy for women was not education but boredom.

The sort of education girls received was largely dependent on class; working-class girls received little or no education at all and for girls who did go to school, teaching was often targeted at skills needed for being a domestic servant or a good housewife. But as suffragists often pointed out, as women were the educators of their children, surely it made sense for women to be better educated?

Not having an education put women at a disadvantage and could leave them vulnerable to abuse as they couldn't read documents or contracts. The records of the Clewer House of Mercy for 'fallen women' show that many of the young women who joined were unable to read and write, sometimes because of itinerant lifestyles. The Community of St John the Baptist who ran the House of Mercy from 1852 believed that in order for women to have independence it was essential to learn these skills, so lessons were given in reading, writing and Bible study.

For much of the nineteenth century education was a luxury that few could afford for their children, especially for girls. Although the Factory Act 1833 had required employers to provide half-time education for children up to 13 years old, this was often not fulfilled.

While the Industrial Revolution expanded work opportunities for women and girls, it also deterred many people from sending their daughters to school as they would lose the income the girls could otherwise be bringing in from working.

So Sunday, the only day they weren't at work, was the only day on which they could be educated. Sunday schools sprang up in the eighteenth century to teach poor children to read the Bible on the day of rest. But while these schools kept the children off the streets, they often didn't go as far as teaching them how to write.

Schools were either private (owned by an individual and run for their profit) or public (run by a governing body.) Churches and charitable bodies founded some primary schools for poor children including the National Schools (Church of England) and the British Schools (Nonconformist) but these often only admitted children from the 'right' church or organisations and many children received no education at all.

A Royal Free Trust charity school had been set up in Windsor Parish church (St John the Baptist) close to the guildhall in 1705 for children who, because of their parents' poverty, received no education. The school had provision for forty girls and thirty boys. Heading the list of subscribers was Queen Anne with a gift of £50. Also on the list was Sarah, Duchess of Marlborough giving £10.

The aim was to teach the children to 'read, write, cast accounts and be well instructed in the principles of religion.' A building was put up in the corner of the churchyard to accommodate the school in 1726, which later became a Masons' hall. Each year the children were given clothes and boots, a bible and prayer book.

The girls' and boys' schools moved into a new Gothic style building in Bachelors Acre in 1857. There were now 370 boys and 250 girls according to Kelly's Directory. The elder girls were taught laundry work. The Royal Free Trust school continued in many forms, eventually comprising the Queen Anne Royal Free First School in Chaucer Close, St Edward's Royal Free Middle School in Parsonage Lane, and St Margaret's Royal Free Upper School which closed in 2000. St Edward's would be created through merging St Edward's Catholic Middle School and the Royal Free C of E school in 1986.

The National School was founded in Peascod Street, Windsor, in 1820 with 305 boys and girls 'for the education of the children of the poor in the principles of the Established Church' (i.e., Anglican) and paid for by subscribers. The school was run by Mr and Mrs Stephenson. In 1825, the AGM committee report lamented the death of Mrs Stephenson, a 'most zealous and pious school mistress', and reported that her role was to be taken by her daughter Janet. The following year Mr Stephenson retired and was succeeded by his son-in-law Mr Robertson. In 1842, the National School master and mistress were Mr and Mrs Harvey.

It was quite common in those days for women to be mistress of a school alongside their husband as master but they often hadn't had much education themselves.

Stephen Hawtrey, a master at Eton college and curate of Windsor parish church started St Mark's school for boys in a cottage in Clewer Lane, which in 1861 moved to a new building in Alma Road and eventually joined with the United Services College to become the Imperial Services College in 1906.

In 1841, the British School was built in New Road, founded by Joseph Chariott and paid for by charitable donation. It comprised large, separate boys' and girls' school rooms, with offices and staff accommodation. Although generally thought of as the 'nonconformist' school, it admitted Anglican children as well as other denominations.

Other charity schools included the Royal Horse Guard school which in 1842 was run by Mr and Mrs Casson and consisted of fifty-four boys and forty-eight girls; the Dedworth Green school run by Miss Gardiner, and the 72nd Highlanders school which had forty-nine boys and girls.

In 1845, the Royal School was opened in Windsor Great Park by Victoria and Albert for children of workers on the royal estate. Prince Albert had had cottages built in the Great Park for estate workers and saw the provision of free education for their children as a continuation of this scheme to improve their conditions. The school is still attended by many children of Crown Estate employees.

Some schools in Windsor were founded by generous benefactors – Clewer Green school, for example, was established for the poor children of the parish in 1806 in two converted cottages by Mary, Countess of Harcourt who lived in the St Leonard's Hill Estate. Her husband Lord Harcourt was Deputy Ranger of Windsor Great Park and Deputy Lieutenant of Windsor Castle, and the first president of the Windsor dispensary. When Mary died, the deeds were transferred to the diocese of Oxford and the school was paid for by the parish. In 1842, the school was run by Mr and Mrs Spicer and consisted of 140 girls and boys.

In 1884, the school was run by Mr and Mrs Poynter. Together they received a salary of £165. An inspection report described it as 'satisfactory throughout', but at a parish meeting the school was heavily criticised for being badly run with low attendance. The father of Richard Wellbelove (also called Richard) was charged in 1888 with the non-attendance of his son at Clewer Green School. He explained that he had been out of work for four months and was ordered to ensure the child attend.

It's likely that Richard senior had kept his son off school because he needed him to work and bring in some money. Certainly some children missed school for this reason. In 1898, headmaster George Shorter wrote to the Windsor and Eton Express to highlight the illegal casual employment of children who should be at school. By 1902 there were 270 children in the school.

For boys from wealthy backgrounds there was plenty of choice in Windsor, with Eton, Beaumont Lodge and, for boys with exceptional singing voices, St George's school, which was established to provide choristers to sing at services in St George's Chapel, Windsor Castle.

But with the exception of a few boarding schools for girls whose parents could afford them there was very little secondary education available for girls in the whole country, let alone in Windsor.

Better-off families tended to employ their own governess for their daughters and there are plenty of advertisements in the *Windsor Express* for governesses but the governesses themselves often hadn't had much education so weren't able to teach to a very high standard and were generally regarded as only one step above a servant.

That started to change when Queen's College for governesses opened in Harley Street, London in 1848 with Queen Victoria as its patron. Its aim was to improve the knowledge and qualifications of governesses by providing them with a good education and raise their status within society. The school was open to all women and girls above the age of 12. Classes consisted of lectures by professors from Kings College, and essays. Subjects that had traditionally been considered 'male', like maths, were included and fees were charged for each subject.

Alternatively, there were a few private schools for young ladies where the emphasis was generally on deportment and accomplishments such as music, drawing and needlework rather than academic achievement. In Windsor, Miss Mariana Alice Browning, sister of Oscar Browning, an educationalist and master at Eton, opened a private school for young ladies in 1876 for the sisters of Eton boys. The school relocated to Bexhill in Sussex in 1900 and closed in 1964. The lease on the building in Osborne Road was taken over by Mulgrave preparatory school for boys. Miss Browning died in 1910.

Ragged Schools

In the 1840s, the concept grew up of Ragged Schools run by volunteers within the community. They provided elementary education for the most destitute, outcast children who were rejected by the church and charity schools, such as orphans and the children of prostitutes, convicts and drunks. In 1846, some of these schools were brought together under the Ragged School Union, created by Lord Shaftesbury.

Windsor had several Ragged Schools, the first of which was started in a rickety shed in the wretched squalor of the George Street slums. A visit in 1846 was recorded in *The London Illustrated News* by the Rev. Robin Ainsley who declared himself very impressed with the teaching and behaviour of the children. The school, he pointed out, had been set up not by the wealthy people of Windsor but by a humble chimney sweep.

But the new railway would cut right through the schoolroom so the George Street Ragged School had to be moved to the hayloft of the White Hart Hotel (which later became the Harte and Garter).[1]

People visiting the castle in their horse-drawn coaches or walking down the high street would have regularly seen urchins scrambling up the ladder to their lessons.

The school was later moved again to a barn-like room in Clewer Road, and in the 1850s more substantial premises were found, paid for by generous Windsor residents and compensation from the Great Western Railway. The day school accommodated thirty girls and a twice-weekly evening school for men and boys was established. Persuading teachers to manage such unruly students, however, was an uphill battle for the Windsor and Eton Ragged School committee. Appeals had to be made for teachers because recruiting people to work with children from such a deprived – and depraved – area was not easy.

Another Ragged School was set up in 1863 in Clewer Fields, one of the worst slum areas, by Sister Emily of the Anglican Community of St John the Baptist (Clewer House of Mercy) who founded several schools in the area.[2] Three years later the school moved into the new mission house, and in time became St Stephen's College for Ladies, a fee-paying school for daughters of the clergy. After the Education Act of 1872, when elementary education was made available for all children in separate schools, St Stephens became an exclusive private girls' school.

There were also schools in the workhouse and the barracks. Girls and boys in the Union Workhouse on Crimp Hill were given a basic education in separate schoolrooms. The girls were taught to sew, read and write; older children were sent out to free schools.

A visit by Queen Victoria and Princess Helena to the barracks school on 3 December 1864 is recorded in the *Evening Standard* two days later. The queen looked at the pupils' work and took a keen interest in their welfare.

In 1869, the National Education League began a campaign for free, compulsory, non-religious education for children. The 1870 Forster Education Act allowed religious schools to continue but created a system of non-denominational 'school boards', i.e. locally elected bodies, to set up and manage schools where they were most needed. Another significant step forward was made in 1880 when another Education Act made school compulsory for children up to 10 years old.

St Stephens primary schools (one for boys and one for girls) opened in Vansittart Road in the 1870s, and later became Clewer St Stephen's School. At the turn of the century an intermediate school was set up for the daughters of tradespeople who could afford to pay more than two pence per week.

Girls' secondary education

Girls' secondary education, however, was still woefully inadequate throughout the country; as a result the National Union for Improving the Education of Women of All Classes was set up in 1871 by Maria Georgina Grey to draw people's attention to the need for good schools with moderate fees to provide better education for girls. The movement was supported by many leading figures including Henrietta Stanley, Mary Gurney and Princess Louise who became its president.

The Union raised funds to create The Girls' Public Day School Company in 1872 to provide affordable secondary school education for day girls rather than boarders. To begin with teachers were trained in the schools but in the new century some of the schools offered teacher training departments.

In Windsor, Miss Ingram ran a school for young ladies in Clarence Road called Freston House. Classes included music, drawing and painting, elocution, dancing, and drilling led by a sergeant instructor from Eton college, as well as French and German taught by a resident governess, Madame Rocheron. On Prize Day at the Albert Institute in 1897, four Freston House girls were praised for passing the Cambridge local exams and five for passing junior exams. Songs, recitations and dances were performed to a large audience and the vicar, Rev. Ellison, praised Miss Ingram's 'excellent scholastic training'.

The real breakthrough in secondary education came with Balfour's 1902 Education Act which enabled councils to set up new grammar schools and encouraged them to subsidise existing ones and provide free places for working-class children, giving promising children from poor backgrounds a chance of higher education. The Act also abolished school boards and placed education in the hands of the newly created local education authorities (LEAs).

Twentieth Century

In 1906, St Stephens Senior Girls' School was opened in Vansittart Road, Clewer. It later became Princess Margaret Rose School. However, a larger school was still needed for the Windsor girls. After the First World War, a red-brick gothic house called Elmfield, on the corner of Osborne and Kings Roads, became available and the new school opened in 1920.

Elmfield had belonged to Henry Darville, a wealthy solicitor, but had been requisitioned during the war and left in a sorry state by the Army. Acquiring the site was a battle as it had been earmarked for Windsor Boys' School, which had outgrown its site in St Leonard's Road; there was strong feeling that the girls should be moved into the existing boys' school and the boys should have the new building. Girls' education, it seems, was still seen by some as less important than boys'.

But after much debate Windsor County Girls' School opened. In 1935, with the closure of St Stephens High School in Clewer, the Windsor County Grammar Girls' School was opened to provide free secondary education for girls.

Just after the Second World War in 1947, the Brigidine nuns moved into Queensmead, the former home of socialite suffragist Lady Augusta Spencer-Churchill, and opened a convent school on 10 May 1948. Their first school brochure shows that their fees for girls under 11 years old were 8 guineas a term and over 11 years, 12 guineas a term. The uniform was sold at Caley's.

In the school archives former pupils affectionately recall music and dance and the sight of the nuns playing tennis and riding lawn mowers in their flowing robes. Mary Mantell who started at the Brigidine (as it was then called) in 1956 said:

> I went to school very proudly dressed in my maroon tunic, cream shirt and striped tie. For summer we had a cream dress, striped blazer, and sailor Breton-style hat. We had to have white gloves for when we were walking to the Long Walk to wave at the queen at the beginning of Ascot Week.

Penny Rigden who later taught ballet said of her first week at the convent in 1949:

> I have memories of twirling on a two-seater roundabout to Mother Fidelma's piano playing and my first dance lesson with Mrs Porter. Music and dance: two words that gave me so much pleasure – and a career!

When Penny got married the nuns even came to her wedding.

The Butler Education Act

In 1944, Rab Butler's Education Act split education into primary schools to the age of 11, and secondary schools for children over 11. To get into a secondary school pupils had to take an exam known as the eleven-plus; those who passed went to the grammar school with the prospect of going on to university, and everyone else went to a secondary modern or technical school, after which pupils were expected to go into a trade.

Girls still didn't have equal educational opportunities even then; when it was discovered that more girls than boys were passing the exams for the grammar schools, quotas were introduced to limit the number of places available to girls.

Many people felt this system was unfair and deepened the class divide. In Windsor it wasn't until the 1960s, when Windsor Boys' and Windsor Girls' Schools both became comprehensive schools, that free, non-selective education was made available to all children in the town.

University Education

Very few women in Britain had the chance of a university education in the nineteenth century. When, in 1862, Frances Power Cobbe argued for university places for women she was laughed at and in 1897, when the idea of awarding degrees to women was put forward at Cambridge University, it was met with such a furious protest by the male students it had to be abandoned.

Emily Davies set up Girton College, Cambridge in 1869, with the aim of teaching women the subjects that were highly regarded by men – maths, Latin and Greek. But the college attracted criticism and even ridicule from people afraid that if women were tempted away from the home to study, traditional family life would be destroyed.

Royal Holloway in Egham, near Windsor, which was opened by Queen Victoria, was one of two London colleges (with Bedford College) that started accepting women in 1878. One of its students was Emily Wilding Davison, who would go on to become one of the most famous suffragettes.

In 1871, Millicent Fawcett (who would eventually become president of the National Union of Women's Suffrage Societies in 1897) founded Newnham College, Cambridge, with Henry Sidgwick, as living accommodation for young ladies who could attend the university lectures – even though they weren't allowed to be awarded degrees.

In 1890, Philippa Fawcett, daughter of Millicent, achieved the top score in the Mathematics degree course at Cambridge. But she was not allowed the title of Senior Wrangler which was traditionally given to the highest scoring student – that had to go to the man who came second, 400 marks below. The situation prompted Windsor resident Lady Florence Dixie to say that the restrictions on education for women were enough to 'drown all ambition, hope or energy' to succeed.

As the nineteenth century wore on, other options became available to women besides university including training colleges for governesses, secretarial work, nursing and teaching. However, in the late nineteenth century it became common practice to bar married women from teaching although the practice was relaxed during the First World War when women were needed in schools. It wasn't until the Sex Disqualification Removal Act in 1919 however that the restriction of married women being able to teach was officially lifted. In 1920, Oxford finally awarded women degrees but it wasn't until 1944 that Cambridge followed suit.

CHAPTER FOUR

Work

Key Dates:
1865 – Elizabeth Garrett passes the Society of Apothecaries exam,
     proving women are capable of studying medicine.
1876 – Women are allowed to enter the medical profession.
1908 – Licensing Bill.
1919 – Woman's Emancipation Bill.
1919 – Sex Disqualification (Removal) Act.

Inequality in employment opportunities and shocking working conditions both helped fuel the demand for women's suffrage. The ideal woman in Victorian Britain was 'the angel of the home', a dutiful wife who kept the house clean, looked after the children and put food on the table. But the reality was that working-class women, especially unmarried women and widows, had to work long hours as well as running the home, often with no one to care for their children.

A clause in the 1908 Licensing Bill to abolish barmaids would have put thousands of women in the country out of work had it been allowed to go through. Windsor, with all its pubs, would have certainly been affected if suffragist Eva Gore Booth hadn't spotted the clause and started a campaign against it.

Harriet Cockle told a drawing-room women's suffrage meeting at Mrs Mugford's house in Frances Road[1] that the clause would have set a dangerous precedent. If a large number of unrepresented women workers could have their livelihood taken away by an Act of Parliament then who would be next? Typists? Factory women?

What women were asking for was merely a matter of justice.

Another issue was the discrepancy between men and women's wages. Alice Abadam of the Church League pointed out that women were, on average, paid only a third as much as a man for doing the same work. With such low wages, she told a women's suffrage meeting in Frances Road in 1909, it was hardly any wonder some women were tempted into prostitution.

Although the Industrial Revolution had created more jobs for women this often caused tension between the sexes: some employers chose to give jobs to women knowing that they could pay them less than men because many women workers didn't have trade unions to fight on their behalf for higher pay. Alice Abadam made the point that women worked in the most dangerous industry of all – with 5,000 deaths a year – and yet one that had no representation: motherhood.

Employment in Windsor

The population of Britain boomed during the nineteenth century, rising from 9 million in 1801 to 41 million in 1901, and by 1850 more than half the population lived in towns.

The 1851 census shows popular women's employment in Windsor to have included dressmakers, milliners, seamstresses, straw-bonnet makers, shoe and bootmakers, street sellers, shopkeepers, bakers and domestic servants. Some women found work at the castle, others as maids at Eton College, and – although it's not always obvious on the census as euphemisms were so often used, but is well documented in other records – many women were brothel keepers and prostitutes.

There were probably also women whose jobs weren't recorded because they worked part-time or helped their husband in his work, or perhaps even worked without their husband's knowledge.

A number of women ran beer/boarding houses, some with their husbands, some alone. It must have been a useful income but definitely not a job for a shrinking violet. There are numerous stories of drunken fights and anti-social behaviour in the newspapers. In 1861, a policeman received a complaint from a woman that her husband had turned her out of bed to make way for a prostitute. When he went to investigate, Sarah Grayling, the landlady of the Prince of Orange beer house in Clewer Lane refused to let him in. She said she had soldiers living in her establishment but did nothing to encourage prostitutes.

On another occasion the police called at the Prince of Orange after complaints from the public and found five soldiers and nine prostitutes they knew well in a large room upstairs. Sarah Grayling was charged with allowing prostitutes to gather. The magistrate said that her house had been selected as being one of the worst in the town. She was fined 10s plus 11s costs and warned that if it happened a third time she would have her licence revoked.

Mrs Barton, landlady of The Magpie, was summoned on a similar charge. 'If I refused to allow the soldiers to bring them in I'd get knocked down,' she protested. Unmoved, the magistrate told her she was to serve everyone but not allow women of that sort to congregate in her house. She was fined £5.

Mrs Goodchild, landlady of the Honours of War beer house in Clewer Lane was found to be allowing parties in her pub during prohibited hours. She admitted serving beer to some lodgers, but the policeman said the customers weren't lodgers and they were there with prostitutes. She was fined 8s 6d.

The Castle

The castle, the Thames and development of the railways all had an effect on employment opportunities for women in Windsor over the nineteenth and twentieth centuries as it developed from a market town into a tourist destination.

At the castle there were jobs for women of different classes, from ladies-in-waiting to below-stairs staff. The most important of the above-stairs roles was the Mistress of the Robes, who attended the queen on state occasions. Then came the Ladies of the Bedchamber including Lady Ampthill, appointed in 1885, who were from aristocratic backgrounds. They attended the queen on a rotational basis, one at a time, staying at the castle for a few weeks at a time for their 'wait'.

Maids of honour including Eleanor Stanley were also part-time residents. These ladies came from good families and stayed at the castle for a few weeks a number of times a year. And there were a number of Extra Ladies who had resigned from their post but were called on to wait as necessary, such as the Honourable Emily Cathcart who, having been Maid of Honour, became Extra Woman of the Bedchamber in 1880, and the Honourable Lady Biddulph who was Maid of Honour to Queen Victoria and became Extra Woman of the Bedchamber to Queen Alexandra. Her husband had been Keeper of Her Majesty's Privy Purse until his death in 1878.

The royal children had wet nurses, nannies, governesses and tutors – although some appointments were more successful than others. The employment of Mary Ann Brough as wet nurse for Bertie (Edward VII) in 1841 could have changed the course of history; she was, for some reason, dismissed from service after just eight months. Victoria was horrified to learn a few years later that the woman who had been at her bedside when she gave birth – and had been entrusted with the heir to the throne – had murdered her own six children.

Mary Ann was initially thought to be one of the victims because she was found, with her throat cut, alongside the children in her Esher home. After a doctor stitched up her throat however, she confessed to killing the children with her husband's razor and then trying to kill herself. She spent the rest of her life in Bedlam insane asylum.

Another member of the castle staff who found herself in court was Ellen West. Described as 'ladylike' and around 30 years old, Ellen worked for Lady Phipps, wife of Colonel Phipps, Keeper of Her Majesty's Privy Purse, who lived in Henry III's tower at the castle. In 1865, Ellen was charged with stealing some of her mistress's clothes and belongings, including a splendid Indian shawl which had been given to Lady Phipps by the queen. She had also acquired goods from tradesmen saying they were for Lady Phipps, but sold them on. Ellen said in her defence that she had been driven to crime by poverty, but she was sentenced to twelve months in prison.

But other employees were rewarded for their service and given different roles in the castle as the needs of the royal family changed. Miss Anna Pullman was engaged as a nursery maid at the castle when Queen Victoria's children were young. When the children had outgrown the nursery she was made linen woman at the castle and later promoted to assistant to the queen's dressers. In recognition of her long and faithful service, she was given residence at Kensington Palace upon retirement and lived there until she died in 1924, aged 94.

Baroness Lehzen, Victoria's beloved governess, initially stayed on to teach Victoria and Albert's children, but after falling out with Prince Albert she left and the nursery was taken over by Sarah Lyttleton who had previously been a Lady of the Bedchamber.

Mary Ann Hull ('Nanny May') was nanny to all nine of the children and was held in great affection, Victoria referring to her as 'dear May'. When Nanny May eventually retired she was given a donkey-drawn bath chair and permission to visit the castle whenever she wanted. After her death the royal children paid for her gravestone which can be seen in St Andrew's churchyard.

Queen Victoria had over a hundred below-stairs servants according to the 1881 census including housekeepers, table-deckers, laundry maids, dressers and kitchen maids, most of whom lived at the castle and were given food and medical care. In July 1863, a castle maid committed suicide by throwing herself off Queen Elizabeth's Tower. She was described in the coroner's court as having been a well-behaved girl who had recently been in low spirits. It was thought there was some mental illness in her family but the exact reason for her suicide will probably never be known.

Eton school

Throughout the nineteenth century and early twentieth century there were plenty of domestic service posts for women elsewhere in the town. Eton College employed matrons called 'dames', and 'boys' maids' who cleaned the rooms. A typical advertisement for a boys' maid placed in *John Bull* in 1882 called for an 'active, steady and trustworthy person', who must be at least 30 years of age and an early-riser. Wages would be £18 a year. Another advertisement in 1945 says the job includes taking care of the bed-sitting rooms and linen for fourteen boys.

In 1912, a housemaid employed by an Eton master was murdered by her sweetheart. Annie Davis, 22, had been seeing Eric Sedgwick for a few years and marriage had been discussed, but lately they had had disagreements and Annie told a fellow servant that Sedgwick had told her a dreadful secret that she would take with her to her grave. Sedgwick, 27, a former soldier who was currently employed as a house porter in the National Liberal Club in Whitehall, visited Annie at Cotton Hall House where she worked. Another servant, Edith, who shared a room with Annie remembered that Annie turned white when Sedwick turned up. A quarrel broke out in the servants' hall and he stabbed her through the heart. The motive was thought to be jealousy. He was the last man to be hanged at Reading gaol.

In 1916, a German maid in Eton College, the personal maid of the headmaster's wife Mrs Lyttleton, was fined £5 for trying to send a message to her sister in Germany. In the 1950s, three middle-aged Eton maids died in tragic and mysterious circumstances: 1956 a Swiss maid at Eton was found dead on the floor of the washroom. It was thought she had died from fumes from a gas heater. The following year a bedroom maid, Sara Seal (60) fell 40ft to her death from a window at Corner House, one of the oldest college houses, which she was cleaning after the forty-four pupils that lived in the house had left for their summer holidays. And in 1959 another maid, Dorothy Coleman (65) was found lying dead in the snow. She was thought to have fallen from a fourth-storey window of Dolphin House.

Private houses

Most of the larger houses in the town also had several staff, while middle-class professional houses often had at least one servant.

Being in service gave many women security and somewhere to live but conditions varied and servants were vulnerable to exploitation and abuse. Some maids were given no wages, only accommodation and food.

Records of the Clewer House of Mercy show that many of the 'fallen women' had previously worked as domestic servants and had 'gone wrong', i.e., presumably had been abused by their employer or another servant. Many of them found jobs afterwards as cooks or maids including Marianne George, the first woman taken in by Mariquita Tennant.

One servant who suffered at the hands of her employer was Adelaide Dunton who was only 12. She'd been working for several months for William Robarts, landlord of the Prince of Wales tavern in Church Lane, when she was taken into Windsor Royal Infirmary in June 1865 with terrible injuries as the result of falling from an upper-storey window.

During the night her employer had come into her room and attacked her with stinging nettles and a stick saying, 'I'll murder you.' The assault went on for an hour-and-a-half and she had no idea what she was being punished for. To stop her crying out he hit her on the head, making it bleed. She escaped the only way she could – by jumping out of the window – but sustained serious injuries. A witness who lived upstairs in the house reported hearing the girl cry out. Shortly afterwards she was brought into his shop by his wife, wearing only her chemise and appeared 'insensible'. There was some doubt as to whether she would survive long enough to see Robarts brought to trial. A few weeks later however, Windsor residents thronged to the guildhall to see William Robarts tried. He was found guilty and sentenced to eighteen months in prison.

Domestic servants who lived in poorer areas of Windsor were also vulnerable on their way to and from work. On 15 September 1897, Emma Johnson, a well-respected 19-year-old housekeeper who worked for Mr Briginshaw, a hosier in Peascod Street, took advantage of early-closing to visit her parents at Tithe Barn Farm, Clewer. Emma, who was around 5ft 6in with a fair complexion and grey eyes, left home later that evening to return to Mr Briginshaw's but never arrived.

When Mr Briginshaw's sons came home at that night they were indignant that the servant was not there to let them in. Knowing, however, that Emma's mother was ill they assumed she had stayed longer than planned, and waited for their brother to come over from Ascot with a key. Emma's parents, meanwhile, assumed she was safely back in Windsor so nobody worried until the following day when one of the sons cycled to the police to report her missing.

Her route back to Peascod Street would have taken Emma across a notoriously rough stretch of the Maidenhead Road close to the Surly Hall hotel, which was frequented by vagrants and caravan people stopping off on their way through to different country fairs. Other assaults had been reported and Emma had mentioned an incident a couple of weeks previously when two men jumped out at her from behind a hedge.

Her semi-naked body was found the following day lying in a mill stream with knife wounds to her throat and stomach and grip marks on her wrists. Suspicion fell first on a former boyfriend, and then on a man called Charles Russell who worked at the gas works and had helped with the search.

Discrepancies in Russell's statements made the police suspicious but there was not enough evidence to convict him and he was acquitted, leaving the mystery unsolved.

Prostitution

With no education or benefits system, some women had little alternative to prostitution as a way of earning a living. Others may well have chosen this source of income as it offered a lifestyle they couldn't dream of from 'respectable' earnings. As social reformer Harriet Martineau put it in 1870, the employment situation many women found themselves in tempted them to 'prefer luxury with infamy to hardship with unrecognised honour'.

But prostitution was a high-risk occupation, exposing women not only to the danger of sexually transmitted diseases, but also to violent and abusive clients. The much-publicised series of murders by Jack the Ripper and copycats created a climate of terror during the 1880s so becoming a prostitute was something few women would have chosen, had better alternatives been available.

A Windsor woman, Annie Chapman, became Jack the Ripper's third victim after she moved to London. Her story shows how quickly a woman's life could change in the nineteenth century. Chapman had been married to a veterinary surgeon when living in Windsor. Although they had separated in 1884, her husband had sent her money regularly which had subsidised the income she received from making antimacassars and selling flowers. She had a daughter in the circus and a 10-year-old son with a deformity who was still in a charity school near Windsor at the time of her death. The ten shilling a week payments stopped abruptly, however, in 1886 when she moved to London, presumably in the hope of finding more work. Annie discovered the reason for this was that her husband had died. Meanwhile, her drinking had increased so she worked as a prostitute for two years until she was killed in 1888 aged 47.

Governess

For genteel women in the nineteenth century, being a governess was one of the very few occupations available. Working in a shop or a factory would be humiliating to a young lady, whereas being a teacher had a certain nobleness about it, and although a governess wasn't quite a member of the family, she was more than a servant. Being neither one nor the other could bring its own problems however: some governesses felt they didn't belong and some were viewed with suspicion as being likely to sleep with the man of the house, similar to a high-class prostitute.

A governess seeking a position as her pupils were leaving Windsor placed an advertisement in the paper saying she had 'good music and French in addition to the usual branches of English'.

Medical

Nursing became a career choice in the second half of the nineteenth century, due largely to the efforts of Princess Christian (Helena) who recognised the need for nurses to be trained. As president of the Royal British Nurses Association from 1887 she helped establish registration for nurses. With the opening of the King Edward VII Hospital and the war years, many more nursing opportunities opened up in Windsor.

The King Edward VII Hospital opened in October 1908. A handsome building with the royal arms over the entrance, it was set well back from the road with a lawn in front. Off the main hall was the matron's sitting room and bedroom and a nurses' room next to the children's ward. On the second floor were nurses' rooms with a 'commodious' sitting room, dining room and individual bedrooms. As the number of patients grew, however, a separate nurses' home was built behind the hospital. In 1928, a fire threatened to destroy the hospital and nurses had to evacuate the Queen Alexandra ward and move patients to safety. They were helped by soldiers in the nearby Combermere barracks and patients were taken to the military hospital.

Tapestry work

Other women moved with their husbands to Windsor because of their work. In 1876, the Royal Windsor Tapestry Manufactory was set up at Manor Lodge in Straight Road, Old Windsor, with Prince Leopold as its president. This was around the time of the Arts and Crafts movement when there was a revival of interest in traditional crafts rather than mass-produced products. The Windsor tapestry works was established a few years ahead of William Morris's tapestry manufactory which opened at Merton Priory in 1881.

Weavers were brought over from Aubusson in France, where this ancient craft had been established for centuries and which was widely regarded as the most important town for tapestry production in the world. The weavers were mostly young, married men and brought families with them. The 1881 census shows that Marie Foussadian, (33 years old) worked as a repairer of old tapestry and lived with her husband Jean Foussadian (37) the head weaver, in Walnut Cottage, St Luke's Road with their two sons Antoine (12) and Victor (7). Most of the women including Henriette Dumond (30), married to weaver Joseph Dumont (33) and living in Lorne Villas, worked from home as linen manufacturers. Marie Petureaux (32) who lived with her husband Joseph (38) in Coburg Villas was a dressmaker.

Education was provided for the children at a school in the Lord Nelson pub. Some of the children would follow in their parents' footsteps, including Victor Bruixand (18), son of John and Francois Bruixand. His brother Joseph (15) was an apprentice stained glass manufacturer.

Queen Victoria bought a tapestry from the manufactory in 1878 depicting Windsor Castle with the river and swans in the foreground. The weavers exhibited their work at the guildhall and around the country and won a gold medal for their exhibit at the Paris Exhibition in 1878.

After the tapestry works closed in 1890 most of the weaver families left Windsor. Jean Foussadier and his family moved to New York to work for a new tapestry manufacturer there called Baumgarten. The weavers' hall was used as a village hall for many years but has since been divided into apartments called The Tapestries.

Shops

Because of the royal connection, proximity to London, and the castle, events such as Ascot and fashions during the nineteenth century, millinery and dressmaking were popular occupations.

From small beginnings making hats and dresses, Maria Caley's business grew into one of Windsor's most famous shops[2]. The family-run Caley's & Son shop, which she ran with her brother and his wife, started in Thames Street and in 1826 moved to a new location opposite the castle; The building of the railway brought more visitors to the town and shop. Queen Victoria bought several Caley's bonnets which were brought up to the castle for her to view and as a result other ladies flocked to buy them.

An advertisement Madame Caley placed in the *Reading Mercury* on 27 October 1834 was obviously aimed at the well-to-do as it begged 'to solicit the attention of the ladies of Windsor and Eton' to the millinery, dresses, cloaks and seasonal designs, promising a

The WVS (Women's Voluntary Service) Mrs Leslie Needham, Lady May Abel-Smith, Mrs Dudley Charles, central organiser for Windsor and Rural Area, and Mrs Fisher who, among many other activities, ran an exchange clothing bureau where men of the Forces could take their clothes to be repaired. (Thanks to Barry Swaebe for his wonderful photograph of WVS women during the Second World War)

Above and below: *The banner carried by the Windsor & Eton branch of the NUWSS. Author's images. (The Fawcett Society, Women's Library Suffrage Banners collection, LSE Library)*

Above: *A horse-drawn ambulance makes its way down the Thames Street in 1904 while horse-drawn cabs wait for customers outside the castle where the taxi rank is today. (Royal Windsor Website Archive)*

Below: *Edwardian ladies shopping in Lower Peascod Street. (Royal Windsor Website Archive)*

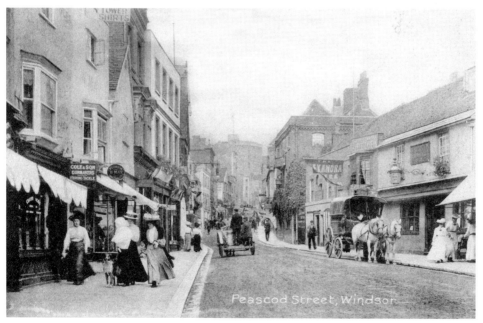

Above: *Windsor Castle from the Brocas. By the turn of the century the river had become a popular leisure spot. (Royal Windsor Website Archive)*

Below: *Nurses in the newly opened King Edward VII hospital, 1909. (Royal Windsor Website Archive)*

MEN'S WARD. KING EDWARD VII HOSPITAL, WINDSOR.

Above: *Peascod Street on a cold day in the 1930s. Typewriting and shorthand services are now offered by the office on the right. (Royal Windsor Website Archive)*

Below: *Women buying whelks from a stall on River Street in the 1940s. (Royal Windsor Website Archive)*

Above: *A blue plaque for Mariquita Tennant who founded the Clewer House of Mercy for 'fallen women. (Author's photograph)*

Below: *A plaque at the entrance to Queensmead school recalls its use as a VAD hospital in the First World War. (Author's photograph)*

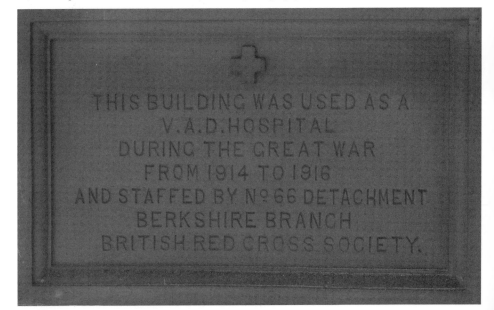

Above: *The convent of St John the Baptist in Hatch Lane, home of the Clewer Sisters who ran the House of Mercy for 'fallen women' (now apartments). (Author's photograph)*

Below: *Women's suffrage rallies were held on Castle Hill by the statue of Queen Victoria which had been put up to mark her Golden Jubilee in 1887.*

Above: *A nurse doing gas-mask drill with the evacuee children from London at the LCC residential school, Windsor. (The Sphere/Mary Evans Picture Library)*

Left: *Emily Wilding Davison (1872–1913), a former student at Royal Holloway college near Windsor, died after being trampled by the king's horse at the Derby in June 1913. (Mary Evans Picture Library)*

Lady Florence Dixie, traveller, author and proponent of women's rights lived in Windsor. (Lithograph, Mary Evans Picture Library)

Queen Victoria (1819–1901) in a portrait from 1852. (Mary Evans Picture Library)

Princess Elizabeth (Queen Elizabeth II), Second Subaltern in the ATS, training as officer, changes the wheel of a vehicle in a maintenance class. (© Illustrated London News Ltd/Mary Evans)

Mabel Knibbs (14) a member of the Windsor Youth Club detachment with a bag she received from the queen. She was parading in front of the castle when she dropped her bag and it was run over by a car. The two princesses saw what happened and told their mother, who sent a replacement. (Mary Evans Picture Library)

Above: *Women at work in the royal potting sheds at Windsor Castle, where four women gardeners were employed since January 1916 in place of men during the First World War.* The Sphere *magazine reports, 'They do all the work that the men whose places they have taken were required to do.'(Unattributed photograph from* The Sphere *8 April 1916). (© Illustrated London News Ltd/Mary Evans)*

Below: *Suffragist rally, Hyde Park 23 July 1910. Emmeline Pethick-Lawrence, Sylvia Pankhurst and Emily Wilding Davidson. Photograph by Mrs Albert Broom (Christina Broom) on a postcard (© The March of the Women Collection / Mary Evans Picture Library)*

Workhouse of the Windsor Union.

Above: *Windsor Union workhouse, 1841.*
Source: (The Penny Magazine 1841). (Mary Evans/Peter Higginbotham Collection.)

Right: *This postcard circa 1912 captioned, 'Kill That Fly' and 'The Fire Fly' reflects public outrage at the numerous attacks on letter boxes by WSPU militants. The suffragette is igniting a cocktail of paraffin oil and tar inside a pillar box to destroy the mail. A pillar box on Frances Road in Windsor was set alight in 1912. (© The March of the Women Collection / Mary Evans Picture Library)*

The Suffragette not at home.

Anti-suffrage propaganda postcard 1908 showing the chaos that ensues when a suffragette neglects her home and family to pursue women's rights. A frequent accusation made by the Anti-Suffrage lobby was that allowing women to vote would signify the end of civilisation. (© The March of the Women Collection / Mary Evans Picture Library)

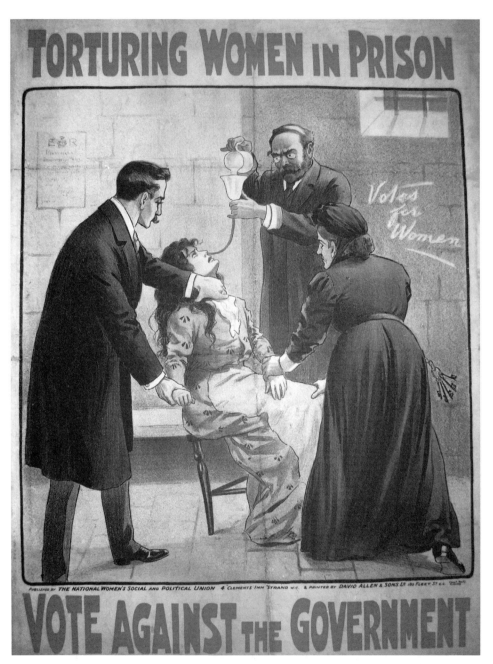

An original suffragette poster 1913 depicting forcible feeding with a doctor pouring liquid into a nasal tube while the victim is held down by a man and a prison wardress. (©The March of the Women Collection/Mary Evans Picture Library)

Second World War poster encouraging the women of Britain to answer the call and go and work in the munitions factories. (Mary Evans Picture Library/Onslow Auctions Limited)

variety of furs, feather and corsets. Presumably she called herself Madame to add a sense of glamour.

In the early twentieth century Caley's was doing so well a second shop was bought in Piccadilly, London, but the business was bought by Gordon Selfridge in 1926 and later became a John Lewis store when Selfridge's was taken over in 1944. Caley's would continue to be at the heart of Windsor's shops until the twenty-first century when, due largely to the building's restrictions, the department store closed in 2006.

Another enduring favourite with Windsor shoppers is Daniel department store which opened in Peascod Street as a draper's shop in 1918. The family already had a shop in Ealing. Former merchandise controller Peggy Bartlett started working at Daniel part-time in 1950 when her daughter started school and stayed for 45 years (some of it spent at the Reading store). Recalling her time there, she said:

> I loved the variety. As you walked through the shop floor you might get called over to give your opinion on the way something looked and staff would come to me with their problems because they knew they could trust me to be discreet. When I was training buyers I had to get them to base their decisions not on their own taste but on what the customers would like. You really felt looked after – I was given a car and driver to help me get in from my village. There was always something different to do and it was so fulfilling. But what I miss most is the people.

Another lady who started work at Daniel in 1950 was Dorothy Morton. She was 17 when her family moved to Windsor from Sunderland:

> After the war my mother wanted to live somewhere different to make a new start. We had no connection with Windsor but we visited Windsor and Kingston and chose Windsor because we liked the countryside around it. We found a home in Winkfield. I'd worked as a nursery nurse for two years since leaving school so I went to the labour exchange in

Victoria Road to ask for nursery work. They had nothing available but told me that Daniel was looking for assistants and arranged an interview with Miss Emily. She was so kind and said, 'Whatever you need to know, we'll teach you.'

Windsor seemed very old-fashioned to me after living in Sunderland. It was still a market town with lots of individual shops. Peascod Street had butchers, a grocer's and little dress shops. Daniel was especially old-fashioned. Tills were only just coming in. Before that, when customers paid for their goods the assistant put their money in a container, pulled a handle and the container shot across the shop on a series of wires above people's heads to the person who did the counting. They then sent the change and the receipt back to the shop assistant who handed it to the customer.

The shop was much smaller in those days and most things were on the ground floor. The first floor was for millinery. When I started we were selling The New Look and huddle skirts – things people wanted. Women used to queue outside waiting to get in.

Mr Charles was always walking around keeping an eye on the staff and there was always someone to ask if you had a problem. The staff were friendly but standards were very high. You had to be welcoming to the customers and the service was very personal. Every counter had two chairs so you could sit and talk to your customer about their requirements. I never dared be late!

On one occasion a pram was delivered to the shop by mistake. Mabel Daniel sold it and had the idea of having a toy department for which the shop became so popular with children. Over the years Daniel has expanded and had several facelifts to keep up with changing shopping trends but is still a family business and held in great affection by Windsor residents.

Sex Disqualification

Women's employment rights in Britain changed in 1919. The Sex Disqualification (Removal) Act enabled women to enter the professions – albeit with quite a few restrictions – and made it illegal to exclude women from jobs because of their gender.

In the early twentieth century, new employment opportunities for women appeared such as typists and secretaries. Advertisements for new businesses such as a Typewriting Office in Peascod Street appeared in the local papers.

In 1937, something happened in Windsor that would have been unthinkable a few decades earlier – the town had a Lady Mayor. Councillor Florence Carteret Carey, however, was well known to the royal family. As widow of Major General Carteret Carey, the Governor of the Military Knights of Windsor, she had been given accommodation in Windsor Castle by George V when her husband died in 1932 and was often a guest of the king and queen.

By 1950, women had shown, through two world wars, that they were capable of doing all sorts of jobs they had not been considered capable of previously, and over the next half century more opportunities would open up for women.

But there is still room for improvement today; Alice Abadam, who talked about women being paid a third as much as men at the Frances Road meeting in 1909, would have been disappointed to find that in the twenty-first century women are still sometimes paid less than men doing the same work, as was shown recently in the row over the gender pay gap at the BBC.

CHAPTER FIVE

Health

Key dates:

1847 – Chloroform introduced in surgery.

1850 – William Jenner, Queen Victoria and Prince Albert's doctor, made the distinction in between typhus (transmitted by lice, fleas, mites and ticks) and typhoid (caused by bacterium ingested from contaminated water).

1853 – Smallpox vaccination made compulsory.

1864 – Louis Pasteur revolutionised healthcare by proving germs caused disease. He invented pasteurisation by showing liquids could be sterilised by heating, and vaccinations for anthrax and rabies.

1864 – Contagious Diseases Act

1870s – Joseph Lister pioneered antiseptic procedures including sterilisation of surgical environments.

1890 – Immunisation for diphtheria invented.

1897 – Vaccine for typhoid.

1895 – X-rays invented by German scientist Wilhelm Conrad Rontgen.

1928 – Discovery of Penicillin

1934 – Free school milk

1948 – National Health Service

The nineteenth century saw a host of exciting medical breakthroughs in Britain, which led to improved hygiene and cures for ailments that had previously only been treated with leeches, laxatives and a change of air. But for much of the century, many women were unable to access good care for themselves or their children, and some of the laws concerning women and health were extremely unfair, which was a major factor in the campaign for women's rights.

While wealthy women could afford a family doctor, poorer women had to rely on charity or their employer. Charities and benefactors often made a distinction between 'deserving' and 'undeserving' poor. Worthy patients might be ones who belonged to the right church, or who were deemed to be of good moral standing. Those who didn't qualify sometimes resorted to 'quack' medicine – remedies sold on the street.

Windsor in the first half of the nineteenth century was a particularly unhealthy place in which to live. Overcrowded squalid slums, black, stinking, open sewers, rubbish heaps in the street and insufficient burial space were just some of its problems. Some of the worst slums on the edge of the Thames were also subject to flooding which washed the waste into people's homes and spread disease.

Edwin Chadwick's report in 1842 on the *Sanitary Conditions of the Labouring Population and on the Means of its Improvement* condemned Windsor as 'the worst beyond comparison' out of Berkshire, Oxfordshire and Buckinghamshire.

From the gasworks at the end of George Street (Windsor Royal shopping centre) to Clewer Lane ran a double line of black, stagnant trenches. 'From these ditches an intolerable stench is perpetually rising, and produces fever of a severe character,' wrote the inspector, Mr Parker in Chadwick's report.

In the 1850s, Dr John Snow proved the connection between cholera and contaminated water – but there was still a suspicion that the smell from open sewers had something to do with it. Florence Nightingale was among those who believed in the great danger of miasma, but although fear of 'The Great Stink' was in itself wrong, it led to measures to improve hygiene and cleanliness which was beneficial.

The Public Health Act 1848 established the Central Board of Health and encouraged local boards of health to be set up to provide sewers, inspect lodging houses and check on food safety. But the black ditch alongside Clewer Lane remained a problem in Windsor and was probably responsible for the outbreak of cholera the following year. The crowded conditions and bad hygiene made it impossible to isolate people when they were sick and consequently fifteen people died in less than a week. The queen was advised to stay away from Windsor until the disease had abated, but most residents didn't have that option.

The worst affected area was Garden Court, down by the river, a few feet away from the open ditch; a cramped little court of small houses let out to multiple families with people packed five to a room. Waste from the privies in Thames Street oozed into the houses which the reporter for *Bell's Life in London* described as 'not fit for a dog to live in'.

A government inspection report by Mr Creasey said there were more cesspools in Windsor than houses. The queen's refusal to return to Windsor may have forced the town council into finally taking action despite their previous reluctance to address the issue of the drains, saying the project was too extravagant. A new drainage system was eventually completed by 1850 and the next year work began on a series of underground sewers but sanitation problems continued throughout the century.

Despite the town council's insistence that an article in *The Lancet* in 1871 highlighting squalid living conditions was wildly exaggerated and out of date, complaints about pollution were regularly made at town meetings and letters to the *Windsor Express*.

One letter writer said in 1876, 'One can scarcely walk in any direction in Clewer without encountering odours which are offensive in the highest degree and as deleterious to health as they are disagreeable.'

There were both 'stinks permanent', like the one from the barrel drain in St Anne's Place, and 'stinks intermittent', caused by the emptying of cesspools, usually at night. The writer suspected human waste was not buried, but spread like manure on land near the road. In some overcrowded houses it was impossible to have the windows open because of the stench.

A refuse collection system was in place in the latter decades of the nineteenth century but the waste, including offal, was taken to a field in Dedworth and left to pile up rather than being burned or buried. Pigs were kept in the same field, so their manure added to the stench.

In 1898, a man in Surly Hall Road complained about the overflowing cesspit behind his property belonging to a row of cottages owned by the Hobbs brothers, which he blamed for the death of his child. Cesspits overflowed into the meadow at the end of his garden where his 2-year-old daughter had been playing before she developed diarrhoea.

In 1853, the town's graveyards were declared full, leading to more health hazards; a few years after that Queen Victoria inspected Clewer barracks and was appalled by the overcrowding and sanitary conditions and demanded improvements. As a consequence, they were rebuilt as Combermere Barracks.

Women's Health

One of the greatest dangers women faced in the nineteenth and early twentieth centuries was childbirth, which carried a high risk of mother and baby mortality. Many Victorian women were pregnant for most of their lives between marriage and menopause. Children were needed as heirs in richer families and workers in poorer ones.

Poor diet, alcoholism and hard physical work during pregnancy all contributed to birth complications, as well as disease and lack of understanding about sterile environments. Pain in childbirth was something women were just expected to suffer nobly until Queen Victoria took chloroform when giving birth to Leopold in 1853, making the concept of pain relief during labour respectable and provoking a surge of interest from women who could afford it.

If a child survived birth it was by no means assured a long life. During Victoria's reign around a quarter of children died during their first year.

Throughout the country consumption (TB), flu, scarlet fever, measles, mumps and German measles (rubella) were common. Before Alexander Fleming's discovery of penicillin in the 1920s, which led to the development of antibiotics, these diseases could often be fatal. Although vaccinations for some illnesses were available, women had no say in whether their children were to receive them.

Harriet Cockle, speaking at a women's suffrage meeting in Windsor in 1909, pointed out that in the eyes of the law only the father could give consent to have his children vaccinated. In Windsor where so many women were married to soldiers who were serving abroad this was a particular problem. A woman couldn't go to court with an objection to her child being vaccinated and neither could she have her child vaccinated if her husband didn't, or wasn't available to, consent.

Despite huge advances in medicine, women's health needs in the nineteenth century were poorly understood. Gynaecological problems were often confused with psychological issues and women could be put away in the asylum for conditions like post-natal depression. Victorian prudery meant there was embarrassment about discussing women's underwear, let alone anatomy.

Unwanted pregnancy

Being pregnant outside marriage was not only socially taboo but for many women unaffordable. Abortion was illegal but some women tried it anyway, with varying success.

In 1858, 25-year-old Charlotte Edmonds discovered she was pregnant. She already had one child with Lyons Morris, a tailor with whom she had lived in Grove Place, Windsor, for four years. Tailor, however, had left her a few months after the birth of her first child and was now living in London. She worked for as long as she could to support herself but eventually wrote to him, telling him about the pregnancy and asking him for some money. His response was that she must go to into the workhouse.

She went to London to show him that she really was pregnant. Lyons persuaded Charlotte to take a concoction of ferns boiled in wine, warning her that the longer she waited the worse it would be. She tried it on 1 August but immediately felt very ill and was too afraid to take any more so continued the pregnancy and had the baby in November. Lyons Morris was tried for procuring herbs to produce an abortion but acquitted. In December he was summoned for neglecting an order to support the child but it's not known if he ever complied.

Unwanted pregnancies sometimes had tragic consequences. One of the residents of Spring Gardens in 1852 made a shocking discovery in a privy behind the houses. Eliza Winchester was throwing down some slops when she noticed a child's foot sticking up. The body of a baby girl was pulled out and a post mortem carried out at the Five Bells in Sheet Street showed that the baby had been born alive a few hours before she was found.

It transpired that the mother of the baby was a young woman called Ann Slaughter. Ann, 20, lived in a small house in Love Lane, close to where the baby was discovered, with her mother, her mother's husband George Merryman who was a plasterer, and his large family. On 15 August 1852, Ann was charged with wilful murder and Mr and Mrs Merryman with aiding and abetting. She at once said that she had acted alone and her parents knew nothing about it. As a result she was kept in custody and the others freed on bail. When her mother came to visit her, she was heard asking Ann how she could have done it. 'I did not kill it,' she replied. 'I was kneeling by the side of the bed when the child was born. It squeaked once but it was dead when I picked it up.' Ann was acquitted the following March for the murder but found guilty of concealing the birth of a child and sentenced to a further eight months' imprisonment on top of the six months she had already served on remand.

Another tragic case is that of domestic servant Annie Simpson who died in October 1891. Annie had lived in Windsor before and come back a few weeks before she died. She took a room in a house in Albany Road belonging to Mary Ann Kenna, saying she had left her domestic service post in Eastbourne because she was about to get married. While living in Mrs Kenna's house she visited a midwife called Mrs Davis several times.

She suddenly became very ill but refused to let Mrs Kenna send for the doctor, begging her to fetch Mrs Davis instead. Dorothy

Davis, 38, came to the house and after a few hours asked for a doctor but one couldn't be found in time to save Annie. When a doctor visited in the morning he discovered an instrument in the room which suggested an abortion had been performed by an unskilled person a couple of days before Annie's death, which had caused peritonitis and blood poisoning. Dorothy Davis was found guilty of manslaughter.

Sexually transmitted disease

Occupational hazards for the prostitutes in George Street and other parts of Windsor in the nineteenth century included syphilis and other venereal diseases which were also passed on through clients to their wives. One of the worst injustices to women was the Contagious Diseases Act 1864 which was a shocking illustration of the double standards of the nineteenth century. Intended to stop the spread of sexually transmitted disease, especially in army towns such as Windsor, and keep the soldiers in a fit condition for fighting, it gave consent for prostitutes to be locked up, forcibly examined for sexually transmitted infections and treated if any were found.

The implication was that while it was natural for men to have dalliances, the women who infected them were at fault. In the first half of the nineteenth century the soldiers had had regular medical checks but in the face of many objections from the men these were stopped. Reports of brutality and maltreatment of women during the inspections and treatment for contagious diseases provoked a campaign led by Josephine Butler with the tacit support of Princess Louise against this 'surgical rape', but it took two decades before it was repealed in 1886.

The Windsor Dispensary

A Dispensary for people who could not afford to pay for treatment had been set up in Church Street in 1818 with support from Queen Charlotte (wife of George III). By 1834 it had moved to larger premises in Victoria Street by Bachelors Acre. As with many nineteenth-century hospitals, it was funded by subscription from the gentry. Subscribers were allowed to recommend one patient per year for each guinea subscribed. Queen Victoria was patron of the Royal General Dispensary, as it became known, and Albert became president.

The Infirmary

By the middle of the century it became clear that an infirmary, where patients could stay overnight, was needed. A lady called Catherine Delavaux who lived in Datchet heard that plans were being discussed to build an infirmary and when she died in 1836 left £1,000 in her will to pass on for the infirmary after her nephew's death if still available. She attached a condition that the money must be used within five years of his death or it should go to St George's Hospital in London.

In 1856, the nephew died and plans for an infirmary were reconsidered and funds raised. It was built in 1858 at a cost of £1,700 next to the Windsor Savings Bank, whose building was later also acquired and over the years several extensions were added.

But the infirmary wasn't open to all. Pregnant women were barred from treatment, along with children under 6, people of unsound mind, those with smallpox, scarlet fever, measles or cholera, and those 'in a dying condition'. They would have to go to the workhouse infirmary.

Destitute women in Windsor were treated in the workhouse infirmary where they lived, which had several wards and a building for 'foul and disagreeable cases'. In 1867 an inspector, Dr Smith, noted that hygiene in the Windsor workhouse was poor, the women's venereal wards were overcrowded, and the lying-in room in which women gave birth was far too small. There was also concern that some of the medicine bottles were not labelled, which could lead to patients being given the wrong treatment.

Workhouse nurses were often not trained and in some cases weren't fit to do their job. In 1883, the Master of the Windsor workhouse was shocked to find one of the nurses, Marion Russell, in a drunken state refusing to go to bed or allow the matron into her room. When they did finally get in they were met with an unbearable stench and found the room in an appalling state, with containers full of filth, vomit and urine. The nurse was dismissed instantly but it took three days to clean up the room.

Smallpox in Windsor

The fear of smallpox was ever-present in nineteenth-century Windsor, especially as it could spread so rapidly, although not everyone took advantage of the free vaccinations. In 1865, William Parsons, a labourer living in Clewer, was fined 10s for neglecting to have his 2-year-old child vaccinated against smallpox. That child died, but two other children living in the same house who also had the disease recovered. As well as being a personal tragedy, not having a child vaccinated was seen as a serious public offence, endangering the lives of neighbours.

William Jenner advised that smallpox patients should be treated in isolation to stop the disease spreading so in 1893, following an outbreak of smallpox, an isolation hospital was set up in tents in a field in Clewer. Efforts were made to find a woman to help the nurses but unsurprisingly none wanted the job. In the end one was found from the workhouse. Eleven patients were taken from St Augustine's Home to the isolation tents and between the 27 and 30 May four cases of smallpox were identified at Clewer and the patients all sent to the tents. By the time the epidemic was over in June it had cost the town £700.

Nursing

As a garrison town Windsor felt the effects of several conflicts including the Crimean War (1854–56). Some 2,116 soldiers' deaths are commemorated in the garrison church of Holy Trinity, and most of these deaths were in fact due to disease rather than the wounds themselves. But nursing standards in the Crimean War were greatly improved by Florence Nightingale (1820–1910) and Mary Seacole (1805–81).

Queen Victoria was a great admirer of Florence Nightingale and at the same time as men were receiving the Victoria Cross sent her a brooch, which became known as the Nightingale Jewel, in recognition of her work. In the accompanying letter she expressed her gratitude for Florence's service which she saw as 'fully equal to those of my dear and brave soldiers'.

Thanking her, Florence wrote about the need for improved hygiene in hospitals. As a result, these measures were adopted by the Windsor Infirmary and hospitals around the country. Florence Nightingale showed that genteel women were quite capable of being good nurses, whereas they had often been considered too fragile for the job. She was a supporter of women's rights and hers was one of the signatures on the first women's suffrage petition to the House of Commons.

Victoria and Albert visited the new infirmary soon after it opened in 1860. The queen described it in her journals as 'excellent, so nice and clean'. After Albert's death in 1861 the infirmary was the first public institution visited by the queen, in 1863. She became an annual subscriber, contributing twenty guineas a year and sending supplies from the castle. A new ward was added in 1897, the year of her Diamond Jubilee.

But it was her third daughter Princess Helena (1846–1923) and her husband Prince Christian who are most closely associated with the infirmary. Princess Christian (as Helena was called) opened the children's ward at the hospital and was for many years president of the Royal British Nurses Foundation, which had been founded in 1886.

It was largely due to her efforts that a Royal Charter in 1893 stated that trained nurses must be enrolled on a public register. Training helped raise the social status of the job, helping establish a new career for women. By the end of the century nurses were better qualified and better paid.

Princess Christian also set up the nurses' training school at 1 and 2 Clarence Villas and in 1894 founded accommodation for District Nurses in two houses in Trinity Place. After her son died in the Boer War she set up a nursing home in his memory in numbers 3 and 4 Clarence Villas in 1904, which she visited regularly.

By the time Queen Victoria died in 1901 it was clear the infirmary was not big enough to cope with the town's rising population. Another site was found opposite Combermere barracks and in 1909 the King Edward VII Hospital was opened by Queen Alexandra and Prince and Princess Christian, who persuaded her friend Henrietta Wedgwood to take the job of matron. Patients were brought to the hospital by horse-drawn ambulance.

Princess Christian helped raise spirits at the hospital by visiting the patients, motoring over from her home in Cumberland Lodge, Windsor Great Park. A Boxing Day visit reported in the *Windsor Express* 1910 describes how she visited the Women's Ward with her daughters, Victoria and Louise, and found it beautifully decorated by the nurses with greenery and paperchains.

A Christmas tree supplied by Lady Spencer Churchill was surrounded by gifts from Princess Christian and the ladies of the Linen Guild, which the princess and her daughters handed round to the patients. These included six watercolour sketches by Princess Victoria, two flannel petticoats from Lady Mary Needham, a turkey from the vicar Rev. Ellison and his wife, and toys, books and sweets for the children. One little boy said he had never spent such a happy Christmas.

The post-First World War period was initially one of financial hardship for the hospital as voluntary war workers left. A new form of subscription was introduced for the working classes similar to health insurance.

In 1948, King Edward VII Hospital became part of the National Health Service, finally guaranteeing free treatment for all. Although women's health was by then much better understood, there was still a way to go. Not until the 1960s would the contraceptive pill become available and abortion decriminalised – and not until the 1990s would working women be given the right to maternity leave.

CHAPTER SIX

Active citizens

Key dates:
1832 – Great Reform Act.
1965 – The Kensington Society formed.
1867 – Second Reform Act.
1884 – Third Reform Act.
1889 – The WFL (Women's Franchise League) formed.
1897 – The NUWSS (National Union of Women's Suffrage Societies) formed.
1903 – The WSPU (Women's Social and Political Union) formed.
1907 – The Mud March.
1907 – The WFL (Women's Freedom League) formed after a split among the leaders of the WSPU. The MLWS (Men's League for Women's Suffrage) formed to support the work of both groups.
1910 – 18 November: Black Friday.
1913 – Cat and Mouse Act.
1918 – Representation of the People Act gave vote to some women.
1928 – Equal Franchise Act gave vote to all women over 21.

The women's suffrage story in Windsor played an important role in the town's history and the lives of the women who lived there, yet has been largely forgotten. Being a poverty-stricken garrison town with breweries and prostitution forming the main industries, Windsor had its own set of problems that very much affected women, and a set of highly motivated and articulate women (and men) who campaigned for and against the vote.

During the nineteenth century, women – along with children, criminals and the insane – were barred from voting. For much of the century so were the majority of men. The best most women could hope for was that their husbands might one day be enfranchised.

Women's suffrage wasn't all about extremism. Militant suffragettes, with whom the movement is most often associated, were only a small part of a huge collection of individual suffragist societies, including political and church groups, who had differing aims and approaches.

The roots of the women's rights movement went back much further than the twentieth century. Some people had been advocating equal political rights for women for decades before the suffrage movement. The educated, middle-class women of Windsor who had time to read would have been familiar with the work of Mary Wollstonecraft's *A Vindication of The Rights of Woman*, published in 1782, in which she called for women to have the same education as men and to be able to have a profession, and be treated as equals within marriage rather than infantilised and kept in a state of ignorance. Other writers and poets including Elizabeth Barret Browning also had strong feminist views.

Lady Florence Dixie

One of Victorian Windsor's most colourful characters and champion of women's rights was the feminist writer Lady Florence Dixie (1855–1905). This 5ft tall Scottish traveller, war correspondent and novelist who lived in the town for several years from 1875 helped develop women's football, and campaigned vigorously for Zulu rights, vegetarianism and Irish Home Rule. She wore her thick brown hair short and rode astride her horse.

Florence was passionate in her belief that men and women should have equal rights in marriage and divorce, and that the eldest child of the monarch should inherit the throne regardless of gender. In an interview with the *Women's Penny Paper* in 1890, she said that women and men 'should have the same aims, hopes and aspirations in life; the same allowances and chances.' She said she would willingly give her life to change the position of women. She argued that man didn't have a divine right to rule alone. 'He has tried it and failed.'

Florence and her twin brother were the youngest children of the Marquess of Queensberry who died when they were three years old. (Her eldest brother was famous for the Queensberry boxing rules and for the court case he brought against his son's lover, Oscar Wilde, which ended Wilde's career.)

Florence and her twin had an unconventional upbringing after their father's death, moving with their mother around Europe so that she could bring them up the way she chose, despite attempts by the authorities to deny her custody.

In 1875, she married Alexander Beaumont Churchill Dixie ('Beau') and moved into The Fishery, a Thameside house close to The Willows near Boveney Lock in Windsor. They were good friends with Bertie (the future Edward VII) who would become godfather to their children.

At her marriage ceremony Florence refused to say the words 'love, honour and obey', substituting 'er, er, er' in their place. That did not, she explained, make her less of a wife, companion and friend, but reflected her belief that women should marry for love, not because they needed to depend on a man for a home, children and money. This issue over the 'obey' clause angered other suffragists too, but it wouldn't be until 1928 that this promise could be dropped during the Church of England marriage ceremony.

Florence had two sons but said that if one of them had been a girl she would have brought up both children in exactly the same way. In 1878 Florence defied convention by leaving her children at home while she embarked on an expedition to South America; there she was attacked by a female jaguar. She shot the animal in self-defence and rescued the orphaned cub, bringing him home with her to Windsor. 'Afflums' liked having trees to climb and the River Thames to swim in, but was considered to have outstayed his welcome when he was caught eating the royal deer in Windsor Great Park, so had to be put in London Zoo. Florence wrote about her adventures in *Across Patagonia* which was published in 1880.

In 1880-81 she went to South Africa as war correspondent for the *Morning Post* during the Boer War. When the Zulu chief, Cetewayo, was taken prisoner and brought to Britain she campaigned on his behalf and as a result he was sent home and Florence wrote *A Defence of Zululand.*

Her most feminist novel *Gloriana* (1890) was a utopian fantasy in which the heroine disguises herself as a man so that she can become prime minister and introduce legislation to give women equal rights to men.

She was a member of the Women's Franchise League, the organisation set up by Emmeline Pankhurst fourteen years before the WSPU, and addressed public meetings on women's rights.[1] Florence continued to speak passionately for women's rights until she died of diphtheria in Scotland in 1905 when she was only 49.

The Reform Acts

The 1832 Great Reform Act is generally regarded as a breakthrough for democracy but for women it proved a big setback. The Act extended the vote to more men, although still only a minority (around one in five). To be enfranchised, voters had to own property and earn more than £10 a year; it also made the struggle for women's votes harder because it specified voters as 'male persons', which would lead to years of political argument.

A petition for an amendment to the Act was presented to Parliament on behalf of Yorkshirewoman Mary Smith, who argued that if she was expected to pay taxes then she should have the right to vote. The petition was dismissed with much laughter.

More than thirty years later, in 1865, the liberal philosopher John Stuart Mill made votes for women part of his campaign when he stood as the Radical candidate for the Westminster seat in Parliament, supported by prominent feminists Barbara Leigh Smith Bodichon, Emily Davies and Bessie Rayner Parkes.

The following year, a group of ladies from the Kensington Society in London met to discuss the issue of women's suffrage and draft a petition for an amendment to the Second Reform Bill which would give women the same voting rights as men. Mill introduced their petition of 1,499 signatures to Parliament on 7 June 1866, arguing that the word 'male person' should be replaced to encompass both genders. The petition was rejected by 194 votes to 73, while the vote was extended to men who rented property as well as home owners.

In fact, one woman did vote in 1867 – but only because Lily Maxwell's name had been added by accident to the electoral register.

During the years that followed, many more bills on women's suffrage would be presented and rejected, but out of this initial defeat grew a campaign for women's suffrage, with individual groups springing up all over the country.

Windsor would have to wait until the next century for its own suffrage societies but the issue was already being fiercely debated some years before. Although there had only been one signature from the whole of Berkshire (from Reading) on the petition in 1866, interest grew over the next few decades, with much newspaper coverage, letters to the paper and meetings.

At a debate at the Reform Association and Working Men's institute in Windsor in 1871, the proposal was made that women who owned property and were ratepayers should have the vote. Although it was initially met with considerable opposition, members ended up voting for women's suffrage by a large majority.

But many other people at the time were concerned that home life would suffer and the fabric of society be threatened if women involved themselves in politics rather than looking after their husband and children. Placing a vote was hardly time-consuming, but anti-suffragist Rev. Keightley described it as 'the thin end of the wedge' that would lead to women invading the male sphere by taking seats in Parliament.

Suffragists weren't initially asking for all women to have the vote, however – only to have the same voting rights as men had at that time. Rhoda Garrett (cousin of Elizabeth Garrett Anderson and Millicent Fawcett) repeatedly made the point that the women who would be enfranchised under the current voting system (i.e. householders) would be mostly widows and spinsters who had no one to look after anyway, so family life would not suffer.

Another common fear among anti-suffragists was that, as women outnumbered men, they would automatically have the majority if they were given the vote (even though it was unlikely that they would all have voted the same way, given all the different societies representing different political and religious views.)

But Miss Garrett argued that Jacob Bright's Bill would only enfranchise 170,000 women, which was one woman in sixty, as opposed to the one man in every six of the population who had the vote at that time.

An amendment to the Third Reform Act in 1884 to include women in the vote was rejected but by now around two thirds of men were able to vote. As more men were enfranchised, more women (and men) began to question the fairness of a voting system which only represented some of the people.

The NUWSS

In 1897 lots of different women's suffrage groups were brought together under the umbrella name of the National Union of Women's Suffrage Societies (NUWSS), led by Millicent Fawcett. The common goal was to obtain the vote through legal and peaceful persuasion including lobbying, leaflets, talks and marches. These societies still operated independently and differed in their opinion on which laws needed changing and whether all women, or just ratepayers, should have the vote, but the initial aim (reflected at the meetings in Windsor) was for women to have the vote on the same terms as men, which at that time required a voter to be a property owner; the suffragists realised they had a better chance of getting this through Parliament.

The New Century

From the turn of the twentieth century women's suffrage would become a heavily-contested topic in Windsor, with passionate advocates both for and against suffrage firing off letters to the local paper in polite but vigorous fashion. But the fight for women's votes was caught up in other political battles. As more men won the vote, the debate over women's suffrage had become a class issue as well as a gender one.

Those Conservatives who wanted women's suffrage generally wanted the vote restricted to female householders, who they hoped would vote for them, whereas Liberals often argued that votes should be granted to more women, but as part of a wider enfranchisement that would include working-class men (who would be more likely to vote for them).

Some suffragists felt that there was very little chance of votes for all women getting through Parliament and saw the Liberal argument as a way of withholding votes from all women. Meanwhile, some working women questioned why they should support women's suffrage if they were to be excluded from the vote.

The Windsor Suffragists

One of the interesting things about Windsor is that, being such a small town, members of one society were often close neighbours of members of an opposing group.

In Frances Road, Lady Mary Needham of the Anti-Suffrage Society looking out of her window at number 52, would doubtless have seen suffragists flocking into Trebartha at number 51 across the road, home of Miss Street of the Church League for Women's Suffrage, and venue of monthly Suffrage At Home meetings.

A short walk away in Claremont Road lived Florence Gibb, secretary of the Windsor and Eton branch of the London Women's Suffrage Society. In Trinity Place, just around the corner from her home it's easy to imagine Florence bumping into the staunch anti-suffragist Rev. Keightley, with whom she had several spats.

Florence Gibb

Florence Gibb set up the Windsor and Eton branch of the London Women's Suffrage Society in 1907 when she was 48. She was an artist and author who worked tirelessly to promote women's suffrage in Windsor until she moved out of the area in June 1912. A prolific letter-writer, especially to the local newspaper, she organised numerous drawing room meetings, debates at the guildhall, and took part in open-air meetings outside the castle, which attracted up to 300 people.

Florence lived in Claremont Road with husband William, an accomplished Scottish artist (best known for his collection of chromolithographs of naval and military trophies which he dedicated to Queen Victoria) and their son, also called William, born in Scotland in 1891. William senior was a reticent man whereas Florence was energetic and passionate and, one suspects, not shy of anyone. Her letters and conduct during debates show her to be a highly articulate and persuasive person. In response to the argument that women couldn't expect 'to have it both ways', she retorted that that was exactly what women wanted: 'justice and chivalry, the vote and respect of men'.

She may well have inherited her bullish charm from her father Archibald Ramsden, a self-made musician entrepreneur from Leeds who made his money from giving singing performances in different towns and selling musical instruments, including a harmonium which he sold to Queen Victoria. His name can be still found on some pianos.

In addition to the suffrage meetings, which usually included a well-known speaker from the London Women's Suffrage Society or another organisation such as the Church League or Men's League, Florence organised fundraisers including suffrage plays and concerts and 'hard-up socials' at her own house, which included a sale of work with tea and a game of clock-golf.

The society had their own banner which they carried on marches. At 136 x 166cm it must have been heavy to carry. The green cloth has Windsor Castle on the front and on the reverse, words from the hymn *Jerusalem:* 'I will not cease from mental fight, nor shall my sword sleep in my hand till we have built Jerusalem in England's green and pleasant land.' (The banner is kept at the Women's Library at the LSE and can be viewed by appointment.)

Florence welcomed debate with the anti-suffragists, seeing this as an opportunity to prove them wrong. On occasions this confidence backfired, such as the guildhall debate where she supplied the anti-suffrage organiser with a list of local anti-suffragists to invite – with the result that a good number of them came along and opposed the speakers, defeating the suffragists by a large majority.

On other occasions it was more successful. One ardent anti-suffragist was Miss E.K. Thomas; in 1910, however, she was converted to the suffrage cause. In fact she not only converted, she became Florence's right-hand woman and took over the running of the society with Rose Miller in 1912 when Florence moved out of the area.

But it would be a mistake to think there was a single suffrage or anti-suffrage society. There were several in Windsor alone. Mrs Everett of The Cloisters, Windsor Castle, wife of the minor canon of St George's, was branch secretary of the Church League for Women's Suffrage (CLWS). The National Church League was found by Claude Hinscliffe, a curate and member of the Men's League for Women's Suffrage, who spoke at the inauguration of the Windsor branch in 1912.

Mrs Everett said at several meetings that women should not be lumped into the same category as children, lunatics and criminals. Because of their experience they were better suited than men to shape many laws that concerned children, homes and many social issues.

The Men's League for Women's Suffrage was also formed in 1907 to support the work of the WSPU and the Women's Freedom League. Speaking at a Women's Suffrage Society meeting in Windsor in 1910, Theodore Guggenheim of the Men's League said that the government could not justify the term 'representative of the people' if it didn't include both male and female voters.

The WSPU

In 1903, frustrated by the lack of progress being made by the NUWSS, Emmeline Pankhurst with her daughters Sylvia, Christabel and Adela, founded the Women's Social and Political Union (WSPU). Initially their methods were similar to the NUWSS, but from 1905 onwards their tactics became more militant.

The term 'suffragette' was first used by the *Daily Mail* in 1906 as a derogatory description of militant suffragists, but the WSPU took ownership of it with pride and used as the name of their newspaper.

The first arrests of suffragettes were made in October 1905 when Christabel Pankhurst and Annie Kenney disrupted a political meeting in Manchester and assaulted a policeman. Encouraged by the publicity the event generated, the WSPU adopted increasingly militant tactics while the NUWSS continued peaceful protests with petitions and meetings.

In a letter to the *Windsor and Eton Express* in 1906 a reader said that the actions of those 'well-intentioned but ill-advised and enthusiastic ladies' had done the cause more harm than good.

Supporters on both sides put forward propaganda, with postcards and posters depicting suffragists as harridans, slovenly housewives and neglectful mothers who were ugly and masculine. Pictures of a home without the wife and mother showed the chaos that would ensue if the suffragette were to neglect her duties at home – the poor husband trying to cope in her absence and the child put in danger.

Suffragist propaganda depicted their opponents as brutal torturers, or smug 'fat cats' who didn't care about other, less well-off women. Some of the cartoons had sexual connotations, either implying that suffragists were so desperate for male attention they'd do anything to get arrested, or that they were hideous, trouser-wearing manly women.

In a similar way to social media campaigns today, women on both sides may well have been put off getting involved for fear of what might be said about them.

1907

The Windsor and Eton branch of the London Central Association for Women's Suffrage, part of the NUWSS, was formed in 1907 by Florence Gibb. By 1909 the National Union of Women's Suffrage Societies felt Windsor was important enough to exist in its own right.

The Mud March

On 9 February 1907 a demonstration organised by the NUWSS from Hyde Park to the Exeter Hall on The Strand to demand the vote attracted 3,000 suffragists. Due to the atrocious weather and resultant muddy skirts and shoes, the event became known as the Mud March. After the procession, led by Millicent Fawcett, Lady Frances Balfour, and Lady Strachey, a Liberal MP presented a Women's Enfranchisement Bill to Parliament. It was refused.

The rally did however pave the way for other large-scale demonstrations. A small step forward was made in 1907 with the Qualifications of Women Act which granted women the right to be elected to the position of mayor and onto local councils but it would be another thirty-one years before Windsor had its first female mayor.

Following a disagreement with the leaders, some members of the WSPU left and formed the Women's Freedom League in 1907.

Emily Wilding Davison

Another branch of the NUWSS was formed at Royal Holloway in neighbouring Egham on the edge of Windsor Great Park in 1908, the nearest university college to Windsor. Its most famous student associated with the suffragette movement was a tall, red-haired, green-eyed woman called Emily Wilding Davison, a high achiever who studied English Literature between 1891–93.

She had been born into a comfortable, middle-class family but when her father died leaving very little money, her mother could no longer afford the fees and Emily had to leave and work as a governess until she'd saved enough money to finish her degree at St Hugh's, Oxford. She gained a first class degree but as a woman she wasn't allowed to graduate. She worked as a teacher and governess before joining the WSPU in 1906.

Women's Sunday

In 1908 Asquith challenged the suffragists to prove that there was sufficient support for votes for women. So in June, the WSPU organised one of the largest demonstrations ever seen at that time, with another rally in Hyde Park, this time attracting up to 500,000 activists.

Trains were chartered to bring women's suffrage supporters from all over the country to London. The demonstration was arranged on a Sunday so that working women could attend. When the government refused to alter its position, the suffragists reacted by throwing stones at the windows of Downing Street with some of the protestors chaining themselves to the railings.

In response to the growing militancy the Anti-Suffrage League was founded in July 1908 by author Mary Humphrey Ward, Lord Curzon, and William Cremer, who is famous for saying that women were 'creatures of impulse and emotion' and therefore unable to rationalise things in the way men could.

The WSPU put notices in newspapers and handed out leaflets encouraging supporters to 'rush the House of Commons' and speak to the prime minister on 13 October 1908. Fearing that the law-breaking and violence would set back the campaign and play into the hands of the anti-suffrage organisations, the NUWSS distanced themselves from the militant actions of the WSPU. A few weeks later, in November, the Windsor branch of the Anti Suffrage League was set up under Mrs Montagu Brown (a relation of Wallis Simpson). Several meetings were held in Windsor and Eton during October and November 1908.

On hearing that an anti-suffrage society was being founded, Florence Gibb invited their members to come to her suffrage society meetings where they would be given 'a courteous hearing' and a chance to reply to the society's speakers. She also went to the anti-suffrage meetings and engaged in robust debate.

Florence wrote to the *Windsor Express* in November 1908 to ask people not to confuse her Windsor and Eton branch of the London Women's Suffrage Society, which used 'quiet and constitutional methods', with other more militant organisations.

But she was up against mounting concern about suffragette violence. A former pupil of St George's School was even put off coming back to England for the annual Old Boys' cricket match. He wrote in the school magazine that he feared it would be too dangerous because of those 'conspirators in petticoats' (i.e. the suffragettes).[2]

A letter-writer to the *Windsor Express* said that the behaviour of the suffragettes had made him join the Anti-Suffrage Society and he urged others to do the same. But the parish vicar Rev. John Ellison said that while he condemned the militant methods used by the suffragettes, he couldn't agree that their behaviour was a reasonable argument for abandoning women's suffrage.

In 1909, amid more militant activism, hunger strikes and force-feeding, the debate in Windsor between pro- and anti-suffrage heated up, with politeness giving way to insults, ridicule and accusations of lying.

In March 1909 the Women's National Anti-Suffrage League held a meeting at the guildhall in Windsor, chaired by Lady Caversham, in which the Countess of Desart said that women had quite enough work to do at home without encroaching on men's territory. Lady Caversham believed that caring for the home was 'a duty and a privilege'; women had a 'softening influence' which would be eroded if they got mixed up in politics.

When the audience was asked if anyone had any questions, Florence Gibb handed up some on bits of paper with questions she had written, but these were dismissed as illegible or unintelligible by Mr Calderon and Rev. Keightley. In her usual highly articulate style, Florence wrote to the *Windsor Express* accusing Mr Calderon of bad manners and 'deliberate misstatements', and said that he and the Rev. Keightley were clearly still feeling bruised after receiving 'a verbal mauling' at a previous meeting.

Within a short time Rev. Keightley fired back saying that far from feeling bruised by the earlier meeting, he'd found the experience highly amusing. But if he was correct in reading into the word 'mauling' an implicit threat to physical violence, then he'd have to get police protection as he was 'far too much of a gentleman' to put up a resistance.

That summer the suffragettes adopted a new tactic: hunger striking. Marion Dunlop Wallace was the first to hunger strike. In response, the WSPU under Emmeline Pankhurst, announced that other suffragettes who were imprisoned would also refuse food until they were listened to, because as political prisoners rather than common criminals they should have received first class treatment.

Terrified by the prospect of creating martyrs, the authorities resorted to forcibly feeding the strikers. Descriptions of this brutal and degrading treatment, where women were held down and a tube forced into their stomach, usually through their mouth, sometimes through a nostril, would have revolted many Windsor women reading their papers at breakfast.

In Windsor the battle of words continued. Mrs Bernard Everett made a stirring speech at Goswell House, Windsor in December 1909, rebuffing the argument that women shouldn't be allowed to vote on the grounds they could not fight. If that were the case, she said, then the many men who were unable to fight shouldn't have the vote either.

And Florence Gibb defended her suffrage group by pointing out that different societies had different methods and she couldn't be expected to have control over other, independent and more militant societies. That would be akin, she argued, to asking the Archbishop of Canterbury to control General Booth of the Salvation Army.

Anti-suffrage supporters were quick to jump on the divisions between suffragists as evidence that women didn't really know what they wanted; but while the brutal treatment suffragists received increased sympathy among some people, their militant activities entrenched the anti-suffrage views of others.

The President of the Men's League for Opposing Women's Suffrage complained in 1910 about the 'outrages' committed by some of the suffragists and said that if women won the vote they would form the majority of the voters, outnumbering men by 1 million, and so would have their way on everything.

In her usual robust style, Florence Gibb replied that most of the suffrage supporters in Windsor were willing to accept, at least initially, votes for women on the same terms as men, i.e. women who were householders, so the new voters would certainly not outnumber the men.

The 'At Homes' and drawing-room meetings in Windsor sound rather delightful, with tea being served and tables decorated in the suffrage society colours (scarlet, white and green for the Windsor and Eton Women's Suffrage Society). But they were not always as civilised as they sound and speakers often had to put up with heckling and ridicule.

While insisting that the campaign for votes was not a conflict between the sexes, Mrs Stanbury, addressing a meeting of seventy people in Clarence Crescent, was shouted down by a man in the audience who accused her of vilifying men, until he was eventually called to order.

Black Friday

In July, a Conciliation Bill, which was designed to conciliate the suffragists by giving some women the vote, was carried by 109 votes. But Asquith stopped it going through, saying there wasn't enough time for the reading of the Bill in that parliamentary session. His delaying tactics met with a furious response.

On 18 November 1910, a day that became known as Black Friday, 300 women marched on the House of Commons to protest against this. They were met with unprecedented police brutality.

As they tried to push through the ranks of policemen, defenceless women were punched, kicked, beaten with batons and sexually assaulted; at least two women later died from their injuries. *The Times* reported that several of the police had their helmets knocked off in carrying out their duty. The police were reported to have, on the whole, kept their temper well but were 'kept warm' by the effort of pushing back the women who kept flinging themselves forward. It was also mentioned that Lady Soloman, who was in her eighties, was knocked down and handled roughly by the police.

Despite government attempts to confiscate pictures and stop newspapers being sold, the stories spread, and for many people the excessive police force at what had been a peaceful protest was the last straw. When the Home Secretary, Winston Churchill, refused a public enquiry into the police brutality the WSPU resumed militant activities with a campaign of window-smashing.

Tensions increased in the run-up to the second General Election in December. In Windsor, Louise Waddington, the Hon Secretary of the Women's Liberal Association for Windsor and Eton, pleaded with voters through the local newspaper not to support any society promoting women's suffrage which called itself non-political as it was 'abundantly clear' these societies opposed Liberal anti-suffrage candidates but not Tory ones. Florence Gibb swiftly wrote to correct Louise Waddington's suggestion, saying that her society was not partisan and would support any party that supported women's rights.

The year 1911 was one of frenzied political activity. Women's rights supporters were becoming increasingly agitated with Asquith's empty promises. But a new weapon came their way in the form of the census. For the first time, the head of the family (usually male) was required to fill in details about everyone in the house, including how long he had been married and how many children he had, rather than giving the information to an enumerator.

Suffragists objected to having their personal details given on their behalf when the Liberal government had consistently denied them the right to vote. If women didn't count, they said, why should they be counted? Consequently, many women refused to cooperate with the census. Some households returned their forms blank or incomplete – others with words of protests scrawled on them. Florence Gibb's name, however, does appear on the Windsor census.

Emily Wilding Davison had the distinction of appearing twice. Unaware that she wasn't at home, her landlady marked Emily down at her lodgings. Meanwhile, Emily was found hiding in the now-famous broom cupboard in the House of Commons which had to be given as her address – a triumph for the suffragettes.

On the eve of George V's coronation in June, Windsor women took part in a procession of 40,000 suffragists in London with the aim of enlisting support from the king to get the Conciliation Bill through Parliament. A note of hope came in the re-introduced Conciliation Bill which was passed by the House of Commons in May 1911 with a majority of 157 – but opposed both by Winston Churchill and Lloyd George.

In November, Asquith changed his position and announced he was dropping the Bill in favour of a new measure that would give the vote to more men, but no women. He indicated that they would introduce a Male Suffrage Bill in the next session with an amendment which would enfranchise women too. Unconvinced and feeling betrayed, the suffragettes went on a window-smashing rampage along Whitehall and Fleet Street, seeking to illustrate that the government cared more about broken windows than women's lives.

A less militant but still attention-grabbing act was the interception of the first aerial post that took place in Windsor in September 1911. The first collection of letters and postcards was conveyed by aeroplane from Hendon to Windsor, including official greetings from the king and queen. Among the many thousands of letters and cards were messages to the prime minister and copies of the suffragettes' *Votes For Women* publication, and suffragette Annie Kenney sent a postcard to the king.

In 1911 and 1912, women's suffrage supporters in Windsor held a series of outdoor rallies right outside the castle by the statue of Queen Victoria. Visiting speakers came down from London and addressed crowds of up to 300 by loudspeaker from their motorcars.

This didn't please all the residents. In 1911, Lady Mary Needham set up the East Berkshire Branch of the National League of Opposing Women's Suffrage in Windsor. Lady Mary was also Hon Secretary of the Berks & Bucks Needlework Guild. She made donations to the endowment fund for students at the Imperial Service College and was a supporter of the Red Cross.

The Wild Period (1912–1914)

The period 1912–1914 is sometimes called the Wild Period because of the extreme militant behaviour of the suffragettes.

In January 1912, Emily Wilding Davison was found guilty of setting fire to a letterbox in Fleet Street. At her trial she said there was not much chance of a woman getting justice in a court that was run solely by men. Women at that time were not allowed to sit on juries (They could have restricted involvement but this didn't include helping decide on the verdict) or act as lawyers, judges or magistrates.

In the spring of 1912, another WSPU window-smashing campaign of unprecedented size took place across London in response to the government's refusal to include women in their new Reform Bill. Hundreds of women came from all over the country to take part. On some of the stones they threw were the words 'Better broken glass than broken promises'.

Over a hundred arrests were made, with sentences ranging from a few days to six months. Following the protest the police raided the London headquarters of the WSPU. Christabel Pankhurst escaped to Paris but Emmeline and Frederick Pethick-Lawrence were arrested and imprisoned for nine months and sued for the damage caused by the WSPU. Both went on hunger strike and were forcibly fed. After their release they fell out with the Pankhursts when they questioned the wisdom of militant activities such as window-smashing and arson, and were dismissed from the WSPU.

In Windsor, acting on information from the police, St George's Chapel was closed to the public in March 1912 until further notice except for religious services. At a debate in the guildhall the atmosphere was so charged that the mayor, Sir Frederick Dyson, began by asking people not to throw eggs.

The treatment of suffragettes caused widespread revulsion and petitions for the government to recognise them as first-division political prisoners rather than common criminals. Millicent Fawcett, although not condoning some of the extreme methods used by suffragettes, backed the call for them to be treated as political prisoners. But the pleas fell on deaf ears.

June 1912

Emily Wilding Davison, serving her six-month sentence for setting fire to pillar boxes, drew attention to the horror of forcible feeding by throwing herself over the landing railings in Holloway prison and then down some iron stairs. She said afterwards that she hoped her action might draw attention to the torture and save others from the inhumane treatment. But the authorities were unmoved and despite her injuries, continued to forcibly feed her.

As a precaution against suffragist attack, the State rooms at Windsor Castle were closed until further notice, as were the State rooms in Kensington Palace and the Botanical Gardens at Kew and the picture galleries at Hampton Court. In June 1912, the Windsor and Eton Women's Suffrage Society was dealt a double blow. Florence Gibb, who had worked so hard for the cause, resigned because she was moving away from the area. Miss E.K. Thomas and Miss Rose Miller, the daughter of a surgeon, were her successors and had lots of ideas and enthusiasm for the future. But in August, tragedy struck: Miss Thomas died of meningitis. She'd been highly respected for her intelligence and passion for the cause since her conversion from anti-suffragist and had helped carry the banner on marches.

Pillar Box Fires

In December 1912, an incident turned more Windsor residents against women's suffrage; a postman noticed an odd smell coming from a pillar box at the end of Frances Road. When he opened the box he found a small empty bottle without a cork. The letters were coated in an inflammable substance.

Other pillar-box attacks were made in different parts of the country including Bradford, where nearly a dozen pillar boxes contained enveloped stained with ink and paint. Around 1,000 envelopes, mostly containing Christmas greetings, could not be delivered because their addresses had become indecipherable.

This attack on people's letters was the last straw for some. A letter in the *Dundee Courier* stated that, in view of the outrages by the 'vile scum of Britain called the Suffragettes', the country's young men should form a guard to protect the nation's letters from attacks from 'these lunatics'.

Another correspondent said if women wanted to be treated like men then they should behave like men and accept their punishment like men, 'not like silly women', and advocated that they should receive 'a good spanking in public'.

The promised Manhood Suffrage Bill was introduced in 1913 but the Speaker announced that the amendment giving votes to women had to be withdrawn. This provoked more outrage among the suffragists and another surge in militant activity including window-smashing, the destruction of orchids at Kew Gardens, damage to golf links, racecourses, cricket grounds and other male preserves, arson attacks on houses, churches, stations and racecourses, and bombs in newspaper offices, council offices and St Paul's cathedral. *The Suffragette* newspaper reported these things gleefully in its roundup of the year, including a comment that on 28 January 1913, women were sentenced for damaging Windsor Castle.

From January to July 1913 the castle was again closed to visitors because of fear of a suffragette attack. In June, the mayor tried to persuade the castle authorities to reopen but was told it simply wasn't worth the risk, bearing in mind the damage a suffragette could do to priceless objects in minutes with her hammer.

Similar precautionary measures were taken at Cumberland Lodge in Windsor Great Park, home of Prince and Princess

Christian. Owners of house boats on the Thames were warned of the danger of arson attack by suffragettes using a launch. Over the Easter Bank Holiday 1913, traders complained they'd made less than a third of the amount they would normally make.

Windsor residents would have felt the tension as militant activities came closer to home. In February 1913, Lloyd George's home in nearby Walton-on-the-Hill in Surrey was firebombed causing around £500 of damage. The following month, on the night of 19 March 1913, Trevethan, a large brick house in Englefield Green, close to Windsor, was burnt down. The house belonged to Lady White, widow of George White a hero of the Boer War. Neither had a connection with the women's suffrage issue so it's likely the house was targeted because it was empty, which was one of the suffragette policies, as Emmeline Pankhurst said that human life was sacred and should never be taken.

The house had been unoccupied for three years and had a For Sale sign outside. The couple had mostly used it for weekends and holidays and Lady White, who was away on the French Riviera at the time of the fire, spent most of her time when she was in England in a grace and favour apartment at Hampton Court Palace. No one was hurt in the fire but £3,000-£4,000 of damage was caused.

Some papers found in the rockery confirmed suspicions that the fire was the work of suffragettes; on an envelope was written 'Votes for Women', on a piece of notepaper were the words 'by kind permission of Mr Hobhouse', and on another sheet, 'Stop torturing our comrades in prison.' Mr Hobhouse was a member of Asquith's Cabinet who had taunted the suffragettes for lacking the true revolutionary zeal that men had.

Just before the fire was discovered a policeman had seen two women riding their bicycles at furious speed away from the direction of the house towards Egham. Another saw the same women on Staines Bridge. Their description matched those of two WSPU members, Elsie Duval and Olive Beamish (using the name Phyllis Brady). A few weeks later both women were arrested and imprisoned on remand. They went on hunger strike and were subjected to force-feeding.

They were released as part of the controversial Cat and Mouse Act, which had been introduced in April to deal with the hunger-striking women. Terrified of creating martyrs, Asquith's Liberal government brought in the act, officially called the Temporary Discharge for Ill Health Act, to allow prisoners who were close to death to be released on licence and later readmitted when they had recovered sufficiently to serve the rest of their sentence.

Elsie escaped abroad but the following year Olive was later sentenced to eighteen months hard labour. The barbaric Cat and Mouse Act provoked outrage among suffragettes and many members of the public. Rather than deter activists, it led to more militancy and a climate of fear.

The Suffragette reported Elsie's escape, along with others, gleefully saying that the mice had escaped the cats.

The castle terraces were eventually reopened in May under heavy guard. When the State apartments reopened in July new rules were issued which no longer included a free-entry day. Now, regardless of the day, adults would have to pay one shilling to get in, and children sixpence. All bags, parcels, cameras, umbrellas and sticks had to be handed in before entering and the rooms were guarded by Metropolitan police.

On 4 June 1913, Emily Wilding Davison was trampled by the king's horse during the races at Epsom Derby. Speculation continues over what her intentions really were that day. The king's mother, Queen Alexandra, wrote to the injured jockey Herbert Jones expressing sympathy after the accident caused by a 'brutal lunatic', probably reflecting the views of many at the time that this was a deliberate act, especially as the press were reporting that Emily had rushed at the horse.

Given Emily's account of throwing herself over the railings at Holloway the previous year in the hope that one big tragedy might save others, it wouldn't have surprised many people if she had thrown herself at the horse, but it seems most likely that it was a tragic accident. She had bought a return ticket to the races and two WSPU flags were found pinned inside her coat. Slowed-down film footage of the moment she is hit by the horse shows her holding up a Votes for Women sash, so presumably she was hoping to present the sash to the jockey or perhaps throw it around the horse's neck so that it would cross the finish line proclaiming the suffragettes' words, which would have been great publicity. (Although probably not as much as was achieved by her death, intentional or otherwise).

Either way, the government's worst fears were realised – the suffragettes had another martyr and her death sent shockwaves through the country. She died from her injuries on 8 June, four days after the accident. Thousands of suffragettes attended her funeral dressed in white, which made the event resemble a spectacular rally. Inscribed on her gravestone was the suffragette motto *Deeds Not Words*.

Following the funeral, the NUWSS organised a six-week Women's Pilgrimage starting on 18 June and arriving in Hyde Park on 26 July to demonstrate that suffragists could be disciplined and law-abiding. But all this led to a state of high tension at the races at Royal Ascot in June, so soon after the tragedy at Epsom, for fear that suffragettes would stage a demonstration or take revenge for Emily Wilding Davison's death.

Guards patrolled the course throughout the meeting to prevent an attack. As a safety measure, carriages and motor cars were not allowed into the racecourse and an elaborate system of concealed wires attached to alarm guns was installed. One caused panic when it went off by accident. Despite the heavy security, a man called Harold Hewitt, thought to be a suffragist, was able to run out in front of the horses holding a gun and shouting, 'Stop or I'll shoot.' The gun didn't go off however and no one was killed.

Fear of suffragettes increased the following year, in March 1914, when Mary Richardson slashed a painting called the 'Rokeby Venus' by Velasquez in the National Gallery. As a result, the State apartments at Windsor Castle were again closed to the public, as well as the picture galleries at Hampton Court Palace (home of Princess Sophia Duleep Singh) and The National Portrait Gallery.

When the suffragettes tried unsuccessfully to petition the king at Buckingham Palace more arrests and more violence followed.

One of those arrested was Emmeline Pankhurst which sparked a series of protests by the suffragettes.

St Mary's Church in nearby Wargrave was almost destroyed in an arson attack on 31 May. The vicar risked his life by running through the burning building to rescue an ancient register and a few ornaments but was unable to save other treasures. A hammer and some papers saying 'Stop persecuting women' were found inside the sixteenth-century building. People reported seeing two strange women in the area on the night of the fire, but they probably escaped onto a train as the church is just up the road from the station.

On the same night, a house in Windsor called The Willows was set on fire. The building was unoccupied, the owner being in Canada. Some postcards were found in the grounds addressed to Asquith, McKenna & Co, and mentioning the Cat and Mouse Act. But the suffragettes responsible (if it was them) were never found. A male speaker at Hyde Park was pulled from his soap box and threats were made to throw him in the pond. In Windsor a woman selling *The Suffragette* had to be rescued by police after a mob threatened to throw her into the river.

On 11 June 1914, Westminster Abbey was bombed. The device was placed behind the famous Coronation chair. Although the damage was minimal, the bomb was the most powerful yet to be used by the suffragettes and the location was greatly symbolic, threatening the heart of British society.

A service at Windsor parish church, next to the guildhall, was interrupted by two suffragettes on 21 June the same year. When the prayer for the king was about to be said one woman shouted, 'God bless Mrs Pankhurst!' The vicar's sermon was drowned out by shouts of 'Stop torturing women!' The two suffragettes ran off and jumped on a train before they could be caught.

But a few weeks later in August 1914, suffragette activity stopped. When war was declared on 4 August, the WSPU and NUWSS agreed to suspend their activities and use their organisations to support the war effort.

Getting the vote

In February 1918, the Representation of the People's Act saw the enfranchisement of 8½ million women (around forty per cent of the female population in the UK). This included all women over 30 who owned a house or were married to a householder. The Act also gave the vote to all men over the age of 21 regardless of whether they were property owners, and men in the Armed Forces could vote from the age of 19.

The higher age for women voters was partly because, due to the carnage of war, women really did now outnumber men, whereas before the war the difference had been much less significant. However, some people still believed that women under 30 would be influenced by their husbands and be incapable of making an independent decision.

The rejoicing after such a long battle for women's suffrage was somewhat subdued. The war was still raging and the majority of women still did not have the vote. Many women who had struggled and made sacrifices to help keep Britain's social and economic infrastructure going through the war, were now excluded from voting.

So equality for women had not been achieved – but a significant step had been made towards it. Another victory followed shortly after in the same year: an Act was passed in November 1918 giving women the right to become MPs. In December 1918, qualifying women were able to vote in a General Election. In November the following year, Nancy Astor was elected to represent Plymouth Sutton, replacing her husband when he went into the House of Lords. She became the first woman to take her seat in the House of Commons and was met by jubilant suffragists as she stepped off the train in London. With women able to occupy seats in Parliament there was hope of real change in women's lives.

Universal female suffrage was finally achieved in 1928 when, under the Equal Franchise Act, all women were given the vote on the same terms as men, and all adults over 21 were enfranchised.

Emmeline Pankhurst died on 24 June 1928, a few weeks before the bill became law. Florence Gibb, Windsor's valiant suffragist leader until 1912, had died in 1925. Although these two women didn't see the day when all women got the vote they did at least see the Representation of the People Act in 1918 so would have known that their efforts hadn't been in vain.

In 2018, the achievement of the suffragists was finally recognised when a statue of Millicent Fawcett was put up in Parliament Square in London.

CHAPTER SEVEN

First World War

Key Dates:
1914 – 29 June: assassination of Archduke Franz Ferdinand.
1914 – 4 August: Britain declares war on Germany.
1917 – Women's Land Army (WLA) formed.
1918 – 11 November: armistice.

As well as turning lives upside down, the war challenged people's thinking about women's ability to do jobs and take on roles that had been traditionally regarded as men's. The line between home and public life, which had already started to blur, became less distinct.

From being told they were unsuited to the 'man's world' of business, and mocked for being 'unnatural' and 'monstrous' if they dared stray into men's traditional territory, women suddenly found themselves being told it was their duty to step into the breech and keep the country going.

The outbreak of war divided suffragists as some opposed the war, while others supported it, but they agreed to suspend their campaigning activities during the conflict and the NUWSS and WSPU used their organisations to support the country. National treasures and art galleries continued to be guarded but now it was from air attacks rather than suffragettes.

For most women living in Windsor the war came out of the blue. When the heir to the Austrian throne Archduke Franz Ferdinand and his wife the Duchess of Hohenberg visited King George V and Queen Mary at Windsor Castle in November 1913, a large crowd gathered around the station to give them a warm reception. They might have read in the papers about the Archduke taking part in the royal shooting party on 19 November, but could not have had any idea how significant a figure in history this visitor would become.

There was no hint of conflict with Austria or Germany at Easter 1914, which the Royal Family spent at the castle, or during the beautiful summer that followed. Windsor was by now a tourist town with the castle, attractive gardens, river cruises and coach trips – but the threat of suffragette activity still hung in the air and the State Apartments at the castle had been closed again since the suffragette attack on the Rokeby Venus in March.

The situation with suffragettes in Windsor was so bad that the *Dundee Courier* reported that they were the 'most cordially hated' people in the town. The castle had been shut for months and £25,000 of business had been lost.

The summer of 1914 was a beautiful one and Windsor women enjoyed fêtes, performances, garden parties, school prize days, picnics, boat trips and days out with their families. The king's birthday on 3 June was celebrated with the ringing of church bells, flying of flags and a royal salute fired down the Long Walk. Some people attending the Ascot races in June felt anxious about suffragette activity after the attempted shooting the previous year, but tight security had been put in place. The royal carriage was escorted by mounted officers, and police, some in plain clothes, were distributed throughout the course; this time the event passed off without any problems.

The assassination of the Archduke Franz Ferdinand on 29 June 1914 saddened and shocked the country – the royal court went into mourning and the State Ball was postponed for a week. The minds of most people were on other stories though, such as the suffragette bomb in Westminster Abbey or the attempt to throw a male speaker at Hyde Park into the pond, or the wrecking of a church service in Windsor parish church by the two women who shouted 'Stop torturing women' – as well as the arson attacks on the Wargrave church and The Willows.

As a military town Windsor was used to conflict, but previous wars had been distant affairs. This one would involve everyone in the community. When war was declared on 4 August 1914, it was clear this was going to be different from any that had gone before. The *Windsor Express* reported, 'The die has been cast and England is at war with Germany.'

Women in Windsor felt the impact of the war almost immediately as their husbands and sons in the regiments left. Within days of war being declared, 103 men were called up from the Windsor 'A' squadron, (Berks Imperial Yeomanry), 80 from Windsor 'D' Company (4th Berkshire Regiment) and 30 from the 2nd Battalion Coldstream Guards. During the next few weeks more followed, including over 1,000 more men from the Coldstream Guards.

On 9 August, the chaplain of the Household troops at Windsor, Rev. Tower, preached a sermon at Holy Trinity church to the troops preparing to leave, saying that Britain was entering the war with a clear conscience and it was the soldiers' duty to fight to 'destroy the hornets' nest' and restore peace in Europe.

But although women gave the soldiers a hearty send-off, lining the streets and cheering as the band played the regiments out, they must have feared for the future and wondered if they would see their loved ones again.

Life in the town

Life in Windsor changed abruptly. Local shops stopped selling German products, and housewives were encouraged to buy local products to support local businesses. Whereas tourists had previously been welcomed and seen as essential for business, anyone with a Germanic accent now raised suspicion. People from Germany or Austria became official enemy 'aliens' and were interned at camps including Frith Hall near Frimley (which was also used as an army training ground for trench warfare), Newbury racecourse and Holyport.

Crowds of people turned up to a meeting held at the guildhall in Windsor on 15 August 1914 to set up working parties and a fund for supplying training and materials. The mayor explained that in addition to the National Fund they needed a small local fund to pay for materials. Warm clothing would be needed if the war was to continue into the colder months. It was announced that doctors had agreed to treat voluntarily the wives and families of soldiers, sailors and territorials who were away at the front, an offer that was greeted with much applause.

Doctors also agreed to give lectures in first aid and the St John Ambulance Brigade, Territorial Nursing Association, ladies who had experience in nursing and the sisters at the hospital had also offered their services voluntarily. The vicar appealed for funds and a register was set up for employers so that jobs could be found for people who had been put out of work.

The call went out for women to do their bit for the war and ladies' working parties were set up in nursing, sewing and cooking for the sick. The *Windsor Express* reported 'Everyone can be of use and there is much for the women of England to do.' One of the ways women could support the war effort was by making warm garments to send to the troops. In August 1914, Princess Henry of Battenberg, President of the Berks and Bucks Needlework Guild, asked members to provide clothes for the families of soldiers and sailors and the sick and wounded. As winter approached, warm clothing would also be needed for the families of those who had been thrown out of employment by the war, especially if it turned out that the conflict was going to continue beyond Christmas. The dowager countess of Arran, who was president of the Windsor branch, asked members to send in warm clothes of every description for distribution among the poor, the nurses, the Society for Friendless Girls and the Ragged Schools.

On 3 October 1914, the *Reading Mercury* reported that the Windsor ladies' working parties had sent the Windsor 'A' squadron of the Berks Yeomanry at Churn 118 shirts and 272 pairs of socks. They also forwarded to the Royal Berkshire Regiment at the front 123 sleeping helmets, while the Windsor 'D' company of the Royal Berkshire Regiment received 20 shirts, and a large number of blankets was sent by the mayor to troops at Aldershot and Hitcham.

In November, the Women's Liberal Association was also engaged in making clothes for the Belgian refugees, British soldiers and sailors and the British Red Cross society.

Other women supported the war by training in first aid so they could help nurse wounded soldiers. The Windsor Centre of the St John Ambulance organisation had been set up 1879 by Princess Christian and had plenty of enthusiastic members. Over 1,000 students had gained the certificate in first aid and home nursing, one of these being Lady Mary Needham. Lady Mary was a staunch anti-suffrage supporter, while Lady Augusta Spencer, who also became very involved in nursing, was a passionate suffragist, but women on both sides of the suffrage argument had to put their differences to one side and work together.

Within weeks of the start of the war, the troops in Belgium had suffered heavy casualties, creating many widows and orphans in Windsor. By November the rolls of honour published in the local papers were huge. It was clear reinforcements would be needed.

The guildhall became Windsor's recruiting station for the New Army (or Kitchener's Mob as it was sometimes disparagingly called). A poster went up showing Kitchener pointing his finger and calling for men to join this volunteer army and on 22 August a meeting was held to persuade civilian men to sign up.

With wage-earners leaving for the front however, many women were left behind struggling to make ends meet. In case this fear of leaving dependents unprovided for was putting men off volunteering, a gentleman living in Sutherland Grange in Windsor offered to give 5s weekly for up to 50 cases. A relief fund was also set up in Eton to assist local families.

At the same time they had to find ways to help newcomers to the town. When war broke out, thousands of Belgians fled to Britain to escape the German invasion. At the end of October 1914 a meeting was held at the guildhall in Windsor about local Belgian refugees. Several offers of housing were made and a fund started by the mayor. Women who were up near the castle in Windsor in November 1914 would have heard the Slough town band playing on Castle Hill to raise money for the Belgian

Refugees' Fund; Windsor residents raised 11s. A party of fifteen Belgian refugees were given accommodation in an old brewery in nearby Bracknell, and in neighbouring Slough, James Elliman agreed to match the proceeds raised from a badge sale for the refugees fund to £300.

The space left in the town by the Windsor soldiers was soon filled with other regiments preparing for action. At the end of November 1914 as many as 5,000 soldiers of the New Army had to be billeted and thousands more in the surrounding areas of Old Windsor, Sunninghill, Sunningdale and Winkfield. In order to keep the soldiers occupied in their spare time, the Royal Albert Institute and Conservative and Liberal clubs offered them temporary membership at reduced rates.

Accommodating these soldiers must have put a strain on some households, especially those who were grieving for their own family members; Christmas must have been especially hard as many people hadn't expected the war to last that long.

Hurried marriages were organised before grooms went to the front. Leila Benyon married Captain Victor Innes of the Royal Scots Fusiliers in December 1914. The wedding announcement in the *Reading Mercury* on 12 December said that the marriage would take place 'at once on account of the war'. Some marriages wouldn't last long. In December 1915 Frances Blount married Hugh Maynard at St Edward's Roman Catholic church in Windsor. The following September, Hugh, a lieutenant in the Coldstream Guards, was killed in action.

And as well as worrying about those serving in the war, civilians faced the terrifying prospect of being bombed. From the end of 1914 the Germans used Zeppelins to bomb factories and railway stations, with the aim of slowing down production of munitions and delaying soldiers from getting to the front line. These airships weren't very accurate bombers, earning them the name 'baby killers'. They caused panic and chaos, instilling terror in the population. Although Windsor was still a small town, the presence of the castle and the royal family made it a potential target for Zeppelin attacks, so an anti-aircraft gun was installed at the castle.

To keep the town safe, women had to be stringent about blacking out. Ellen Jones Nash, manageress of the International Stores in Peascod Street was fined 5s in 1917 for not blacking out sufficiently. She had been hurrying to catch a train and forgotten to draw the blinds properly. Others used the blackout as cover for misbehaving. Two boys in February 1917 stole chocolate from Ellen King's shop. They were recognised to be part of a gang that took advantage of the dark nights to steal from tradespeople and were sentenced to six strokes of the birch.

Wartime clubs and societies

Patriotic clubs were set up for girls to keep up morale and help them contribute to the war effort. Now that women's work was no longer confined to the home, girls needed to prepare for the world of work. The clubs also provided cheer and support for relations of soldiers during the conflict. In December 1914, a League of Honour Club was set up in Thames Street, Windsor by Mrs Payne-Cook. Speaking to an audience of 300–400 women and girls at Windsor town hall, Mrs Payne-Cook said the club was open to any girl who wanted to join.

In November 1915, a Girls' Wartime Club was also set up in Windsor offering lonely young women shelter, help and food and moral support. As well as educating the girls through lectures, the club offered guidance and help to soldiers' families. One of the leaders recalled an occasion when a young woman came to the club asking for directions to a camp where her husband was stationed; by the time she arrived the troops had been moved on and she had missed the chance to say goodbye. She returned to the club broken-hearted, but the girls were able to give her a cup of tea and cheer her up a bit and make sure she got the right train home.

The club put on performances including a Japanese operetta, *Princess Ju Ju,* at the Royal Albert Institute in 1917 to raise money for the Windsor War Hospital Supply Depot and Red Cross Workroom. According to a review in the *Windsor Express* it was 'an artistic and charming performance', and Miss Bailey, who played the emperor, was 'exceedingly good'. They had social evenings too where servicemen were invited to join the girls for a pleasant few hours.

Thrift

While the men were beating the enemy on the battlefield, women were encouraged to win the war on the home front by running their houses efficiently, 'making-do' and not wasting valuable resources.

In June 1915, The Mothers' Union in Windsor offered advice on household thrift, encouraging housewives to spend wisely and save what they could. In 1916, Mrs Clare Goslett addressed a Windsor Mothers' Union meeting on thrift and household economy in wartime. The three pressing needs of the country she said were 'Men, Munitions and Money'. As women had already contributed their men and were making munitions, they needed to think about how to save money by spending wisely and doing without unnecessary things. Although rationing didn't come in until the last year of the war, as the conflict progressed housewives had to cope with rising food prices and queues outside shops. Food supplies in Britain were badly affected as nearly a third of male agricultural workers left farms in order to fight and distribution was interrupted. Since the late nineteenth century the country had been importing a lot of grain from other countries to meet rising consumer demand for white bread. The grain shortage during the war was increased by a poor harvest in 1916 due to terrible weather, and the need to save food for the troops as well as an increase in submarine warfare which stopped supplies getting through. Britain was left with just six weeks' worth of wheat. Scarcity of food drove prices up, making managing a home more difficult, especially in poorer families which often had more mouths to feed and no garden to turn into a vegetable patch.

Women everywhere were encouraged to grow their own fruit and vegetables. Government posters told women that the kitchen was the key to victory and they should 'Eat less bread'.

Housewives shared thrifty tips such as using burnt bread or nuts as an alternative to tea leaves and buying dried custard powder and soup cubes. The *Windsor Express* carried advertisements for Bird's Custard with the slogan 'Not a particle of waste!'

Darvilles the grocer shop in Peascod Street advertised its flaked maize (3½*d* per lb) with recipes:

> Flaked maize pudding: 2oz maize, 1oz sugar, 1 pint milk. Boil the sugar and milk together and pour over the maize in a greased pie dish. Bake until golden brown.
>
> Blancmange: 3oz flaked maize, 1oz sugar, 1 pint milk, 1 walnut-sized knob of butter. Boil the sugar and milk, pour over the maize and cook, stirring continuously for three to four minutes.

Although voluntary rationing had been encouraged since the start of the war, it was enforced in the final year. Sugar, meat, flour and dairy products were all restricted, and anyone found cheating risked being fined or imprisoned. Recipes were produced for making bread and cakes with mashed potatoes or turnips rather than flour.

Women working at Windsor Castle were already used to a restricted diet. George V took rationing seriously and despite rationing on a national scale not being introduced until 1918, he set an example from the early days of the war by reducing food intake for the royal family and all the castle staff, introducing meat-free days and banning alcohol.

In 1917, a communal kitchen was opened at the old technical school in Bachelor's Acre, which made it easier for women to feed their children. It was run by a committee of ladies organised by Miss Street. Meals were served at cost price. The mayor said in his an opening speech that the aim was to save breadstuffs. The first customer was the mayoress. The king sent down plums and apples to the soup kitchen from the royal gardens.

Women's work

In the early months of the war some women asking for work were met with snubs and discouragement. The feeling was that the war wouldn't last more than a few months so there would be little point in training women to do men's jobs, but by the spring of 1915 the government Board of Trade recognised the need for women to do war service. In April 1915, an appeal was made for 'strong and vigorous girls' to join the Women's Land Army.

By July of 1915 the *Windsor Express* reported that women were taking the place of men everywhere: as bank and post office workers, taxi drivers and ticket officers on the railways. In October, the *Windsor Express* featured an advertisement for recruits for the Women's Army Auxiliary Corps saying 5,000 women were wanted every week including salemakers, storekeepers, cooks, waitresses, drivers and mechanics.

Suffragist journalist and novelist Beatrice Harradean wrote several articles for *The Windsor Magazine* about the many new roles women had taken on since the start of the war. In the July 1915 issue Harradean said she believed women's views on the war were broadly the same as men's – that the conflict had been forced upon Britain by honour and obligation and self-defence and now had to be continued to ensure people would never again have to experience the tragedy. But there was also a determination that with peace should come a new order in which women could be made full citizens 'so that the world may start afresh on new lines with a new experiment, having failed on the old lines and with the old experiment.'

In the November 1915 issue she praised female doctors whose achievements were a source of pride for all women and at last justified 'the claim always put forward but not always understood that the co-operation of women is needed not only for the good of their own sex but for the good of the community.'

The argument over votes for women, however, rumbled on in the background. A letter to the *Reading Observer* in June 1915 from John Massie of the National League for Opposing Woman Suffrage criticised the paper for referring to women as 'war heroes' and for putting 'a suffrage stamp' on work that was being carried out by suffragists and non-suffragists alike to strengthen the case for women's suffrage. Although women were performing a useful service it was not 'war work in any proper sense of the term' and women should not be rewarded with the vote because the battle for the nation's survival depended on men alone.

Munitions

The Munitions of War Act 2 July 1915 opened up a different employment opportunity for women. A Munitions Bureau opened in Clarence Road, Windsor and women were invited to enrol for work. Munitions work suited some women who had young children because the government provided nurseries for munition factories, whereas women working in other areas had no childcare provision so had to rely on friends and family to help out.

From 1916, women reading the local papers would have seen urgent appeals to apply at their nearest Labour Exchange for work at the munitions factory in Middlesex. Refined, well-educated women were employed as overseers in some factories. Mrs Carteret Carey, wife of General Carteret Carey the acting governor of Windsor Castle, organised a weekly party of ladies from Windsor to work in the munition factory canteens in Hayes.

The Women's Land Army

In 1917, some women came to Windsor as part of the Women's Land Army. The organisation was set up to help maintain the country's food supplies. With the men away fighting, women were needed to grow food, look after the animals and drive tractors. As well as providing an essential service, the WLA also offered women a healthy outdoor life for those who didn't want to be stuck in a munition factory. Advertisements appeared in newspapers showing cheery, healthy-looking girls dressed in dungarees and boots. They were issued with a uniform of outdoor clothes with a WLA armlet and metal badge.

Bessie Ziman from London who was 19 at the start of the war and had ambitions to be a concert pianist joined the WLA and was sent to Windsor to work as a dairy maid at the Royal Dairy Farm near Frogmore House in Windsor Home Park. She delivered milk to the king and queen at the castle and sometimes sang in the choir there on Sundays. Other WLA women were employed as gardeners on the royal estate in the king's gardens at Frogmore, by Windsor

Castle, working in the glass houses from January 1916. They did all the work that men in their places had been doing previously and were accommodated in houses in the royal gardens close to their work. According to the *Sphere* they were reported to be 'giving every satisfaction'.

Clothing

In order to do many of the new jobs required by the war, women needed different clothes; ladies' fashions during the war took on military references, with high collars, boots and military braiding. Out went the Edwardian corsets and in came dungarees and overalls. Clothing advertisements appeared for garments that were hardwearing but also attractive and included farm smock coats, long boots and hats with brims that could be turned up or down.

Fundraising

Other women supported the war effort by fundraising and voluntary work. The Ascot Women's Suffrage Society held a sale of 'useful and fancy articles' in All Saints village hall in December 1915, raising £50 towards a bed for one year at Royaumont, a hospital set up by Scottish women in a French abbey for treating war casualties. Lady Augusta Spencer-Churchill, who opened the sale, said in her speech that women were able to serve the war in many different ways, including as drivers, lift attendants and munition workers, but one of the best things they could do was nursing which was 'valuable and heroic work'.

Lady Augusta had been to one of the field hospitals near the front when visiting her son Edward, a captain in the Grenadier Guards, who had been wounded, and spent some time with patients, writing letters home for them. One of the men asked her to explain to his family how he had been wounded while crossing from one trench to another to share some Christmas pudding.

Another fundraising event in Windsor in the run-up to Christmas 1915 was the White Elephant exchange at the guildhall on 11 December. People brought in unwanted gifts or articles they had no use for ('white elephants') and paid a fee of 2s 6d in return for a raffle ticket which entitled them to a surprise item. A large crowd of women turned up to do their Christmas shopping. There was much laughter as the tickets were pulled out and prizes announced which included 138 'white elephants' from a piano to a chicken. The event raised £60 for the Windsor War Hospital Supply Depot which had just opened.

The Windsor War Hospital Supply Depot was set up in a house called Clydesdale in Osborne Road belonging to Mrs Deane Butcher. Around ninety women worked there. In June 1916, they received a visit from Princess Christian who presented war office badges and certificates in First Aid and Home Nursing. Lady Augusta Spencer, who did a lot of work for the depot, said that they had sent out nearly 11,000 articles to military hospitals in England and France, including 2,800 articles sent to the French wounded at Verdun the previous week because they had heard the men were badly in need. Lady Augusta, a staunch suffragist, and Mary Needham, a committed anti-suffragist, both received certificates in Home Nursing on this occasion.

The depot was open on Tuesday and Friday and women could work for all, or a portion, of the time. By January 1917 they had 220 volunteers and 133 ladies had earned War Office badges. They had made 27,806 articles, making use of whatever material they could find. Pieces of felt, tapestry and old blankets could be used for slippers, cork carpet for the soles, almost any used material could be used for making soldiers' bags and old linen was used for splints.

In October 1916, an Australian lady, Mrs Rita Dennistoun Fiske, organised a huge fête in the Great Park for wounded soldiers. The event was held in marquees by Queen Anne's Gate for around 6,000 wounded servicemen from all over the empire to commemorate the departure from Australia of the first convoy in 1914. Soldiers from King Edward VII Hospital in Windsor, the Duchess of Connaught's Hospital at Clivedon and many local hospitals were brought to the event by train, bus, ambulance and even steamer, while others were driven by lady volunteers. The weather was fine, the food was plentiful due to lots of donations, and the men were entertained by music from the 2nd Life Guards band. Lady Augusta Spencer supervised 250 volunteer waitresses for the fête including many soldiers' wives.

Changes in lifestyle

The First World War changed life for everyone in Windsor; in 1915 the 'London season' of events was dropped from the social calendar – there was no boat race, no cricket at Lords and no Henley Regatta. At Ascot, however, the races continued despite some objections that celebrating at a time when so many were dying for their country was inappropriate.

Despite the bleak times they were living through, however, there was plenty of entertainment in the town during the war. Fêtes, sales, parties and performances were put on to help raise money for the war effort. These events were even more successful when the women organising them managed to secure support from the castle. The royal family involved themselves in lots of ways: opening sales, making donations and presenting prizes.

The king and queen also visited soldiers at the hospital, entertained wounded soldiers at the castle and went out to France several times, including a ten-day visit in July 1917. The queen spent most of her time there visiting and cheering the wounded in hospitals, while the king was taken to the battlefields and talked to the troops.

In 1917, Queen Mary and her children drove through the streets of Windsor in their coach to boost morale. Church bells were rung and the street was decorated with flags of the allies. Their daughter Princess Mary visited hospitals and charities with her mother and came up with the idea of the Princess Mary Christmas Tins. These decorative gift tins contained items such as tobacco, pencils, a Christmas card and a picture of the Princess and were sent to members of the Armed Forces, nurses at the front in France and the widows or parents of servicemen who had been killed.

Towards the end of the war Princess Mary also supported the Women's Land Army, attending a rally in Oxford to encourage new recruits.

Hospital work

The King Edward VII Hospital was put under a lot of pressure during the war as many of the medical staff joined up to fight. With Windsor being a military town, the hospital was identified as a suitable town for receiving wounded soldiers.

Pressure was increased as the town's population swelled and in the latter years of the war the hospital was so short on staff that the matron had to double as the anaesthetist. A contingent of Voluntary Aid Detachment (VADs) nurses was brought in to bolster the depleted staff.

In September 1916, twenty-seven wounded men arrived at the hospital from the front. In spring there was such pressure on beds an outdoor ward had to be added, providing another eighteen beds, funded by a collection run by Lady Spencer Churchill.

Nursing

In 1915, Lady Augusta Spencer set up a Women's Red Cross VAD hospital at her home, Queensmead, with Princess Christian as commandant and Dr Hathaway as medical officer. In a speech Lady Augusta said that many women who had been involved in making garments and sending gifts to men at the front would welcome the chance to become more personally involved in the war, looking after wounded men who had been defending the country.

A field hospital was also set up in Windsor Great Park in 1915 for the treatment of wounded soldiers straight from the battlefield. Called The Princess Christian Military Hospital, it comprised a semicircle of wooden huts with verandas where patients were wheeled out to get fresh air.

Many of the nurses at the field hospital were volunteers from the Voluntary Aid Detachment set up by the Red Cross.

Coming from middle- and upper-class families many of them had never worked before so being thrown into life in a busy field hospital must have been a big shock for some of them. Florence Caswell, a debutante from London with a country house near Great Fosters, Egham, went along to some Red Cross lectures on First Aid and Home Nursing and learned skills such as how to make a bed and roll a bandage. She joined as a VAD and was sent to Old Windsor workhouse infirmary for a year to get some experience. Although she was working in the maternity ward, it was useful training as she found herself working with patients from the poorest backgrounds.

'I learned more about life there than in all my twenty years,' Florence said in a recorded interview for the Imperial War Museum in 1974. When she was ready she was transferred to the military hospital to work with soldiers, cycling there each day from her Egham home.

She had expected her duties to include cleaning the ward and giving the patients meals and bed baths. As soon as she arrived, however, the hospital was besieged by a convoy of wounded soldiers and she was thrust straight into helping with operations. The hospital was run along strict military lines and the staff were stringent about sterilising the wards with disinfectant but there was no penicillin and little by way of anaesthetics. But the patients when they weren't in too much pain were 'very jolly, wonderful people' from all walks of life.

CHAPTER EIGHT

Second World War

Key Dates:
1938 – ATS (Women's Auxiliary Territorial Service) established.
1939 – 3 September: Britain declares war on Germany.
1941 – December: National Service Act – conscription for women was introduced.
1945 – 8 May: the war ended in Europe (VE Day).
1945 – 2 September: the Second World War officially ended following the surrender of Japan.

In the Second World War, as with the First, economic conditions made it essential for women to do men's jobs. In 1938, with the growing likelihood of another war, the Women's Auxiliary Territorial Service (ATS) was established. Posters showed glamorous women in khaki uniform making the job look exciting, although some of the work was very mundane and included potato peeling, cooking and cleaning. But some women learned new skills as welders, mechanics, electricians and anti-aircraft gun operators.

With the National Service Act in December 1941 Britain became the first country to introduce conscription for women. Single women aged 20–30 were given a choice of working in industry or one of the auxiliary services of the armed forces. Married women and women with children under 14 were exempt but many joined anyway out of choice.

The most famous ATS member in Windsor was Princess Elizabeth. Her involvement showed girls everywhere that no one was too privileged to get their hands dirty. Although women weren't allowed to take part in armed combat they undertook many other duties.

Elizabeth joined as Honorary Second Subaltern, rising after a few months to Honorary Junior Commander. Photographs of the Princess changing a truck wheel, working on car engines and driving an ambulance appeared in newspapers everywhere. Her younger sister Margaret was a Girl Guide and later joined the Sea Rangers.

One of the most dangerous and exciting jobs in the ATS was Ack Ack duty. Although women weren't allowed to fire the anti-aircraft guns themselves, Ack Ack Girls worked alongside the men who loaded and fired them to defend British towns from German bombing raids. The name comes from the sound the anti-aircraft guns made when fired. Women would act as Spotters, looking out for enemy planes; Range-finders who would determine the distance a gun shell would have to travel to hit its target; or Predictors who calculated the length of fuse needed to ensure the shell hit its target at the right height.

Eva Hoe from Hull joined the 591 Ack Ack Battery in Datchet, next to Windsor. Telling her story to the BBC People's War project, she described how they had shifts of 24 hours on the gun site followed by 24 hours on fatigues, which included working in the cook-house and officers' mess. When the Ack Ack Girls got their 10*s* weekly pay they would spend it on cigarettes and shampoo and going out for tea. They usually provided their own entertainment such as putting on a fashion show at Christmas. On days off they would walk into Windsor but someone nearly always stopped and gave them a lift. Looking back, she described her ATS days as the happiest in her life.

The Home Front

Other women played an essential role on the home front, running the household on tight rations, growing food, running fund-raising events for the war effort, and taking in evacuee children.

Some joined the WVS (Women's Volunteer Service) helping out in all sorts of ways including fundraising, serving tea to firefighters, clearing up after a bombing raid and offering support and refreshments to bomb victims.

Munitions factory

As men left factories to enlist, women were called upon to take their places. Unlike in Germany where Hitler forbade women from working in munition factories as they weren't considered skilled enough, in Britain posters went up urging the women of Britain to 'Come into the factories.'

The Slough trading estate just up the road was requisitioned by the government and every factory was used for war work including making parts for Spitfires and incendiary bombs. Kathleen Beck and her sister Peg worked in the gas mask factory in Slough. Kathleen married a Royal Horse Guard at Clewer Church, Windsor, the day after war broke out and a month later her sister Peg married a Scots Guard at the same church. Kathleen recalled for the BBC People's War Project that in the final year of the war when Peg was expecting her first baby, she received a letter from the War Office to say her husband Duncan was missing, presumed killed.

Duncan had in fact been taken prisoner and was allowed by the Germans to make one quick radio call. He asked anyone who was listening if they could let his wife know he was a POW. Luckily for Peg a young man in Maidenhead who heard the message wrote it down on a cigarette packet and cycled over to her home in St Andrew's Crescent, Windsor, to give it to her.

Land Girls

With the prospect of war looming, the Women's Land Army that had proved so effective in the First World War was reintroduced in June 1939 to ensure that the country would be self-sufficient, especially as Hitler's U-boats threatened to starve Britain out by blocking food supplies from America.

Posters went up everywhere showing healthy-looking, rosy-cheeked women in trousers cheerfully carrying out their tasks, giving the impression it was quite glamorous work. In fact, it was no easy option. Women worked long hours and accommodation was often basic in huts or old farm cottages with no services – a shock especially to girls who had grown up with servants. Jobs included looking after animals, milking cows, ploughing fields, harvesting crops and in winter breaking up frozen earth for sowing crops. Farm equipment was quite basic so most things had to be done by hand. By 1943, 80,000 women were part of the WLA, working fifty hours per week and earning 28s.

Three women from the WLA worked on the king's farm in Windsor Great Park. The deer park was ploughed for growing crops and the deer relocated to Balmoral. The crops provided a bumper harvest of barley in 1942 and the biggest wheat harvest in the country, and was proclaimed a model of how properly managed agriculture could be used as a weapon of war.

Other women took to the skies or supported the WAAF from the ground, working in radar stations, helping to track enemy bombers. Just a few miles up the road from Windsor in White Waltham, Maidenhead, the first female pilots were flying for the ATA (Air Transport Auxiliary) in 1940. Their chief job was to fly warplanes including Mosquitoes, Wellingtons and Spitfires from the factory to the RAF squadrons or transport personnel, freeing up RAF pilots for combat flying.

Although these women weren't flying in combat, they risked their lives constantly, flying unarmed with no radio (in case of interception), sometimes in bad weather and sometimes flying faulty planes to repair centres.

Living in Windsor during the Second World War

Although Windsor was considered a safe place to live and many people were evacuated to the town during the war, life was far from worry-free for women living there. The sandbags stacked up against and around Windsor Castle and the blacked-out windows were a daily reminder that the town was a target for bombing. The town's proximity to the munition factories in Slough was another worry as it was known to be a major producer of explosives. As a precaution from enemy bombers, Slough and its trading estate were surrounded by drums filled with oil-soaked rags to create a smoke screen when lit at night but there was always the fear bombs missing the target might fall on Windsor.

As soon as war broke out, residents were given instructions to cover their windows with blackout material and use only candles or torches upstairs. The local papers carried urgent reminders of the need to black out and remember gas masks alongside advertisements for cleaning materials and school uniform, reminders that life carried on. Mothers had to ensure their children always carried their gas masks to school and knew how to use them.

Gas mask drills and air raid rehearsals became part of everyday life for school children and they had to get used to practising their times tables in the air raid shelters. Teachers had to help pupils identify different aircraft by their sound. They supported the war effort by getting the children to help grow vegetables and perform in many fundraising events organised by the borough including War Weapons Week in 1941, Warship Week in 1942, Wings for Victory Week in 1943 which later became the Royal Windsor Horse Show, and Salute the Soldier Week in May 1944.

These events brought some cheer to the town and boosted morale as well as raising money for the armed services. Perhaps throwing themselves into organising or taking part in them also helped take women's minds off the conflict for a short time and provided some camaraderie. Flags, bunting and posters went up in the weeks before and shops were filled with attractive window displays. The programme for the Salute the Soldier Week included an opening ceremony at the guildhall, singing by the County Girls' School and County Boys' School, concerts, dances, exhibitions, a children's rally, a display by the Women's League of Health and Beauty and a circus.

Women living in Windsor during the war kept up with the news on the wireless, at the cinema and in the local paper. They became used to seeing searchlights in Windsor Great Park and hearing bomber planes swarming over the town heading for London or Slough.

Rationing

Petrol was rationed from September 1939 and drivers had to find their way around without road signs in the dark during blackout, which could be hazardous. Stories of road accidents due to the blackout were quite common in the local newspapers, including Alice Osborne who died in King Edward VII hospital, Windsor, after she came off the back of a motorbike as she was travelling back from Bracknell to London after visiting her evacuee son.

To help people manage on restricted food and anticipating food rationing, the Conservative Club in Peascod Street ran a series of free practical and healthy cookery demonstrations from 10-15 October 1939 which promised to show how the toughest of meats could be cooked within a few minutes. Examples of meals made included a shin of beef stew with two vegetables and a pudding which could all be made in fifteen minutes.

Rationing began officially in January 1940 but books were being sent out in the run-up to Christmas with reminders in the paper that books would need to be registered in a shop. In December 1939, 300 ration books had already been reported missing in Windsor. Police believed they had been stolen by people who thought that by registering at several shops they would be able to obtain extra supplies. Some women were fooled into handing over their ration books to people who called on their door saying they were from the Food Office and demanding the books. As a result Food Office representatives were issued with a special warrant card.

The ration cards had to be registered at a shop. Each purchase was marked off in the book. Rations per person per week included one fresh egg, 4oz margarine, 2oz butter, 3 pints milk, 4oz bacon and ham, 2oz tea, 1oz cheese and 8oz sugar. Fish wasn't rationed but became very expensive because of the dangers of sea fishing in wartime.

Windsor residents were used to a military presence but now the town and Great Park were full of soldiers. Public halls and private houses were taken over by the armed forces and open spaces were dug up for growing food, and for accommodating and training the armed forces in camps. Buildings were requisitioned or lent for military use. Clewer Park, a manor house near Windsor racecourse that had once belonged to Sir Daniel Gooch of railway fame and was also the site of Clewer Barracks, was taken over by the Royal Navy and used as an administration centre for the Wrens.

Queensmead which had been used as a VAD hospital in the First World War was used again in 1945–46 by the Red Cross for repatriated Commonwealth POWs. Zelda Dunlop was one of the Red Cross nurses working at Queensmead when the ex-POWs who had been liberated from camps in Germany and the Far East at the end of the war arrived. In Queensmead school's archives Zelda recalls her enjoyment working in the house and the warm reception they gave the soldiers who had nowhere else in England to go: 'As nurses we were very excited. It brought us very much into the front line in a way. We thought it was marvellous to have these chaps come back.'

The VAD nurses at Queensmead treated around fifteen patients at a time from different Commonwealth countries. When not working they had the Great Park to walk in on one side of the house or they could wander around the town, and see the castle and Eton college.

Green spaces previously used for recreation were also taken over for war use. Land on Ascot Racecourse near King's Ride that had been the winter home of Bertram Mill Circus was turned into an internment camp for aliens in 1940 as fear of an imminent invasion grew and Churchill adopted a more stringent approach to foreigners. From 1943 this camp became a POW camp for German and Italian prisoners. Smith's Lawn (now the polo field) in Windsor Great Park was used for accommodating troops and planes, and as an assembly centre for Wellington bombers.

Not only did the women of Windsor live in fear of losing their husbands, sons or sweethearts, they also had to contend with the fear of enemy bombing. During the war there were forty air raids over Windsor and Eton, and over 2,300 bombs. The first bomb fell on 23 October 1940 near the barracks, destroying a pub. It was followed shortly by several other bombs including one on the GWR railway station. Bombs also landed on Princess Christian Nursing Home, Eton College, the Great Park and the city's dust destructor, which resulted in sixty people injured from flying glass.

A woman in St Andrews Avenue was getting out of the bath at the time the dust destructor was hit and narrowly escaped being hit by shards of glass which were blown out of the front door and embedded themselves in the bathroom door.

More bombs fell on surrounding areas including Slough, Datchett, Ascot, Sunninghill, Sunningdale, Binfield and Bagshot. In Windsor 9 people were killed and 111 injured.

Mary Kerridge

Some women took over the running of their husbands' businesses during the war. One of these was actress Mary Kerridge who ran the Theatre Royal in Windsor while her husband John Counsell was away fighting. She judged correctly that the audience wanted light-hearted plays to brighten up the bleak time they were living through and keep up morale. Managing the business and being a single mother to twins while her husband was away must have been hard work. She would get up, join the queue for her rations, spend the day rehearsing for the next show and in the evening perform in the current show, while looking after her babies, Jennifer and Elizabeth born in 1943 when John was with the Royal Artillery.

Mary, who was born in London in 1914, had worked as a secretary and receptionist before becoming a repertory actress. She married John on August 5 1939, a few weeks before war broke out. He had attempted to establish a repertory theatre at Windsor in 1933 but had run into financial difficulties. Meeting Mary, however, inspired him to try again, this time with more success.

In 1940, the lease on the theatre ran out and John was called up but Mary was determined to keep the theatre going. As well as acting and running the repertory company she directed plays. As a result they were a success and she built up a loyal following.

Pretty and charming with a gentle humour, Mary could also be firm and refused to allow critics to review her productions.

In 1941 she toured with Sir Donald Wolfit's travelling Shakespearean company and played in a whodunnit while still running the theatre in Windsor.

After the war she went on to make a series of appearances at the West End, played Queen Elizabeth in Laurence Olivier's film of Richard III and appeared in an episode of Miss Marple on television. She also wrote several pantomimes before her death in 1999.

Evacuees

In the summer of 1939 nearly 3 million people were evacuated from towns and cities to suitable receiving areas during Operation Pied Piper. Windsor was designated a receiving area for evacuees from London and residents were told that they must take in 10,000 evacuees, although the number that arrived was closer to 9,000. Most of these were school groups travelling with their teachers.

A former evacuee telling her story for an exhibition at Windsor Museum described her experience as a happy one although she missed her mother and had to wear a raincoat in bed because of rain coming in through the ceiling.

Doreen Crowhurst, who was evacuated from London to Windsor, told her story to Windsor Museum[1]:

We had to get up very early because we had to be at the school at nine o'clock. We had to take packed sandwiches with us and a change of clothes. Being from a very poor family we didn't own a suitcase so everything was put into a pillow case and we had a gas mask with us. My dad went to work so he couldn't come and my sister was crying too much to come. So it was my mum and my big brother who was 21. We got to the school and had a roll call. There must have been about 300 of us and as the buses rolled up – big red, double decker buses – some of the kids had never been on a bus. Everyone was crying – mums, dads, kids, everyone.

When the children arrived in Windsor they were met by Boy Scouts who gave them little paper bags full of treats – barley sugar, biscuits and a few sweets. They were walked through the town, eventually arriving at King Edward's Court which is now the main shopping centre but was then three rows of terraced houses – Edward Square, Denmark Street and Goswell Road.

Householders in these roads who were willing to take evacuees had displayed numbered cards in their windows indicating how many children they were able to take and the children stood in the road waiting to be allocated to a house.

Doreen was taken in by a couple she called Aunt Maude and Uncle George. Aunt Maude gave her fresh sandwiches and told her to put her old sandwiches in the pig bin.

'I thought, "Ooh how lovely, they've got pigs in the garden," but unfortunately it was just a bin to collect the food.'

Later, Maude and George's daughter took Doreen on the ferry over to the fairground at the Brocas.

'Everything was lovely until it was bedtime. Straightaway I wanted my mum.'

The house had no lights, just flickering candles. The rain came in through the chimney so to avoid getting wet Doreen had to wear her raincoat in bed.

Evacuees were dispersed around the Windsor schools, using their classrooms and facilities and taught by their own teacher during the afternoon whereas the resident Windsor children were taught in the morning. Clapham High School for Girls was evacuated to Windsor Boys' School and the Carlyle School, Chelsea, to Windsor County Girls' School.

At the Windsor County Girls' School, a branch of the Junior Red Cross was set up under the patronage of Lady Spencer Churchill[2] so the girls could learn the basics of nursing and support the volunteer nurses.

Housewives taking in evacuee children were responsible for their food and board and received 10s 6d week for one child, 8s 6d for additional children, plus a small laundry allowance for bed wetting. Being an evacuee must have been a horrible experience in some cases – homesickness aside, children were vulnerable to abuse and being treated as unpaid domestic staff – but taking in strangers into your home wasn't always easy either and complaints from housewives about poor behaviour and bad hygiene among their new charges were common. A tribunal committee was set up in Windsor for women and evacuees who weren't comfortable with their situation.

Within months of the first evacuees arriving, as there was still no sign of any bombs, some of the children returned home before Christmas. A second evacuation in February the following year was much less successful with the majority of households refusing to take the evacuees, so billeting was made compulsory. Even then some people got out of it by showing medical certificates stating that having evacuees in their home would be bad for their nerves.

Some small children were evacuated with their mothers. In these cases the allowance only covered lodging not food, so the evacuee mothers had to buy and cook their own food which could potentially cause tension with the homeowner. Joan Benbrook who was initially evacuated to Windsor as a child with her mother said they felt like intruders in the house so she and her mother spent as much time out as possible, taking long walks in Windsor Great Park after school. The next-door neighbours who worked in the castle were much kinder, however, and made her a cuddly toy. Both parents of another girl, who had been evacuated to Ascot with her mother, were killed in an air raid in London when her father was given leave and her mother went to greet him.

A 10-year-old evacuee from London was housed with her 15-year-old sister at Savile House, Eton college with Dr Ley, one of the Eton masters, and his wife. They were just sitting down to supper in the kitchen on 4 December 1940 when a bomb fell on the college.

The child's experience is described in a letter belonging to the Eton Wick History Group which formed part of a wartime memories project in 2005, marking sixty years since the end of the Second World War. Unfortunately the name of the letter writer has been lost.

'I suppose the air raid warning had gone, we were so used to gunfire we just carried on, the planes were always making for Slough. After the initial shock we tried to make our way to the back door over heavy beams and debris. Savile House being a low house, it seemed miles away. We finally made our way to the brick shelter at the bottom of the garden which we shared with other houses in Westons Yard.'

Mrs Ley and another evacuee were taken to hospital but their injuries were not serious. Later that evening the children were transferred to Bekynton house.

'On the way, passing through the school yard, we just missed a large hole in the ground by the school office – little did we know it was a timebomb. It went off the next night. Eventually we managed to salvage most of our possessions but were never able to return to Savile House.'

The child returned to London in 1943. 'The events of 4 December 1940 remain very clear today. Evacuated and bombed out when my home in London remained safe!'

Evacuees in Windsor did enjoy some privileges, however, such as visits to the castle. The king sent bunches of grapes from the ancient vine at Cumberland Lodge and venison from the royal deer park to be distributed among the evacuees and the princesses invited evacuee children from a London school who were billeted in the Great Park to a tea party at the royal lodge. Afterwards the children saved up their pennies to buy the princess a handbag for her birthday.

The Royal Family

The most famous evacuees in Windsor were the two princesses who stayed at Windsor Castle. The public was initially told only that the princesses were at a secret location in the country but residents soon became used to seeing the royal children riding around the Great Park in their pony and trap.

Their mother, Queen Elizabeth, refused to bow to pressure to send the children to Canada for safety saying they couldn't go without her and she wouldn't go without the king – and the king would never leave his country.

The king and queen visited bombed areas of London during the Blitz. Buckingham Palace was an obvious target, easily visible from the air, and it was hit nine times during the war. After the first hit in 1940 the queen famously said she could 'at last look the East End in the face'.

After the war

Without the contribution of women, the Second World War would have been considerably harder to win. Afterwards, however, a lot of jobs connected to the war obviously disappeared and, as with the First World War, there was strong feeling, backed by Trade Unions, that returning servicemen should be given back the jobs they had vacated in order to defend the country.

After all their work the Land Army girls were denied a part in the victory parades, although in the summer of 1945 a Women's Land Army rally was held in Windsor Great Park, attended by the princesses. Some 700 Land Army girls marched through the streets of Windsor led by the band of the Royal Horse Guards.

CHAPTER NINE

Charity and Good Works

Key Dates:

1848 – Revolutions in Europe.

1853 – First Windsor Mothers' Meeting.

1858 – St John's Home for Girls (orphanage) set up by the Clewer Sisters.

1862 – Windsor almshouses founded in 1503 were rebuilt.

1886 – Formation of the Society for the Assistance of Ladies in Reduced Circumstances (Princess Helena was patron).

1914 – Baby Clinic set up in Eton.

Without a welfare state, vulnerable people in nineteenth century Windsor were reliant chiefly on the church, charitable institutions and the generosity of a few wealthy individuals. Women in the nineteenth century were generally on the receiving rather than the giving end of this charity, especially if they had been abandoned or had children to care for. Certain occasions, such as Christmas, were likely to bring out goodwill, for example the elderly poor received free coal from the castle at Christmas, but in general, handouts were unpredictable and often subject to personal judgement about the worthiness of the recipient.

As women were mostly dependent on men for their money they weren't usually in a position to give money to charitable causes although they might have been able to influence their husbands to do so. Widows, however, had the freedom to make their own decisions and wealthy women sometimes made provisions for the poor in their wills.

Sophia Bonnell from Pelling Place in Old Windsor, for example, left an annual sum of £10 in 1841 to give Christmas Dinner to as many people of the parish as the sum would pay for. Forty-one years later the tradition was still going strong, with Miss Bonnell and James Bonnell, the trustees, presiding over dinner for seventy-five people, which consisted of roast beef, potatoes, plum pudding, ale and bread.

From the 1840s there was a growing awareness of social problems throughout Britain and a willingness to become involved among better-off Victorian women who were well-read and had time on their hands. Novels by Charles Dickens, Mrs Gaskell, Charles Kingsley and Charlotte Brontë brought home to readers the poor living conditions endured by poor people, and also showed the poor to be relatable human beings who were simply less fortunate than the wealthy.

The educated Windsor residents who had time for reading, who were generally women, would have had some idea of workhouse conditions through reading books like Charles Dickens's *Oliver Twist*, which was published in monthly instalments from 1837–1839. This may be in part why a group of Windsor ladies made regular visits to the Union workhouse, spending time with the ill and elderly, and reading to the children.

Altruism was one driving force. But another was fear – fear of social change. In the mid-nineteenth century people in Britain were fearful of the working class rising up in revolution as had occurred in other European countries in 1848 including Italy, France, Germany and Austria.

In nineteenth-century Windsor, as in other towns, some charitable causes were deemed more acceptable than others. Well-bred ladies who were happy to donate to the infirmary might balk at entering the stinking slums because of the perceived health risks of miasma, or the damage to their reputation by associating with women of ill repute.

The mothers of poor children at the Ragged School, however, were helped in Windsor at mothers' meetings. A couple of women, Miss Devonshire and Miss Hall, started holding meetings there in 1853 and others soon rallied round to give advice and practical help such as how to make clothes for the children. The Windsor Mothers' Meetings were still going strong fifty years later when they had a tea to celebrate the anniversary and seventy-eighth birthday of Miss Hall.

Princess Helena

For some women in Windsor, the Society for the Assistance of Ladies in Reduced Circumstances (formed in 1886), of which Princess Helena was patron, was a lifeline. Princess Helena (1846– 1923) also set up an infant nursery in Grove Road in 1876 for the children of destitute mothers who were ill or at work during the day. The nursery took children from 1 month to 3 years old from any parish and was open from 7.30 a.m. to 7 p.m. and cost 4*d* a day. Food was provided and the children were under the care of a matron. The nursery was visited every day by one of the ladies on the committee.

Lots of Windsor women supported the nursery with money and gifts. A fundraising garden fête was held at Abbey House, the home of Miss Hunter, in the summer of 1917. Many women were involved in running the fête including Lady Augusta Spencer Churchill, Miss Hunter and Mrs Broadbent. The band of the 2nd Life Guards played, and wounded soldiers from King Edward VII Hospital were entertained at tea. A group of young ladies danced, including a floral dance by Miss Chaplin.

Princess Helena also set up a fund called the Free Dinner and Relief Fund and spent £150 on meals, coal and blankets for the poor. In April 1914, the royal borough created Helena Day for residents to show their appreciation of Princess Helena's good work and raise money for the charities she supported.

The Clewer Sisters

Many women in Windsor were helped by the Community of St John the Baptist, the Anglican Sisterhood in Hatch Lane which had been started by Mariquita Tennant. After ill health forced Mrs Tennant to give up running the House in 1852, she was succeeded by Harriet Monsell, a warm-hearted, energetic, red-haired Irish woman who was known for her strong principles and fair-mindedness. She and Rev. Thomas Carter set up the religious community which supervised the House of Mercy and, in time, many other charitable institutions.

The Clewer Sisters set up several orphanages or children's homes including, in 1858, St John's Home for Girls, an orphanage for the daughters of 'respectable parents' in Windsor (i.e. children who were legitimate) and St Augustine's Home for boys with troubled pasts.

They also founded St Andrews Convalescent Hospital for the poor in Clewer and St Andrews Cottage, an Almshouse 'for invalid poor ladies'. In addition to these they founded other Houses of Mercy, schools, orphanages and Mission houses around the country.

The Windsor soup kitchen

In the coldest months soup kitchens helped poorer mothers ensure their children had at least one hot meal, and it was mainly women who worked in them. Various soup kitchens were set up in Windsor. One is described in the *Windsor Express* 10 February 1883 as being on the premises adjoining the National School, while another was under the guildhall and there was a third in Eton.

In 1886, Windsor residents donated money, meat, flour, bread and peas to the guildhall soup kitchen which was open daily for eleven weeks during bitter weather. An army of women were involved in ladling out the soup. The mayor thanked the Misses Bloom eating house, Church Street, and Mr and Mrs Bourne and their employees at the Three Tuns who waited on the poor.

In November 1902, at a meeting in the guildhall it was decided another soup kitchen should be started as soon as possible and the soup kitchens in different parishes should be merged into a concerted effort. As well as soup the new Windsor soup kitchen under the guildhall provided coffee and cocoa for young children who would otherwise go to school without breakfast. 'Already pain and suffering are beginning to be felt owing to the inclemency of the weather and the lack of work for those who have to depend on odd jobs for their living,' said Mayor Shipley. He appealed through the *Windsor Express* for the public to give generously to the fund for the kitchen.

Mayoress Carter (wife of the mayor) was always busy at the guildhall kitchen, serving out soup according to the *Windsor Express* 1909. She and the mayor gave a garden party at Suffolk Lodge in Bolton Road in the summer to thank the many people who had helped at the soup kitchen during the winter. Lady Dyson, the next mayor's wife also put in many hours every week at the guildhall kitchen.

In April 1911, the *Reading Mercury* reported that the Windsor soup kitchen had served over 8,200 meals to hungry children, men and women during the winter period. In December 1911 the kitchen was whitewashed and some improvements carried out ready for another Christmas.

The *Windsor Express* made clear they wanted to see 'wasters' weeded out. The mayor's soup kitchen, however, said the report, was essential for hungry children and men who were willing but unable to find employment. An anonymous donor had sent the mayor half a guinea towards the fund that week and it was hoped others would follow the example.

Fundraising events

While some families disapproved of women doing paid work, voluntary work and fundraising was considered acceptable. During the wars, most of this activity went to support the war effort but Windsor women were busy fundraising for other causes too. In November 1917, the Windsor Ladies Swimming Club put on a concert at the Royal Albert Institute to raise money for a YMCA hut in France to be given by ladies' swimming clubs of the southern counties.

Archbishop Laud's and Theodore Randue's Charity

A rather unusual 'marriageable maidens' charity had existed in Windsor since the seventeenth century to provide a dowry to poor women who wouldn't otherwise be able to attract a husband, the recipients being chosen on May Day and their names printed in the paper. By the turn of the twentieth century however, there were complaints that some of the women were taking the 'marriage portions' without actually getting married, so it was decided the money should be withheld until the ceremony had taken place.

Baby clinic

Poverty and poor housing conditions during the First World War contributed to high infant mortality. Nurse Orchard, a midwife, set up a clinic called 'Babies Welcome' in the Eton Wick village hall in 1914, with a committee of ladies including masters' wives from Eton college.

The clinic, funded by donations and subscriptions, provided support for women with young children. A doctor gave free consultations. The babies were weighed and the mothers received advice on subjects such as feeding and making children's clothes. They could also buy milk, knitting wool, needlework patterns and second-hand clothes, and enjoy a cup of tea and a chat while their toddlers played.

CHAPTER TEN

Leisure

Key dates:
1849 – The railways are built.
1866 – Windsor racecourse first meeting.
1880 – Royal Albert Institute opened.
1884 – First ladies championship at Wimbledon sparked an interest in tennis.
1895 – Women's football was invented.
1900 – Female athletes first took part in the Olympic Games.
1902 – Alexandra Gardens opened.
1943 – First Royal Windsor Horse Show.

A large part of Windsor's transformation into a tourist town had to do with the improved leisure facilities. In the early nineteenth century some people had very little opportunity for leisure, but by the end of the century many improvements had been made.

How much leisure time someone had and how they spent it depended largely on class and gender. But women of all ages and class could enjoy walking in the Great Park and along the Brocas riverbank. On Sundays in the nineteenth century the Long Walk was filled with people dressed in their best clothes to promenade and enjoy the fresh air.

In the nineteenth century the annual Windsor Revel that took place on Bachelors Acre was a chance for women to let their hair down and eye up the town's eligible young men. The event which took place in August and October from 1810 included tented stalls, sideshows, gambling tables, cricket, wrestling, climbing a soaped pole, tightrope walking and blindfold races. Entertainment included band music, dancing and fireworks. But the Clewer House of Mercy and the boys from Eton College banned their residents from going to the fair for fear they would be tempted into misbehaviour.

Fairs had been held on Bachelors Acre since the Middle Ages. The Bachelors Revel started in the time of Queen Charlotte; Windsor's young men would assemble on the field called the Acre and process around the town with a band and flags before the cricket game and roasted ox back at the Acre. The Revel was abolished in 1857 when behaviour was judged to have got out of hand but revived on a larger scale in 1875.

The circus

Wombwell's Menagerie caused great excitement when it came to the town with its performing elephants. Queen Victoria was so delighted by this travelling zoo that on more than one occasion it was invited to the castle, the townsfolk running alongside as the animals were marched up the hill.

Mothers would also take their children to Sanger's circus, a hugely popular circus which also processed through the town and performed for the queen. In 1852, a stupendous procession was advertised in the paper 'on a scale of grandeur never before attempted in the world', through the principal streets with a magnificent cage of lions, monster Egyptian serpent carriage, horses, ponies, camels and an elephant. In April 1890, the tent was packed and the audience was 'amused and delighted', according to the *Windsor Express*. Crowds of 4,000 people would turn up to the shows featuring acrobats, trapeze artists and clowns. Acts featured Miss Lavinia Sanger with a splendid jumping horse, Black Eagle, and Blondin the pony who could balance on a narrow plank.

While the circus tent was being set up in 1898 a young man who was cleaning out a cage was attacked by a bear and taken to the infirmary. George Sanger, a Berkshire man, was known as king of the circus world and awarded himself the title of lord. His wife

Ellen had performed at Wombwells. People who had enjoyed the circus as children would have been shocked to read in 1911 that 'lord' George Sanger, the owner, had been shot dead by a man who had been a bareback rider. The killer then shot himself.

During cold winters many women enjoyed skating and sliding on the frozen ponds. In January 1908, a large number of people skated on the frozen lake at Virginia Water and ponds in Windsor Great Park, Englemere Lake, Ascot. In the Long Walk, a pipe leading from Cranbourne to Windsor Castle burst creating a series of mini lakes. One accident was reported in the *Windsor Express* – Miss Laney slipped on the ice and bumped her head but wasn't seriously hurt.

Days out

The building of the railways brought with it the option of daytrips including Brighton and Bournemouth. In July 1850, a cheap excursion from Windsor to Oxford on the Great Western Railway in covered carriages was advertised at the unprecedented price of 3*s* 6*d* per person. Low fares were also available to bring people to Windsor the following weekend for the annual Revel on Bachelors Acre, the last train back not departing until after 10.30 p.m. so there would be time to see the fireworks. Low fares were also offered every Monday for visitors from London wanting to visit Windsor and vice versa. In 1920 Windsorian Coaches was established, offering more opportunities for days out.

At home

Taking afternoon tea was a pleasant way to spend the afternoon for ladies who could afford the time and was a pleasant social occasion. It was invented in Windsor by the Duchess of Bedford, a friend and Lady of the Bedchamber of Queen Victoria, who found it helped to solve that problematic empty feeling between luncheon and dinner.

Educated ladies could also while away a few hours reading. In 1841, Edgar Allan Poe published *Murder in the Rue Morgue,* often accepted as the first detective story. Arthur Conan Doyle's first Sherlock Holmes story, *A Study in Scarlet*, was published in 1887.

Sport

When it came to sport, Victorian women's clothing was too restrictive for many games but croquet, which is thought to have been introduced to England in the 1850s, was a sport they could join in because it didn't require too much movement and, for those with a large enough garden, could be played at home. It was a social sport that men and women could play together on any flat lawn so was ideal for house parties. In the 1870s the local paper carried several advertisements for Jacques croquet sets and for creating and repairing croquet lawns and lawn tennis courts. Croquet tournaments including ladies' open singles were played at Ascot heath. Lawn tennis also became popular in the 1870s. Perhaps inspired by the Ladies' Championship at Wimbledon first held in 1884, many large houses had tennis courts in their grounds. As tennis became established, women's fashions changed.

One of the women at the 1884 Wimbledon tennis tournament fainted during a match, quite probably because she was wearing a corset and long, heavy dress. Edwardian ladies wore lighter dresses and from the 1920s and 1930s, skirts got shorter.

But the sport that really came to symbolise female emancipation was cycling. While clambering onto a penny farthing in a crinoline would have been fraught with difficulty, the invention of the safety bicycle with its two equal-sized wheels and a chain in the late nineteenth century brought women the freedom of the road. Long skirts and bicycles didn't go well together so women began to embrace a more relaxed style of clothing and corsets gave way to bloomers (named after American women's rights advocate Amelia Bloomer).

Before bicycles, a woman had mostly had to rely on men for transport. The bicycle put her in control. She might have got some shocked stares and even the odd missile thrown at her – riding astraddle rather than side saddle was considered risqué and quite possibly dangerous to her reproductive health – but she could pedal anywhere, unchaperoned.

At first, female cyclists tended to be wealthier women but as the price of bicycles came down, working-class women could own bicycles too, especially as second-hand ones became available. Riding was taught free to customers of Royal Windsor Cycle Company at 24 High Street in 1897. In 1898 the auction galleries in Peascod Street were advertising a pneumatic bicycle for ladies.

In 1900, a resident of Arthur Villas, Arthur Road placed an advertisement for a second-hand lady's bicycle in 'splendid condition', only ridden a few times, and in 1906 a resident of St Leonard's Road advertised a Lady's Royal Sunbeam bicycle, 23in frame with brakes and free wheel in an 'as new' condition for £8.

American suffragist Susan B. Andrew said that the bicycle had done 'more to emancipate women than anything else in the world.' Bicycles enabled women to get to suffrage meetings and demonstrations, and to escape quickly after militant acts such as the firebombing of Wargrave church.

The River

Whereas in the first half of the nineteenth century the river had been chiefly used for commercial purposes, the building of the railways brought a faster transport system so the river started to become a leisure amenity. By the end of the century the river was filled with rowing boats and steamboats and the riverbank at the Brocas on the Eton side became a popular place to sit and watch regattas.

Women also took part in rowing. The up-river regatta in August 1897 featured Lady and Gentleman double sculling. N. Ogilwy, Miss M. Ogilwy and Miss F. Bradley (cox) from Eton came first. M.G. Atkins, Miss Atkins and Miss F. Atkins (cox) from Windsor came second. It was apparently a fine race to within 30 yards of the finish when the Ogilwys got ahead and won by two lengths.

The promenade along the River Thames beside Barry Avenue was first created in the 1890s although several alterations would be made over the years. Before the steps were constructed from the promenade to the bridge in the 1930s the easiest way to cross from one bank to the other was to pay the ferryman to take you across the water in one of the punts.

Plans for a riverside garden in Windsor had been discussed in Victorian times but on 15 July 1902 the public pleasure gardens were finally opened by Princess Christian on the fields adjoining the river formerly known as the Goswells. Alexandra Gardens were named after the Queen Consort and soon became a favourite spot for families on sunny afternoons.

Crowds of people, many of them women with parasols and children in their Sunday best, poured through the gates on a sunny afternoon to admire the bandstand, flower beds, tennis courts, lawns and fishpond.

A piece of land between Alexandra Gardens and River Street was bought by public subscription in 1910 and given to the National Trust, of which Princess Louise was president, to prevent it being built on, blocking the view of the castle from the river. This became a bowling green and tennis courts.

By the turn of the century the River Thames had become a popular place for relaxing and the river was packed with boats including the *Empress of India, Queen of England* and *Windsor Belle* as well as an assortment of smaller craft. In July 1903, when Prince Christian rang from the castle to reserve a launch, he was told there were none available and he had to borrow the Prince of Wales's boat. Salter's steam launches offered trips to Cliveden.

Swimming in the Thames was also popular and there were several bathing places along the river including Baths Island, as well as changing rooms by the railway arches. Whereas swimming was a part of Windsor boys' lives, it wasn't until the late nineteenth century that women became involved in competitive swimming. Although ladies' swim sessions and courses were advertised in the paper, the headline 'A Windsor lady wins a swimming prize' in 1900, marking Miss Downay coming second in a gala in London, shows how much of a novelty it was. But as the report explained, getting dressed and undressed was considered too troublesome for many fashionable ladies. The instructress of the London club, Ada Lewin, recommended stockinette in place of serge for swimming costumes. She made her own costume which fastened at the shoulders.

In 1908, a competition for ladies was held at the corporation baths under the GWR bridge, for young ladies who had learned to swim there. The hon. secretary Mr Duly said he believed all ladies should be taught to swim and that there were probably more lady swimmers in Windsor than any other town of its size. The Windsor Ladies Swimming Club Gala became a popular event. In 1912 the winner of the 150 yards was Miss Muriel Parsons, whose sister Miss Gladys Parsons came second.

Medals and prizes were presented in a ceremony at the guildhall to members of the Ladies Swimming Club on 30 September 1916. The occasion was presided over by Mayor and Mayoress Carter, Mrs Sheppard, the president of the club, and Lady Dyson. Miss Ivy Strange won medals in life-saving, diving and the half-mile swim. In his speech, the mayor said that not only was swimming beneficial for ladies, it gave them the chance to do a great act if needed. A number of drownings were indeed prevented by members of the Ladies Swimming Club including in May 1920 a woman who had got into difficulty at the swimming baths and was rescued by Marjorie Dickinson.

On 28 August 1930, two girls aged 10 and 12 were swimming in the river when they got into trouble. Winifred Norton, a mother of two and a member of Windsor Ladies Swimming Club, had been sitting on the promenade by the riverside when she heard their cries for help. She plunged in fully clothed, but when she reached the spot where the girls had been they had disappeared. She dived down, found both of them, held one under each arm and kicked her way to the shore. In their panic the girls clung to her clothes, pulling her back down into the water, but she eventually got them to safety, cheered on by a crowd lining the promenade. Although she refused to give her name and address, Winifred was followed when she went home to change in her house in Sudan Terrace and was identified. The previous year she had also rescued a boy from drowning in the river.

Nora Brown, captain of Windsor Ladies Swimming Club in 1924 was also an instructress to the Windsor Ladies Gymnastics Club and was described in the papers as a 'very good, all-round sportswoman', who was a brilliant hockey and tennis player as well as a swimmer.

Gymnastics

By the twentieth century, Windsor women were also taking part in gymnastics. Miss Winnifred Palmer started a Windsor gymnastics and drill class in 1906. In December her class put on a display at the Congregational Hall in Windsor. 'Ten thousand thanks are due to anyone of any class who can attract Eve from her tight lacing habits, her high-heeled boots, her slavery and dependence on dress,' said a report in the *Windsor Express*. Recent efforts in hockey, cricket and golf and lawn tennis had been in the right direction but best of all was gymnastics. All ages took part in a fancy march with high jumping. The ladies showed off their expertise on the parallel bars, and free exercise while their dumbbell drill was pronounced 'a masterpiece'.

In April 1908 the Windsor Ladies gymnastics team took part in a display in Slough Public Hall of Slough and Windsor Ladies' and children's gymnastics including floor exercises, vaulting horse and drill. The president Dr Frank Hathaway hoped the performance would persuade other people of all ages to take part in gymnastics and drill halls would be turned into gymnasiums. He assured the audience that the exercises weren't made in Germany and asked the young ladies to confirm that the exercises didn't leave them feeling tired but energised.

Other pastimes

In 1900 the first female athletes took part in the Olympic Games in Paris. Another sport that was attracting women was football and the first ladies' football club was started in 1895 under the patronage of women's rights activist, Lady Florence Dixie who had previously lived in Windsor. It's not known if there was a ladies football team in Windsor but by the 1920s there was a Windsor Ladies hockey team and Windsor Ladies polo team.

There was also a Ladies Royal Household bowling team captained by a Miss Brown which played on a bowling green at Royal Household Club at Frogmore. In August 1948 they played the Crawley ladies team. Miss Brown escorted the Crawley team through the State apartments pointing out objects of historical interest. The two teams had lunch at the Royal Oak hotel before going to the club at Frogmore. The Crawley ladies won by one shot. The game was followed by tea at the club.

Plays and concerts

Many women enjoyed a visit to the Windsor Theatre Royal for plays and circuses. Some also performed there. Chorus girls in 1926 had to squeeze past a large bear on a chain whose outstretched paw very nearly reached them. The actor Geraldine McEwan, a student at Windsor County Girls' School and daughter of a print worker, lived in Old Windsor. She used to be taken by her mother to the theatre during the war. In 1946, aged 14, she made her first stage appearance there as the attendant to Hippolyta in Midsummer Night's Dream. After a few years with the Windsor Repertory company she went on to appear in London's West End in 1951 and for many people is best remembered for playing Agatha Christie's Miss Marple on television.

Plays, concerts and recitals were also performed at the Royal Albert Institute in Sheet Street. In February 1911, the Windsor and Eton branch of the London Society for Women's Suffrage put on a concert and a play called 'How the Vote was Won', which was entirely performed by women, all of whom were professional actors. The play, organised by Florence Gibb, was about women agreeing to call a general strike and all turning up on the doorstep of their nearest male relative, insisting that he support them until they were granted the vote.

Those less fortunate women who didn't have a male relative on whom they could rely had to go straight to the workhouse. So at the start of the play Ethel Cole, an anti-suffrage supporter, finds that her servant has disappeared and the maid-of-all-work is cheerfully leaving for the workhouse. Ethel's husband is horrified to discover his wife's sister, his own sister, his niece, a distant relation, a first cousin and an aunt, all turning up to claim him as their nearest male relative, demanding his support and hospitality until the happy day when the vote would be granted to them and they could once more support themselves. Horace gives in to the pressure and as the curtain falls, he is seen bedecked with the suffrage colours, waving a Votes for Women flag and hurrying off to join a men's march to Westminster to force the government to grant women the vote.

The *Windsor Express* reported a good turnout for the evening with local suffrage supporters turning out in strong force. The play 'went excellently and elicited much merriment from the audience'. Special praise was given to Miss Cicely Hamilton as Winifred and Charles Thursby as Horace, while 'much credit' was given to Florence Gibb for the organisation.

Windsor en fête

During the summer, women were customers and stallholders at a variety of fêtes and outdoor events. These generally raised money for charity and during the wars many of these were held to raise money for the war effort. The Royal Windsor Horse Show was first held in 1943 against the spectacular backdrop of the castle as part of the Wings for Victory event in order to raise money to buy war planes. The king and queen, queen mother and two princesses were present at the first show and Princess Elizabeth won in the pony and dog cart class.

The first show was a single-day event called the Windsor Horse and Dog Show and included a dog gymkhana. But unfortunately, or so the story goes, a dog stole a piece of chicken from the king's plate which put an end to dogs being allowed to take part.

Over the course of the twentieth century many leisure and sporting opportunities were opened to women and helped free them from the narrow confines of being the angel in the home although in the twenty-first century equality in terms of prize money was still a long way off.

Across the century 1850–1950, life for women in Britain had changed dramatically. They had proved that they could run the country, excel in sport and take part in politics. Windsor women contributed to that change and continue to do so.

Acknowledgements

I couldn't have researched this book without reading through hundreds of newspapers, including the wonderful *Windsor Express* and many papers in The British Newspaper Archive – it's such a useful and valuable resource and saved my eyes after many hours of peering at microfilm. I'm very grateful to the staff at Windsor and Slough Libraries, Windsor Museum, Windsor History Group, Eton Wick History Group, Berkshire Records Office and the Women's Library at the LSE for their guidance and help. I found Kelly's Directory in Windsor library extremely useful for identifying who lived where and the jobs people did, and ancestry. com and findmypast.com helped set me on the right track for tracing individuals on the census. I've found a number of websites very useful especially Thamesweb who also very kindly supplied some of the photographs. I must also thank Barry Swaebe for his wonderful photograph of women during the Second World War supporting the war effort, John Daniel from Daniel department store for putting me in touch with his former staff and Queensmead school for letting me use their archive. And Amanda Bryett for her inspirational 'Conspirators in Petticoats' walking tour around Windsor, which I'd thoroughly recommend to anyone who has an interest in suffragist history.

Endnotes

Introduction
1. Windsor Express, 1909

Chapter One: Queen Victoria and Princess Elizabeth
1. Florence Gibb used the argument about the queen wishing she had Florence Nightingale in the War Office in a letter to the Windsor Express on 15 January 1910.
2. For further interest *The Mystery of Princess* Louise by Lucinda Hawksley (Vintage) is a fascinating read.

Chapter Two: Home
1. 1908 British Newspaper Archive *Windsor Express* Saturday 14 November 1908.
2. Lecture delivered by Lady Florence Dixie, 21 April 1891.
3. Peter Higginbotham www.workhouse.org
4. For a full and fascinating study of the home for fallen women see *A Place in Life: Clewer House of Mercy 1849-83* by Valerie Bonham
5. The Black Horse www.twobrewerswindsor.co.uk

Chapter Three: Education
1. Ragged school, British Newspaper Archives *Windsor Express* 1856
2. A full and very interesting history of St Stephen's can be found in *The Story of St Stephen's College* by Jenny Balston

Chapter Four: Work
1. British Newspaper Archive *Windsor Express* Saturday, 14 November 1908
2. More information on the history of Caleys can be found on www.johnlewismemorystore.org.uk

Chapter Six: Active Citizens
1. Lecture at the Christian Institute, Glasgow
2. St George's College archives

Chapter Eight: Second World War
1. By kind permission of the museum. Copyright Windsor & Royal Borough Museum
2. *Girls in Green* by Susan Mercer

Index